Exiles, Eccentrics, Activists

Exiles, Eccentrics, Activists

Women in Contemporary German Theater

Katrin Sieg

Ann Arbor

THE UNIVERSITY OF MICHIGAN PRESS

1997   1996   1995   1994   4   3   2   1

A CIP catalogue record for this book is available from the British Library

Library of Congress Cataloging-in-Publication Data

Sieg, Katrin, 1961–
   Exiles, eccentrics, activists : women in contemporary German
theater / Katrin Sieg.
      p. cm.
   Includes bibliographical references and index.
   ISBN 0-472-10491-8 (alk. paper)
   1. German drama—20th century—History and criticism. 2. German
drama—Women authors—History and criticism. 3. Authors,
German—20th century—Political and social views. 4. Theater—
Europe, German-speaking—History—20th century. I. Title.
PT668.S535 1994
832'.91099287—dc20   94-19407
                                                            CIP

To my mother

Acknowledgments

In the three years of preparing this book, I have relied on the encouragement, support, and friendship of many people. I would like to thank a few of them. Most of all, my parents have made this study possible—by instilling in me a delight in the arts, by cheering me on through graduate school, and by financing much of my research when I was just scraping by. They generously supplied trans-Atlantic plane tickets, mailed me books, invited Ginka Steinwachs for dinner, and even paid some of the copyright fees for photographs in this book. Janelle Reinelt has been a wonderful teacher and friend who saw (and was largely responsible for) my transformation from a women's libber into a feminist scholar and from a German exchange student to an international graduate student. She has also been there at crucial times when I was stranded and broke, for which I will always be thankful. Sue-Ellen Case, my graduate advisor at the University of Washington, has most profoundly shaped my thinking, guided me through my dissertation, and oversaw early versions and revisions of this book. I have been most inspired by her wit, wisdom, and integrity, as well as her dedication to feminist criticism and theater scholarship. I wish to express my appreciation and affection to her, for introducing me to communities of feminists in academia, as well as showing me a side of German culture I had not known before (including certain bars). She made possible many personal contacts and friendships with women critics and artists in Berlin that have become very important to me—and, in that way mend my sense of great dislocation toward my country of origin.

Finally, I wish to thank my friends who lured me out of my study after long days of writing in the gray Seattle winter: Almuth, Holly, Rachel, Ursula, and Carolyn. My heartfelt thanks and appreciation also to my fiberoptic family who have continued to provide love, gossip, and laughter: Antje Wischmann, Angelika Czekay, Esther Beth Sullivan, and Karin Herrmann.

I wish to acknowledge Ginka Steinwachs for granting me copyright and the translation rights to her manifesto, "Das Theater als oralische Anstalt" (1984); the Verlag der Autoren for permission to cite Emine Sevgi Özdamar's unpublished plays *Karagöz in Alamania* and *Keloglan in Alamania;* and *Theatre Studies* for permission to reprint portions of my article "The Representation of Fascism: Gerlind Reinshagen's Play *Sonntagskinder," Theatre Studies* 36 (1991).

Contents

Introduction

The present study is the first book-length examination, in either German or English, of twentieth-century plays written by women in German. It attempts to rewrite the history of modern German theater through a series of exemplary readings. Rather than insisting on women's essential difference of experience and aesthetic practices that, properly accumulated and narrated, would amount to a discrete female history running alongside its patriarchal counterpart while never touching it, I imagine a history of women's theater contiguous to and engaging with the dominant tale, exposing its biases and mechanisms of exclusion at each intersection, simultaneously inscribing itself into the extant text and eroding it. Such a genealogy of precursors traces specifically "female" traditions insofar as those early texts not only register the conditions of their effacement from patriarchal theater history but also suggest strategies of subversion, resistance, and, possibly, attack.

The first part, "Fluchtwege—Lines of Flight," discusses the work of three playwrights of the Weimar Republic, Marieluise Fleißer, Erika Mann, and Else Lasker-Schüler. It examines the conditions underlying their relative invisibility in the canon of twentieth-century German theater. The title of this part compounds a material analysis of both literal and figurative exile with the notion of a genealogy of German women's theater. The aesthetic and political models that these three authors developed provide the ground for the analysis of texts written during the last twenty years.

The second part, "Inroads," investigates contemporary women's dramatic texts in terms of the strategies they deploy to inscribe and secure a place for the female subject as the author of her own images. At the same time, these plays contest and deconstruct the theatrical

institution as a "technology of gender" (de Lauretis 1987) that has traditionally cast women in the role of object, not subject, of representation.
In Gerlind Reinshagen's play *Eisenherz* [Ironheart], the heroine, Bublitz,
sets out on a precarious journey toward self-determination, a utopian
project that cannot be represented in positive terms but appears in flashes
of "anticipatory illumination" (Bloch 1986). The poetics of pleasure that
Ginka Steinwachs articulates in her "palatheater of the mouth" emphasizes the power of the erotic to challenge and undermine the phallocentric order. The dramaturgy of the Austrian author Elfriede Jelinek is
caught in the negative gesture of deconstruction, which insistently forces
women's status as nonsubjects in the patriarchal economy, and, more
specifically, in the discourses of liberal humanism and fascism, to the
foreground. The author's high visibility and the invisibility of women
her work underlines create a productive tension and a spectatorial space
from which the misogyny of the German master texts becomes apparent.

Several factors determined the selection of authors represented here:
Apart from personal preference and availability of scripts, the most important concern was the accessibility of the texts in English translation.
In many ways, this book complements Sue-Ellen Case's anthology *The
Divided Home/Land: Contemporary German Women's Plays,* published in
1992. That volume includes many of the plays examined here, and presents almost all of the authors. However, there are some exceptions to
this general rule. Whereas *Home/Land* introduces Friederike Roth to
American readers, this study provides only a brief account of that
author's work in the introductory section to part 2. I was reluctant to
include a chapter on Roth, who is regarded as an important figure in
contemporary German women's literature, because I believe that this
writer offers less than others in terms of particular historical or national
articulations of gender and sexuality that could challenge and revise the
American reader's understanding of feminist theater practice. Of all the
plays included in Case's anthology, Roth's representation of heterosexual relationships requires the least critical work in terms of recontex-
tualizing it.

Secondly, one of the chapters in the second part of this book is
devoted to Elfriede Jelinek, who most critics would agree is both a major
new voice and a most decidedly feminist one in the German-speaking
theater, despite a sparse production record. This playwright is not represented in Case's anthology. Although I admit it is somewhat awkward

to include one Austrian in an otherwise all-German group of playwrights and thereby risk obscuring important national differences, my choice seemed justified because the reception, publication, and production of Jelinek's work occurred (with few exceptions) in West Germany rather than in Austria. This has changed to some degree, since several of her plays have been staged in Austria and her work has entered the curriculum at Austrian universities. In addition to Jelinek, there is now a whole group of Austrian women playwrights whose work has been anthologized, wanting more critical attention. References to these writers, as well as others who are not discussed in the chapters, can be found in the introductions to parts 1 and 2. These introductions sketch the work of those individual theater artists discussed in the six chapters onto a broader map of the Weimar Republic and of contemporary West Germany respectively. The introduction to "Inroads" is especially designed to aid those seeking an extensive bibliographic listing of contemporary German women playwrights.

A history of German women's theater addresses and contributes to the major debates that have successively shaped dramatic theory and practice in this century. Women have participated in the antibourgeois movements during the first two decades of this century. They took part in large numbers in the redefinition of the medium as an instrument for social and political change in the Weimar Republic. After World War II, women authors found allies in the New Left and its project to intervene in dominant constructions of national identity. Finally, women are at the forefront of postmodern theater scrutinizing its own history as an apparatus of ideological (re)production.

So far, the narrative of German theater history, as projected from these debates, has been constructed solely through the achievements and contributions of male authors. American theater historians have merely replicated the androcentric perspective of the German theater scholars. While providing rich material for the many studies on images of women in men's work, the dominant texts reveal little about women as authors of their own representations. In this critical vacuum, women's texts have remained invisible; only very recently have feminists begun to chart the work of women in German theater, beginning with the actress (Möhrmann 1989). Many of the authors in this study have questioned the gender-coded hierarchy of writing as "active" and male, over the performative arts as "passive" and female. Moreover, a documentation of the work of German women dramatists challenges one of the most tenacious misconceptions in theater history and criticism, namely, that the high art of playwriting has been mastered by only a few, isolated women.

The few exceptions are well known: the tenth-century nun Hrotsvit von Gandersheim is generally named as the first German playwright (although her plays were written in Latin); and the work of Karoline Neuber in the eighteenth century signals the emergence of the professional director. However, Neuber's innovations in production techniques and stage practices and her contribution to a national theater in Germany are frequently represented as secondary in comparison to the impact of her partner in this project, Johann Christoph Gottsched, a scholar from Leipzig and, in one critic's words, "intellectual leader of Germany" (Brockett 1982, 392). Likewise, Gottsched's wife Adelgunde, author of numerous comedies, many translations of French plays, and one tragedy, appears as a minor figure overshadowed by her husband. The genre differentiation evidenced by husband and wife—he wrote and theorized on the tragedy, while she wrote comedies—prefigured the dismissal of a host of nineteenth-century women playwrights as the authors of trivial, inferior ware.

The story of Karoline Neuber and Adelgunde Gottsched appears paradigmatic for almost all of the authors in this study. This book reinscribes a viewpoint that has so far been effaced by the traditional, historiographical focus on great men. Else Lasker-Schüler's fantastic and grotesque outcasts who defy the bourgeois moral and sexual codes have been eclipsed by critical attention to Frank Wedekind's precocious and voracious sexual outsiders. Theater students and audiences in Germany and the United States are more likely to associate radical sexual politics with Wedekind's *Spring Awakening* or *Lulu* and Bertolt Brecht's early plays like *Baal*, rather than the representations of queer sexuality in Lasker-Schüler's and Christa Winsloe's work. The reception of Marieluise Fleißer's 1920s plays began as late as the late 1960s and has been overshadowed by her more successful contemporaries Brecht and Ödön von Horvàth. Erika Mann, a member of one of Germany's most famous literary families, is better known as her father's secretary and her brother's editor than as artistic and administrative head of a cabaret troupe. The German New Left and its New Subjectivist aesthetics are generally associated with male authors such as Botho Strauss, rather than Gerlind Reinshagen. Elfriede Jelinek has only very recently begun to garner popular and critical attention, after long being neglected in comparison to the great men of the Austrian avant-garde such as Ernst Jandl, Peter Handke, and Thomas Bernhard. Ginka Steinwachs, because she inhabits a very unique, francophile-aesthetic model, has been all but ignored in androcentric, literary-dramatic criticism.

In 1899, critic Amalie von Ende published "Nine Hundred Years of Women's Drama," an essay that demonstrated the need for a burgeoning feminist movement to uncover and lay claim to a tradition and to trace genealogies. Feminist literary histories have largely ignored the contributions of women playwrights, but von Ende's proud retrospective contested the common assumption that women had not tackled the drama.[1] Even feminist theater historians frequently locate the so-called beginning of women's dramatic production around the turn of this century in conjunction with the first women's movement.[2] In the last three years, a great deal of archival research on eighteenth-century women's plays in German has brought to light a wealth of texts that help correct the perception of women's inability to write dramas as well as redefine questions of periodization and genre (von Hoff 1989; Wurst 1991; Kord 1992). Anke Roeder, editor of the only book about contemporary German women playwrights to date, contends in her introduction that women began to write around the end of the eighteenth century and that their texts were shaped by and thematized autobiographical experience.[3] With this assertion, Roeder replicates not only the view that women came late to the theater (with the exception of the actress), but also the assumption of women's affinity with the "interior spaces of the soul" (Gerhardt 1986, 8, 9). In social terms, that aesthetic domain corresponds to women's relegation to the private realm of the home. Conversely, the association of women with subjectivism traditionally produced the dichotomy between femininity and drama, which served to legitimize women's exclusion from the stage as a public space.

That same figure, women's alleged affinity with, and assignment to, the subjective sphere of soul and sensibility and lack of comprehension for larger social and historical processes, marks Marieluise Fleißer's essay "Women's Dramatic Sensibility," published in 1930. There she asserts that women lack the ability to structure, to construct, a drama in accordance with Aristotelian rules. However, Fleißer formulates an alternative dramaturgy characterized by "masterful condensation" of images and language and organized around "the mounting pressure of the atmosphere" rather than the linear development from exposition to resolution (Fleißer 1986, 16). Fleißer, whose work enjoyed a renaissance during the

1960s and 1970s, is, along with Else Lasker-Schüler, one of the few women playwrights mentioned in the context of Weimar culture. Fleißer's experience of the "frosty freedom" in urban Berlin and its male-dominated theater scene has been treated as paradigmatic of the problems encountered by women artists.[4] Although I would not discount the traumatic effect of Fleißer's encounter with the avant-garde on her work and on her life, the horror and the scandal of it have, until now, tended to overshadow her accomplishments as well as the range of dramatic strategies of other women in theater during that era (Führich 1992).

While some of the authors in this study, Fleißer, Lasker-Schüler, and Reinshagen, use the subjective perspective as a point of departure, as a lens for the perception and representation of the world, others, like Mann, Jelinek, or Steinwachs, cannot be subsumed under this category. Mann's cabaret addressed current, political events, and provided a platform for the emigrants' warning voices against the Nazi regime. Jelinek not only constructs large, historical mosaics in her plays but explicitly refutes the notion of a private, subjective space proper to the liberal, humanist individual. Likewise, Steinwachs rejects the theater of psychological realism with its focus on bourgeois domesticity and sides instead with the bold, allegorical figures of baroque drama. The critical conflation of subjectivism and femininity appears at best as a simplification and at worst as the reinscription of women's historical exclusion from the masculine, public spaces of the theater.

By tracing topical debates through women's texts, this study analyzes the theatrical representation of German history from a feminist perspective. The first section introduces a historical context that determined the conditions of cultural production not only during the Weimar period but also in a similar political constellation during the 1960s—namely the polarization between fascist, patriarchal state apparatuses and an increasingly powerless opposition. "Inroads" explores the similarities between these two historical moments, and discusses the emergence of the student movement and the formation of the New Left in relation to political activism and aesthetic practices of resistance. Reinshagen's socialist-feminist politics links a critique of oppression, which is indebted to Marxism, with a focus on women's concerns, experiences, and political practices. The plays of Jelinek and Steinwachs, two authors who (in contrast to Reinshagen) identify themselves as feminists, more explicitly address and participate in the debates around feminist aesthetics and strategies of resistance against patriarchal oppression, which took place within the women's movement and among feminist theorists and critics in academia. The second part thus performs a shift in historical referent and context from a focus on the New Left to a German feminist counterculture.

Fleißer and Lasker-Schüler and, in the second part on contemporary drama, Reinshagen and Jelinek, are at opposite poles of feminist theory—the politics of essentialism and poststructuralism. Although in feminist discourse *essentialism* often denotes the assumption of sex as innate and biological, I am using this term more loosely to describe a theoretical position that rests on *identity* as a stable concept, whether conceived of as organic or as social/cultural. Since both Fleißer and Reinshagen were trained in Marxist thought, both represent identity as a cultural construct; from that position, they describe the victimization of women in dominant, patriarchal culture (Fleißer), or envision an alternative, female counterculture (Reinshagen).

In contrast to Fleißer's and Reinshagen's tendency to represent the female German subject as a stable, historically and socially determined position, Lasker-Schüler's work prefigures the contemporary feminist politics of positionality. Her play *IchundIch* [IandI] shows a German-Jewish subject in crisis and highlights the instability and tenuousness of any social-political position in the context of exile. Jelinek, who approximates the poststructuralist position within contemporary feminist discourse, not only assumes the social constructedness of the subject but also debunks the category of identity with its liberal humanist baggage. Woman appears as a sign in discourse having accumulated historical meanings but making no claim to truth. Steinwachs, the subject of the last chapter, deploys the tactics of "operational essentialism" by navigating between the poles of essentialism and poststructuralism.[5] Her play *George Sand* performs feminist coalitions with various social-political groups and arguments and manages to carve out multiple, shifting positions of resistance.

While the debate around essentialism and poststructuralism, which has dominated feminist theory for the past decade, provides a recurrent reference point in my discussion of women's plays, the acceptance or contestation of "women's experience" as a stable category also informs formal considerations—specifically the question of realism versus nonmimetic styles of representation. The texts in this study register the tensions between realism and its abandonment in favor of liberating fantasies. The representation of utopia versus the analysis of oppression, and the attendant question of the usefulness of realism for a feminist aesthetics, is an important theme within this study.

Both Fleißer and Jelinek present closed ideological systems that offer no escape routes, whether exemplified by the suffocating hold of the Catholic small town on Fleißer's bright young women, or by a postmodern discourse that knows no outside. Resistance in these all-encompassing systems can only be thought of as self-destruction: either as the condemnation of the misfits, or as the unraveling of the binaries sustaining the master texts. Reinshagen's "subjective realism" is marked by cracks and leaps in the language. These fissures provide glimpses of the imagination and open up utopian possibilities while maintaining a focus on the realistic representation of material oppression. The work of Steinwachs and Lasker-Schüler makes use of the fantastic and grotesque to convey bold visions of a utopian realm in which differences and oppositions are peacefully and pleasurably reconciled.

The emphasis of the present book on written texts reflects in part the scarcity of feminist performance traditions in German theater, as well as my own geographical distance from the off-scene in the German cities where women performance artists can be found. Nevertheless, I thought it all the more important to sketch in feminist performance practices in the chapter on the Peppermill and trace them to contemporary acting and dance. Unfortunately, mainstream German theater now has little of a feminist acting tradition—unlike Britain, the United States, or France—and despite the emergence of women directors in the last decade, most of them have not professed an interest in or commitment to feminism through their work. Many plays by women deplore the lack of a feminist production context: Reinshagen's play *Die Clownin* [The She-Clown] ironically juxtaposes a classical heroine, the amazon Penthesilea who flaunts her power over men, with the actress who portrays her while being brutalized by an authoritarian male director. Reinshagen seems to advocate non-text-centered performance traditions, such as clowning, as less damaging to women—an argument that the history of women in cabaret proves to be true to some extent. Likewise, Jelinek's *Clara S.* calls attention to the immense energies devoted to compensatory, placating gestures demanded of women who trespass on the turf of high art and its institutions. Steinwachs' *George Sand* borrows from popular and subcultural performance traditions in order to revise the representation of women. The state-subsidized German theater and the constraints put on the few women directors who do make it into the upper echelons seem to bear out these playwrights' mistrust of the legitimate, bourgeois stage as a site of feminist intervention.

In order to ensure control over the presentation of their texts, some playwrights chose to perform and/or direct their own work (Steinwachs and Specht) or, with varying success, assisted in its production (Fleißer). Yet there is another sense in which the woman playwright turned player. Her attention to gender issues, her artistic departures from established models, and the very act of writing plays, were often interpreted as *social* transgressions against feminine modesty and virtue. The amount of popular attention generated by a woman's texts in some cases created such strong public pressure that the drama of her perceived gender deviance at times obscured her plays. The representation of aesthetic and social transgression as personal, psychological, or moral failure in the popular media almost destroyed some women playwrights; Fleißer's biography provides an apt example. Others, like Lasker-Schüler, achieved some measure of control over the meanings of their bodies, even reveling in a queer defiance of social roles. Likewise, Jelinek's image in the mass media and her public flaunting of femininity must be seen in relation to the outrage created by her writing. Her depiction as a psychologically dysfunctional yet sexually desirable woman plays out the trope of the "illness of modern woman" she so furiously deconstructs. Jelinek's example attests to the dominant culture's refusal to imagine or represent women as intellectually competent; it also points to the limits of masquerade as a source of empowerment. The author is made to act out the hegemonic notions her texts challenge: that woman can never transcend her physical existence through art and can only exist as a vessel for men's ideas. Jelinek's rigorous, philosophical attacks on the Western masters have a ricochet effect, rendering her body ever more central until it is turned into a centerfold. Lasker-Schüler's erotic personas, too, came up against ideological boundaries they could not exceed, forcing her to leave Germany.

While the foregoing cannot replace an analysis of feminist performance practices, it points to some performative aspects of women's theater that cannot be separated out from the study of their texts.

The revision of German theater history that feminist scholars have begun to chart is an interdisciplinary project, as the imbrication of aesthetic, philosophical, social, political, and historiographical discourses in the following chapters demonstrates. Opening up the discipline in scope and focus resituates performance practices within the emerging field of cultural studies in which the achievements and contributions of marginalized groups are no longer confined to the wings of the social theater.

In tracing oppositional social, political, and cultural practices, it has been important for me to insist on German identity and culture as sites of struggle and contestation. I believe that it has become all the more urgent to challenge hegemonic notions of what it means to be German since the fall of the wall has prompted a resurgence of nationalism and xenophobia as well as women's reconfinement to the so-called private tasks of housekeeping and childraising. The return to traditional gender roles and the curtailing of options for Germany's female population has been especially difficult for women from the erstwhile German Democratic Republic (GDR) who had benefited from the socialist state's doctrine of egalitarianism and the sociopolitical measures that implemented it.

There remains a large amount of work to be done for a critical revision of German theater history. When I finished my dissertation in 1991, scarcely any plays by East German women were available, and almost no scholarship on them.[6] Since then, my sense that GDR culture, including women's drama, is rapidly being forgotten, denigrated, and erased in the post–cold war era, has prompted me to conduct archival research and undertake a critical evaluation of women's theater and performance under socialism (Sieg 1994). One of the theses I advance is that with the diminishing public sphere as a space for political debate and controversy in the GDR during the 1970s, the discourse that allowed women (and other oppressed groups) to address gender issues and voice criticism was that of the so-called protocol, a quasi-documentary genre of personal testimonials that became charged with dissident meanings. The collective, subjective, anonymous voices gathered in these volumes instigated private dialogues on political questions. Women's development of this performative genre, however, made it impossible for me to incorporate that research into the present study, organized as it is around individual authors. One may hence view the format of this book as an effect of the German division and the different strategies of feminist intervention it produced.

This study, like many others in the area of women and theater, traces the multiple inscriptions of gender in the theatrical institution, dramatic conventions, and criticism, yet its emphasis on women playwrights continues to privilege the written text in its examination of the theater. Therefore, future studies are needed that would address non-scripted performance in order to include performance artists like Elisabeth Bohde, who works in Flensburg, clowns such as Carla Drops from Berlin, and those artists who fall in between the categories of performance art and *Tanztheater,* such as Brigitte Markland (also from Berlin). The work of feminist theater companies like ANNA KONDA (documented in *The Divided Home/Land*) also deserves critical attention.

Feminists will also have to account for the theater by Turks and Afro-Germans that, unlike these communities' considerable impact in other genres, is just emerging.[7] The traditions brought to the stage by these established ethnic minorities, together with the dramatic styles coming from recent immigrants from far-flung regions in Eastern Europe, will change culture and theater in Germany in ways that are, as yet, difficult to imagine.

PART 1

Fluchtwege—Lines of Flight

The title of this part compounds multiple critical approaches to the writing and performances of Marieluise Fleißer, Erika Mann, and Else Lasker-Schüler, which will be unraveled in the course of the three chapters. The reading of the texts follows the itineraries of their authors into exile and "inner emigration," providing the material ground for analysis. The biographies of these playwrights and the history of the Weimar Republic was marked not only by defamation, deprivation, and persecution but also by resistance and open opposition. Their literal banishment from Germany by Nazi authorities, however, has been replicated by dominant theater history. Exile constitutes the major trope in this section as it also signifies the exclusion of women from male literary production that defined itself as urban, avant-garde, and objectivist, thus relegating women to the margins, the provinces, the subjective. The itineraries of Fleißer and Lasker-Schüler register their movement toward the capital, the male bastion of exclusive dramatic and critical discourses neither of which they came to inhabit. As women playwrights, they were exiled to the interstices of dominant theater history, their writing located within and outside male dramatic models.

This precarious position necessitates a critical double focus that charts the dominant discourses of theater criticism and practice as the critical context for textual analysis while questioning their validity for the specific situation of women playwrights and measuring their distance from the dominant models. The work of Fleißer, Mann, and Lasker-Schüler, three of the most prominent women dramatists, falls outside many of the male-biased categories, as well as exceeds the historical and geographical boundaries that the term *Weimar Republic* implies. After the scandal that ensued over the Berlin production of *Pioniere in Ingolstadt*

[Pioneers in Ingolstadt], Fleißer was all but forgotten; literary historians situate her in the late 1960s to the early 1970s, when her plays were rediscovered. Mann emigrated with her cabaret shortly after it started and spent the following years touring other European countries and the United States. Likewise, Lasker-Schüler had to go into exile; her play *IandI*, written in Jerusalem in 1940–41, was first produced in 1979.

The lines of flight within the dramatic texts of Fleißer, Mann, and Lasker-Schüler also delineate the search for a utopia in which contradictions will be resolved—or the impossibility of reconciliation will be recognized. The three authors differed in their evaluation of the use of mimetic and nonmimetic models. While Fleißer insisted on a material analysis of gender relations in prefascist Germany that denied the possibility of an autonomous female subject, Lasker-Schüler abandoned the naturalist elements apparent in her earlier plays for utopian visions that allowed for the reconciliation of material contradictions in the realm of fantasy. Mann's cabaret called attention to the dangerous operation of mimetic art in and to fascism, while deriving its political effectiveness from the critical use of mimesis. The troupe's activist pleas to oppose Nazi ideology were linked to an appeal to refuse conventional narratives of victimization.

Finally, this part maps the lines of flight connecting dramatic models and strategies developed by Weimar women with contemporary feminist theatrical practices. Fleißer's appropriation of the traditional *Volksstück* [popular theater] as a vehicle for social criticism established a form that is still vital today, as Kerstin Specht's feminist plays *Lila* and *Das Glühend Männla* [The Little Red-Hot Man] demonstrate. The Peppermill deployed materialist performance traditions such as physical comedy and grotesque dance that inform contemporary women's theater and dance. Therese Giehse's acting style provides the link among the cabaret, the tradition of comic acting in the socialist productions of the Berliner Ensemble, and the West German political theater of the 1970s, while Lotte Goslar's dancing can be seen as a precursor to postmodern *Tanztheater*. Contemporary women's performance art in its exploration of a socially constructed subject-in-process, situated at the intersections of gender, sexuality, race, and class, can claim Lasker-Schüler as a precursor. That author created and performed personae whose identity was emphatically fictional, while maintaining a notion of material oppression.

Fleißer, Mann, and Lasker-Schüler based their art on the part of

their identities that was most oppressed, demonstrating a direct relationship among their experiences, their politics, and their aesthetics. As an
underprivileged woman from the provinces, Fleißer's critical *Volksstücke*
investigated the impact of material power relations on male-female relationships. The humanist socialist Erika Mann engaged in a persistent and
courageous critique of Nazi fascism through subversive humor. And the
Jewish bohemian Lasker-Schüler created complex representations of the
tensions within a subject who straddled Jewish-German, male-female,
and heterosexual-queer differences.

This part attempts to convey the diversity of political positions and
dramatic strategies that Weimar women developed vis-à-vis dominant
ideologies of gender, sexuality, race/ethnicity, and class, and to examine
the degree to which they carved out agency against oppressive systems—
patriarchal power, the threat of Nazi authorities, as well as intersections
between Christian, bourgeois, and heterosexist ideologies.

Since this study examines women's dramatic production in the
twentieth century, it is necessary to briefly lay out the cultural terrain
around the turn of this century, a time marked by massive socioeconomic changes resulting from industrialization that drastically affected
the social position of women and broadened their radius of action. In
1933, an article entitled "Women Dramatists: Women Conquer the
Stage," appeared in the magazine *Die Dame* (Kafka 1933). Although the
term *conquest* may seem exaggerated, the plays written by Anna
Gmeyner, Christa Winsloe, Lasker-Schüler, and Fleißer indicate an unprecedented incursion of women into the theatrical institution.[1] While
their predecessors are judged to be exceptions—isolated cases—these
playwrights were perceived as a group, a new generation of authors that
enriched the stage with a gender-specific perspective and brought
women's issues to the theater.

The change in gender roles and relations that occurred during the
last decades of the nineteenth century registered in a great number of
discourses. Feminists of various persuasions voiced their dissatisfaction
with the reproductive functions assigned to women that denied them any
intellectual or professional competence. Around the turn of the century,
women militantly demanded a place in cultural production.

Amalie von Ende's article "Nine Hundred Years of Women's
Drama" contested the traditional territorialism that claimed the drama
as a male preserve. With great enthusiasm, knowledge, and critical engagement, women playwrights attacked naturalism's favorite topos: the

bourgeois-patriarchal family. The concentration on this social and dramatic space, however, while providing the opportunity to represent
gender oppression and so potentially liberate women from their imprisonment in the private sphere, in fact resulted in a reinscription of their
exclusion from public agency. The production of their first plays at the
experimental theater clubs (*Vereinsbühnen*) and matinées, which had
served as the springboard for the male theatrical avant-garde around the
turn of the century, became an impasse for women playwrights. In
contrast to their male colleagues' productions, productions of women's
plays at the theater clubs did not provide avenues into the regular theaters. The resistance against women's work was shared by conservative
stages and their avant-garde counterparts alike. Otto Brahms's Freie
Bühne and Max Reinhardt's experimental theater Schall und Rauch,
with one exception each, remained exclusively male. The plays that
were performed generally conformed to gender stereotypes that challenged neither women's social role nor the dramatic traditions and
forms which inscribed this role in the dramatic structure. The traditional *Bürgerliches Trauerspiel* [bourgeois tragedy], dating from the eighteenth century, with its highly standardized characters, plot, and arsenal
of dramatic resolutions such as murder, suicide, and infanticide, repeti-
tively rehearsed the image of woman as victim, thus functioning as a
straitjacket as well as a target for the dramatic efforts of women playwrights. In her overview of turn-of-the-century women's plays,
Michaela Giesing measures the success of these texts to challenge traditional role models, by their distance from the bourgeois-tragedy format. Within this general trend, Fleißer, Mann, and Lasker-Schüler developed three specific forms.

Before proceeding to a more general discussion of women in the
cultural landscape of the 1920s, a few words are in order here about
Anna Gmeyner (born in 1902 in Austria), a playwright not included in
this part though well known and critically acclaimed in her time. As a
Jew and a playwright aligned with socialist politics and agitprop theater
in Berlin, Gmeyner's career was cut short by Hitler's coming to power.
In 1933, she emigrated first to France and later to England. She never
returned to Germany or Austria after the war. Gmeyner wrote three
plays: *Heer ohne Helden* ([Army without Heroes], 1930), *Zehn am
Fließband* ([Ten at the Assembly Line], 1930), and *Automatenbüfett* ([The
Automat], 1932). In exile, she turned to writing film scripts, novels, and
poetry. The author also moved away from the socialist politics with

which she had earlier aligned herself. While her first two plays, socially critical docudramas, were performed by socialist collectives in Berlin, *Automatenbüfett* is written as a *Volksstück*, pitting Eva, an outsider, against the philistine community of small-town patriarchs that frequent the restaurant. Eva is the catalyst who exposes the moral double standard prevailing in this milieu, a Lulu of sorts who serves as the projection screen for the town fathers' desires and the jealousy and hatred of their wives. The piece was produced by Moriz Seeler's experimental theater, which also staged Fleißer's first drama. Gmeyner's plays have strong female protagonists who steer the plot toward social change. However, Angelika Führich, the only critic so far who has dealt with Gmeyner's dramatic oeuvre, argues that the playwright only half-heartedly emancipates her heroines by letting them find happiness and dramatic closure in the private idyll of love relationships (Führich 1992, 93–94). In *Automat,* for instance, Eva leaves with Herr Adam, the now disinherited manager of the restaurant. Although somewhat ironized, these endings reassign the private as the heroine's proper domain, leaving political concerns and their solution to men. Nevertheless, *Automat* in particular is noteworthy, because it applies the *Volksstück* form to an urban (albeit small-town) setting, one that examines the processes of mechanization and commodification in regard to personal relationships and the way that gender operates within them.

Women in Weimar Theater

Fleißer, Mann, and Lasker-Schüler practiced their critiques in allegiance with social-political movements, from the antibourgeois Bohème and Marxism to liberalism. For the first time in German history, these diverse and oppositional voices had gained parliamentary representation and access to power.[2] The ideological landscape was populated by an immense range of political agendas with a large potential for conflict. The Weimar Republic emerged from a failed revolution. The German communists' attempt to install a government modeled after the Soviet Republic was thwarted not only by the still-intact monarchist administrative and military apparatuses but also by the social democrats who were in power during the first postwar years. The communist *Spartacist uprising* (1919) and the Munich *Putsch* attempt organized by the National Socialists (1923) marked the extremes of an ideological spectrum, the tensions between which were to intensify.

The changed socioeconomic conditions after the first World War, and the efforts and achievements of the first women's movement impacted gender roles and relations in the culture at large. Although neither Fleißer nor Lasker-Schüler called themselves feminists, their work cannot be evaluated apart from the changing place of women in society.

The economic boom during the Bismarck era—the so-called period of promoterism inaugurating the newly unified nation—and the fast-paced industrialization that preceded and accompanied World War I resulted in fundamental economic and social reorganization. The Weimar Republic was thus characterized by high capitalism, particularly in the industrial and urban centers, and the concurrent emergence of a new class, the petite bourgeoisie. This class, consisting of employees with low-qualified jobs, was located between the proletariat and the middle-classes and grew rapidly. The petite bourgeoisie, characterized by extreme conservatism and an "authoritarian personality" (Horkheimer 1968) became the object of literary and sociological analysis, particularly since it was this social group that would constitute the majority of the National Socialist voters.

These socioeconomic refigurations produced a high amount of paranoia, frustration, fear, and aggression, which was directed against social change (Buck 1985, 10). The popular imagination attached itself to representative images of change, like that of the "new woman." Decades of feminist struggle had brought access to the universities, suffrage, and the recognition of women in public positions, albeit mostly in "feminine" professions like nursing, teaching, secretarial, and social work. In 1908, Prussia was the last state to grant women the right to academic education and qualification; in 1919, women gained the right to vote and be elected. The percentage of women in the workforce rose only imperceptibly, but there was a significant redistribution of women within the professional market: While their employment in the agrarian and domestic sector decreased, they increasingly took over industrial work and found employment in the trades and the service sector (Frevert 1986, 171). This shift in work patterns registers, at the same time, a move from the provinces toward the cities. The drift to the cities that occurred during the 1920s can be observed in the biographies of two of the authors in this chapter: Fleißer left her native Ingolstadt (Bavaria) for Berlin just as the Westfalian Lasker-Schüler had done twenty years earlier. Erika Mann grew up in Munich, the cultural capital of southern Germany. The new visibility of women in the white-collar professions drew attention and disapproval. Fascination and fear of the new woman crystallized itself in the image of the flapper, the young urban woman who smoked, wore her hair short, earned her own money, traveled alone, and loved promiscuously.

The city, particularly Berlin, became associated with the new woman, with modern lifestyles, intellectual vitality, and avant-garde art. However, the flip side to the cultural capital of the Roaring Twenties with its coffee houses, theaters, bars, and dance halls was the increase in unemployment, poverty, suicide, crime, and abortion (Frevert 1986, 171). In Berlin, the gap between old and new, between radical ideas and traditional practices, was the widest. The city was also the place where the disparity between the claim of equality between the sexes and the reality of women's continued oppression and exclusion, particularly in the arts, became most clearly visible and exposed that claim as a myth. Fleißer described the dilemma between the theory and the practice of women's rights: "In terms of legislation, the so-called women's rights had long been obtained. But the real fight for the personal dignity of the creative woman had only just begun."[3]

It was the city that presented consumers with an urban, popular culture, in part imported from the United States, with the glitter of girl revues and nude dancing performed for the newly rich who had to spend their money quickly before it was devalued by the rising inflation. While the entertainment industry, including the cabaret, offered women easier access to cultural production than did the classical and bourgeois theater, it also commodified every gesture of defiance or rebellion. Women like Erika Mann, Anita Berber, and Valeska Gert performed political interventions in popular forms looked down upon by leftists who disregarded the possibility of contestation within mass culture, ceding the ground to the growing clout of fascists who did realize the importance of the entertainment industry for political control.

Women artists participated in the theater's redefinition of its own place within a rapidly changing society. Fleißer addressed such topical issues as unwanted pregnancy and abortion. The actor Erika Mann played the leading role in a lesbian drama, making lesbian love visible on stage. Lasker-Schüler explored marginalized sexualities and pitted visions of Christian-Jewish communion against growing anti-Semitism. In the recently founded republic, theater took over the task of political education and agitation. The founder of the Tribüne Theater in Berlin announced in its manifesto: "We have a standpoint and a direction. . . .

We will not play, but get serious" (Rühle 1967, 133). The rise of anti-illusionism and the involvement of the theater in topical political issues indicates the changing function of the medium, which is epitomized by the *Zeitstück* [topical play]. Performance practices moved away from the sole ownership by the middle strata of society; much experimental and topical theater was done in the service of the working classes. The Berlin theater scene became the nexus connecting the political, intellectual, and artistic avant-garde; a new consciousness of political imperatives resulted in an increased awareness and critique of representational forms and structures imbued with an ideological baggage many wanted to leave behind. Expressionists, bohemians, workers, and women were among those who abandoned and worked against the separation between art and life and redefined the theater as an arena in which new models of social relations could be tested.

Chapter 1

The Critical Volksstück: Marieluise Fleißer and Kerstin Specht

The life and work of Marieluise Fleißer, born in the Bavarian town of Ingolstadt one year into this century, registers in exemplary fashion the zigzag course of German history and reflects the promises and perils a woman writer encountered in a lifetime spent under four different regimes. She belonged to the first generation of German women to profit from the newly achieved educational opportunities in the waning days of the monarchy. The Weimar Republic saw her succeed as a playwright and taste the libertarian atmosphere of Munich and Berlin, where she associated with the theatrical avant-garde around the young Bertolt Brecht. The radically changed ideological climate of the Third Reich forced her into "inner emigration" and marriage, both of which almost destroyed her. The silence imposed by Nazi agencies outlasted that regime, however, and grew into forty years of oblivion. She only recovered in the 1960s, when her work was reclaimed by a new generation of political theater artists.

The bulk of this author's work was written in the 1920s and illustrates the conditions with which a gifted young woman from the provinces had to contend in order to assert herself as an artist at that time. Her writing, comprising five plays, one novel, and numerous short stories, progressively records the predicament of young girls, domestic workers, intellectuals, and independent women severely damaged by their social, sexual, and intellectual relations with men. Fleißer's writing, which always revolves around "something between men and women" (Rühle 1973, 349), painfully dramatizes the oppressiveness of "love" as an ideology that ensures women's continued allegiance to mysogynist structures and institutions in the personal sphere as well as the sphere of artistic production. In her writing, Fleißer throws the Berlin avant-garde of the 1920s into relief as a haven for social, political, and artistic experimentation and rebellion at the same time that it denied women access to a liberating space outside bourgeois institutions and conventions.

Fleißer is the only author in this study whose work has been accorded canonical status in the history of German theater.[1] Her choice of the *Volksstück* was informed by her personal experiences in her Bavarian hometown; her revision of that form—which Susan Cocalis terms the critical *Volksstück*—was determined by her perspective as an urban woman allying herself with Marxist politics (Cocalis 1992). Fleißer came in touch with the New Objectivist avant-garde around Brecht in Munich and Berlin during the early 1920s, and was associated with that circle until 1929. At the same time, her critical use of the *Volksstück*, a genre that affirmed "the normative social order [and its] patriarchal customs," was motivated by her female perspective and continuous focus on gender relations (Cocalis 1992, 107). The representation of the oppressive power relation between the sexes and the sympathetic concern with women's issues together make up Fleißer's female signature in her oeuvre. This commitment to a patriarchal critique complicated her relation to the Berlin avant-garde that privileged the analysis of capitalist oppression over other "peripheral" issues. Fleißer's plays *Fegefeuer in Ingolstadt* [Purgatory in Ingolstadt] and *Der Tiefseefisch* [The Deepseafish], which are discussed in this chapter, and *Pioneers in Ingolstadt* register both her alignment with and her distance from the avant-garde, which eventually played itself out so spectacularly in the scandal surrounding Brecht's *Pioneers* production, leading to her alienation from the Berlin theater scene and her return to her native Ingolstadt.

In the 1920s, before her rediscovery in the 1960s and 1970s, Fleißer's work fell between the cracks of hegemonic theater practice and what the avant-garde deemed "political" theater. On the one hand, her departure from the traditional *Volksstück* rendered her suspect in the eyes of conservative critics who furthermore viewed her deviance in social terms, namely as unladylike, lewd, and immoral. During the Third Reich, that suspicion, on the one hand, translated into the proscription to write and publish. On the other hand, her insistence on the category of subjective experience, on the "secondary contradiction" of gender, and on the "provincial" milieu prompted her artistic allies to dismiss her as less politically committed and as "backward" because she aligned with the outmoded aesthetics of expressionism. Her plays are informed by a

Marxist critique of oppression without subscribing to a party program as Brecht's aesthetic demanded.

Because Fleißer's life and work are singularly intertwined, I would like to situate the discussion of her writing in the context of her biography. Fleißer, one of five children, early on distinguished herself through her intelligence, creativity, and love of theater. After her graduation from high school, she enrolled as a student of theater in the newly established drama program at Munich University. She moved from her provincial hometown to Schwabing, a lively bohemian neighborhood in Munich, and became part of a clique of artists including Lion Feuchtwanger and the young Bertolt Brecht, both of whom became her intellectual mentors. In the move from Ingolstadt to Schwabing, the dutiful daughter Luise Maria first became the bohemian Lu and finally the writer Marieluise, a name which Feuchtwanger chose for her (Pfister 1981, 29–31). Her mentors' remaking of her persona, which this act of naming signals, extended to her writing as well. Fleißer's association with the avant-garde began with an act of censorship:

> He [Feuchtwanger] asks her to show him everything she has written so far [she reported later]. He calls it expressionism and rubbish. Nowadays one writes 'new objectivism.' Enraged, she burns everything she has written, including the essay 'Is Rebellion Sin?' of which she was so proud. (Rühle 1973, 413)

Her submission to the judgment of men she respected and their intervention in her work continued throughout her career; the producer of her first drama changed the title of the play to *Purgatory in Ingolstadt* and only asked for her permission after the fact. In 1930, Brecht prevented the publication and production of her play *Deepseafish,* which dealt with their relationship. As late as 1968, Rainer Werner Fassbinder adapted and retitled *Purgatory* without her approval. Only toward the end of her life did Fleißer defend her work against men's interference, insisting on her rights as an author.

In 1926, Brecht, who had moved to Berlin, persuaded Moriz Seeler, the director of the Junge Bühne, an experimental theater, to produce *Purgatory in Ingolstadt*. The play received rave reviews from both of the city's most influential, and continually feuding, theater critics. Fleißer's success earned her a contract with a publisher, and the pension she received guaranteed her a modest income as well as some degree of security. In the same year, Brecht proposed to Fleißer the material and form of a second drama that she was to write. The entire process of creating *Pioneers in Ingolstadt,* from the early writing stages to his production of the play in 1929, was overshadowed by her feelings of inadequacy and resistance. Although unfinished, the play went into rehearsal in Berlin with Brecht as the unacknowledged director. Fleißer felt violated by Brecht's disrespect for her style, her writing technique, and her authority. She suffered from writer's block and, terrified, refused to attend the final dress rehearsal. At opening night, she realized that Brecht had intentionally provoked a scandal; spectators appeared armed with whistles. When the young author appeared on stage to take a bow, she was traumatized by the audience's violent reaction. The police president ordered that several scenes be cut due to obscenity, causing an uproar around censorship issues. Fleißer felt she had been used as a pawn by two opposing political camps. However, the scandal surrounding *Pioneers* had consequences far beyond warring factions in Berlin. Her hometown turned against its notorious daughter; the mayor of Ingolstadt wrote an open letter in which he renounced Fleißer and her "smut," her father forbade her to set foot in his house again, and even her fiancé warned her to stay away. At this point, Brecht turned against Fleißer as well. She soon became involved with Hellmuth Draws-Tychsen, a journalist with literary aspirations and an eccentric to the far right. *Deepseafish,* the most autobiographical of her theater pieces, dramatizes her relationships to both Brecht (Chief Tütü) and Draws (Laurenz). She wrote it shortly after becoming engaged to Draws and read it in front of a small audience but refrained from publication or production at Brecht's behest. Fleißer's destructive four-year relationship with Draws not only drained her emotionally, exacerbated as it was by her alienation from her former friends and colleagues, it also ruined her financially.

Fleißer's return to her hometown in 1933 coincided with the end of the Weimar Republic and the beginning of fascist rule. It marked the end of her brief career as a noted writer, and the beginning of a forty-year period of silence, enforced both by the adverse political climate and her marriage to a tobacco merchant. In Ingolstadt, Fleißer was not merely ostracized, but physically threatened by a population embracing the Nazi party and ideology who had not forgotten the scandal that had soiled the name of their town. Moreover, as an educated woman and a leftist artist, the author was a target of harrassment in a climate of anti-intellectualism, red-baiting, and narrowly defined gender roles. Her books were among the first to be burned, and she was forbidden to publish more than six articles per year. In addition, her husband, contrary to his earlier promise, forced her to work in his business, leaving her little time to write. Fleißer went into inner emigration, working for six years on a historical drama entitled *Karl Stuart,* with no expectation of ever being published again. Her fear, despair, self-doubt, and exhaustion resulted in a nervous breakdown and hospitalization. After the war, which left the couple physically and financially depleted, Fleißer had difficulty re-orienting herself in the literary marketplace. At best she was ignored; at worst her writing style with its regional resonances and use of dialect was mistaken for the Nazis' populist literature (Rühle 1973, 423). Only after her husband's death did she slowly regain confidence as an artist, writing some of her strongest short stories about her years in Berlin, her inner emigration, and the hardships of the postwar era. In the late 1960s, when a new generation of theater artists rediscovered her work and claimed her as their inspiration, the almost seventy-year-old Fleißer be-gan to review and substantially revise her entire oeuvre. In 1972, the prestigeous Suhrkamp Press published her collected works. In the few years before her death in 1974, Fleißer finally achieved public recognition in the form of critical attention and many awards—one of which was the city of Ingolstadt's Prize for the Arts—and garnered from that, at last, a sense of satisfaction and pride in her accomplishments.

Purgatory in Ingolstadt

Purgatory tells the story of two adolescents, Olga Berotter and Roelle, who are outsiders in the closed Ingolstadt universe of strict rules, con-trolled by peer pressure, Catholic rituals, and small-town surveillance. The play is divided into six sections composed of short episodes arranged as a multifaceted collage of fear, paranoia, and hate rather than as a linear narrative. In the course of the play, Olga, who is pregnant by Peps, seeks help in vain, tries to have an abortion, and attempts suicide. In the end, she renounces all hopes to escape her narrow world where she is cruelly taunted by her peers, and prepares to beg her father to take her back. The ugly, sweating Roelle vacillates between pathos and pleading, ag-gression and submission, in his conflicting desires to assert an elevated distance from his tormentors and beg for their acceptance. When he fails to attain their friendship and that of Olga, he condemns himself to a state of eternal sin by ingesting a list of his confessions.

The outsider status of Roelle and Olga is the result of their transgression of conventional gender roles. Roelle does not comply with traditional notions of masculinity because he refuses to smoke and because he is hydrophobic. Christian, Olga's brother, derides him as a coward. Similarly, Olga is punished because her intelligence and education have set her apart and made her incompatible with her family and peers' expectations of her. Unlike her sister, Olga is exempted from household chores because she has to do homework. Her privileged position gives rise to the other girls' hate and envy; the men feel threatened by her. When the father of her unborn child leaves her for another girl, the couple sneer at Olga:

> HERMIONE: He really would be stuck with you.
> PEPS: She'd have her man get up first in the morning and grind the coffee quietly. [. . .]
> HERMIONE: That's what you get for being so smart.
>
> (Fleißer 1992, 39)

Olga's pregnancy and attempted abortion render her prey to her peers' aggressions, which they cloak in religious language. Her pregnancy, the sign of her sexual transgression that brands her as a loose woman and "damaged goods," delivers her to the aggressions of her peers. In their eyes and her own, it provides the justification for their taunting and tormenting her. Because Roelle has found out about her attempted abortion, he blackmails her into submission and tries to molest her. The group, in an effort to establish a universe of strict order as a hellish caricature of the bucolic world portrayed in the traditional *Volksstück*, uses religious values and rituals to mask the desire to punish.

Purgatory's treatment of women's issues such as unwanted pregnancy and abortion intervened in hegemonic discourses on women's social role and sexuality. Women's right to control their own reproductive functions was prohibited by section 218 of the penal code, which, though modified, is still in effect and under contestation today. The decline in the birthrate during the 1920s, which triggered allegations of a "birth strike," and high abortion statistics contributed to conservative fears in regard to a woman's role. *Purgatory* examines abortion and reproductive rights as part of a general social analysis rather than merely as a secondary contradiction, and thus participated in a reevaluation of women's issues within a political critique.

Fleißer's Ingolstadt is marked by the absence of patriarchal power structures such as "intact" families headed by authoritarian father figures or maternal role models (Cocalis 1982, 64, 65). Cocalis speaks of "decalcomanias on the city-walls of Ingolstadt" (Cocalis 1979, 68), the lingering images of a regime of repression no longer bolstered and enforced by social agencies. The Marxist philosopher Ernst Bloch coined the term *Ungleichzeitigkeit* [discontinuity] to describe the coexistence of modern and premodern elements in the culture, which he deemed typical of German history.[2] Bloch's analysis of this phenomenon calls attention to the self-perpetuating function of the superstructure that not only mystifies the operative principles of the material base but also masks a significant change of its mechanism.[3] The notion of discontinuity, which he developed in 1932, also stressed the necessity for a counterhegemonic critique to address the production and dissemination of power on the level of ideology instead of focusing solely on economic structures. Whereas Bloch was concerned with economic shifts, Fleißer focused on changes in the patriarchal system.

In Fleißer's writing, Ingolstadt serves as a model for a community on the threshold of modernity where the old authority mechanisms preserved by the nuclear family have largely vanished but linger on in the subjective expectations and everyday behavior of the characters. Berotter's weakness and impotence highlight the power hierarchies among the teenagers themselves, whose group dynamics, revolving around the establishment of norms of behavior, replicate the operation of the now defunct agencies of repression on the individual, psychological level. The absence of traditional patriarchal figures, be they strong fathers, fertile mothers, or prosperous employers, expands the frame of Fleißer's "naive gaze" to include not merely the material base of an oppressive system—the object of analysis for a Marxist dramaturgy—but also its subjective components that reproduce heterosexual ideology. In Fleißer's world, the patriarchy is kept in place not by the vitality of its institutions but by the emotional investment of those who participate in it, including its most abject victims. The poor girls, ostracized adolescents, and battered young women are riveted to their exploitative lovers, employers, collaborators, and tormentors from whom they expect solidarity, protection, and "mercy."

Yet it is not merely the brittleness of a crumbling order in transition to the industrial age that denies the female protagonists the reward for their compliance and submission, a reward they might formerly or otherwise have attained. Rather, there is a sadomasochistic dynamic at the heart of gender relations that emerges more and more succinctly with the advancing age and increasing urbanization of Fleißer's protagonists. In *Purgatory,* Olga rejects Roelle precisely because he alone shows sympathy instead of the violence she believes necessary in a man who could offer her protection. What she finds attractive in Peps, the father of her unborn child, is the brutality with which he takes whatever he needs and that is inevitably turned against her.

Where authority structures of the family have collapsed, the group has taken over the function of maintaining collective discourses of power and repression in order to guarantee conformity. Fleißer has referred to this dynamic as "the law of the pack" (Rühle 1973, 364). It is characterized by a high degree of aggression against outsiders who simultaneously threaten the established order and perpetuate it as scapegoats.

The pack's power resides in the outsiders' desire to be part of it. Thus, norms and values are kept in place not only by the group but also by those who are excluded from it. By accepting the right of the group to torture misfits, Roelle and Olga forfeit the possibility to rebel against pack terror. However, both waver in their relationship toward the group. The boy, humiliated by the other teenagers' rejection and by his mother's grotesque overprotectiveness, attempts to glorify his difference from his peers by claiming to be "a real saint" because angels speak to him (42). His efforts fail; he cannot convince his audience of his divine power and therefore is unable to persuade them of his superiority. Yet, even in the moment of his deepest shame, Roelle possesses two avenues out of his abjection. On the one hand, he can still pass on the humiliation he experiences to an even weaker creature, and the dog he reportedly tortured as well as the vulnerable Olga offer him the opportunity to "have power for once" (36). On the other hand, Roelle is the prototype of Fleißer's heroes in that he accepts his state of damnation by literally eating a list of his sins—thereby claiming evil through a deliberate and defiant gesture. Through this action, Roelle, the first of Fleißer's "fallen angels," gains a new freedom—his pride is able to cancel out his dependency and fear.[4]

Olga, who inhabits the lowest place in the social hierarchy, can neither pass on the pressure she receives from above nor embrace her state of sin as a possibility of liberation. Pregnant and alone after failed attempts at abortion and suicide, she has incurred the community's wrath: the pack derides her, and her father banishes her from his home.

She hesitates between her desire to belong and her wish for freedom, torn between her masochistic love for Peps, the "leader of the pack," and her fascination with the ostracized Roelle. She is faced with the choice of either submitting to the community or to the outcast; she never considers the option of leaving and asserting her independence, though she entertains fantasies of freedom and escape. Olga chooses to return to the fold. But acceptance must be bought at a high price: She demonstrates her repentance by confessing her sins to her father and she proves her conformity by renouncing her only ally, Roelle. Without him to assure her of a place outside community protection, she abdicates all hopes of liberation or escape.

Olga admires Roelle because he allows her to experience rebellion—and pride—vicariously. When he is most defiant, she shows her support for him and calls him "my Roelle" (54). Any profession of weakness, however, prompts her disavowal of him as a way to realign herself with the group. His attitude toward her becomes a gauge of his independence, highlighting the trap Olga creates for herself: Only if he ignores her can she place herself under his protection; any indication of his need or desire for her proves his unworthiness in her eyes. When Roelle asks her, "Who or what am I to you?" she replies: "That shouldn't matter to you" (45). By insisting on her own erasure, Olga is complicit with producing masculinity as autonomy and femininity as dependence. Again and again, Olga and Roelle attempt to cast each other in roles neither is willing to enact: Roelle, who needs Olga's recognition to prove his manhood, lacks the independence she requires to perform as a girl. Ultimately, each tries to stage their own death as a performance of gender: Roelle wants to die as a martyr, Olga as the fallen woman. Neither can persuade the other to assist in their respective fantasies. Their conflicting desires remain fixated on each other in a stalemated struggle: "On a heap of revulsion we have mounted two faces so that they shall stare at each other for all eternity" (65). Fleißer represents this stall in biblical terms of purgatory as the place where the gender struggle occurs most fiercely and remains eternally unresolved.

The language of religion operates in conjunction with the repressive, petit-bourgeois mechanisms in a small town where everyone and everything is under close surveillance. Olga's statement "I can't bend my little finger without being watched from heaven" (54) displaces community control onto the metaphysical category of "heaven," which mystifies power relations and fosters a fatalistic stance. The slippage from small-town control mechanisms to religious discourse reveals how both conspire in order to keep authority structures intact. The community and its laws appear immutable and inescapable to Olga: "Oh, that we fall every day into a world of viciousness, just as we fell into our bodies, and now we're stuck with them," Olga exclaims (61). Her transgression of social norms signified by her swollen belly locks her in the traditional narrative of the fallen woman who, like Friedrich Hebbel's classic heroine Maria Magdalena, must drown herself so as to restore the normative heterosexual order (Case 1992, 26, 27). Likewise, she is incapable of leaving the purgatory in Ingolstadt: Although it is her social isolation that prompts her wish to escape to America, she cannot imagine emigrating alone. She is stuck with her marked body in a world that condemns her for it.

Accordingly, any rejection of the social order is conceptualized in the religious term of blasphemy. "I am the devil," Roelle boasts, claiming hell as a counterspace vis-à-vis the bourgeois world (heaven), a domain to which Fleißer's female protagonists have no access. Hell and purgatory thus designate gender-specific social sites that illustrate the difference of agency available to male and female outcasts. Pfister points to the complicated location of a position simultaneously outside of and within hegemonic structures, which is occupied by Fleißer's male outsiders and "fallen angels," but remains closed to women:

> Like Satan who was promoted to Prince of Hell, while Eva's sin—namely her insubordination against God—was punished with her subordination to man, the male rebel in a patriarchal world can achieve a new, autonomous, "free" position, while the female rebel is not only persecuted but also, and especially, held contemptible. (Pfister 1981, 49)

For a woman, there is no place outside patriarchal ideology. Barred from hell, she is condemned to the intermediate space of purgatory.

Unlike expressionist drama, which frequently uses Christian imagery in order to imbue its antisocial heroes with mystic powers,[5] Fleißer highlights the social functions of religious discourse to rehearse the control of individuals' behavior and thought (confession) and orchestrate their compliance with social norms in public rituals (prayer, penance), to authorize or deny positions of resistance to the social order according to gender, and to initiate narratives such as the prostitute's damnation or the martyr's validation, which assign male and female meanings to death. The author thereby demystifies the church as mere administrator of a divine will and exposes its active production of gendered power relations that the institution represents as God-given and therefore unchangeable by human beings.[6]

Fleißer's focus on the individual and gender-specific production of conformity and deviance shifts the material analysis of power relations from the level of institutions to the level of subjectivity. It prefigured the concept of the "authoritarian mentality,"[7] and called attention to the misogyny lodged in protofascist attitudes and behaviors. *Purgatory* responded to a gap in contemporaneous Marxist theories, namely their inability to account for the Nazi rise to power on individual, domestic, and psychological levels, because they privileged macrosocial processes and class conflict. After the premiere of the play in 1926, Herbert Jhering wrote that "one understands Hitler and Kahr" and stressed the topicality of this play, seemingly so remote from the urban centers where the Nazis staged their political spectacles (Rühle 1973, 41). In a program note for the 1972 production in Frankfurt, Fleißer commented on this aspect of *Purgatory:* It represents an

> unredeemed society that kicks in order not to be kicked itself. This condition of denied redemption produces the obsessive longing for a Savior, which later made possible a fake savior and political pied piper. (Rühle 1973, 364)

Prefiguring more recent feminist analyses of fascism, Fleißer identified the hierarchical organization of society that was perfected by the Nazis, as patriarchal, homosocial, and misogynist.[8] In her work, gender became a primary category within a political critique previously blind to its patriarchal bias. At the same time, her departure from the epic dramaturgy developed by Piscator and Brecht empowered the latter to impose a "politically correct" viewpoint on Fleißer's writing. The terms of her exclusion from hegemonic as well as avant-garde theater practices became legible in the scandal surrounding Brecht's production of *Pioneers.* Despite the differing critical reception of each play—one mostly positive, the other overwhelmingly negative—the uproar around *Pioneers* was organized around categories that *Purgatory* had already set up.

The reaction that *Pioneers* provoked was largely due to the heating up of the political climate at the end of the republic. John Willett's chronicle of art in the Weimar Republic, which traces the emerging discourse of New Objectivism (or "the New Sobriety," as he terms it),[9] marks 1929 as a turning point in the politics and organization of the avant-garde. The economic crunch following the stock-market crash, along with the renewed polarization of the political spectrum, precipitated the emergence of a militant counterculture outside main-stream institutions. In this situation, experienced as a political reinvigo-ration by many leftists, Fleißer's play became a vehicle of attack on the bourgeois order that propelled its author into isolation. Her double marginalization—in the social order that Ingolstadt represents, and in the avant-garde world of outsiders—went beyond the personally tragic. It exemplifies the conditions of women's exclusion from the arena of cultural production during that time.

In order to evaluate the manner in which critical and theatrical practices conspired to effectively exclude women, it is necessary to map out the intersection of the dominant discourses on style (expressionism, New Objectivism, and the critical *Volksstück*) with the politics of loca-tion (the urban avant-garde and southern province) as well as examine the congregation of these discourses around gender.

Inge Stephan examines how the association of avant-garde and ur-banity functioned to exclude women from the vanguard of the literary and theatrical scene in Berlin; the dominance of the Brecht circle rele-gated them to the margins and therefore provincialism. Berlin became the battleground for the patricidal poetics of the young iconoclasts:

> On this literary battle-ground, the daughters have no place. They stand at the margins of the drama which plays itself out between fathers and sons and which ends with the gradual disappearance of the fathers. Even the work of those few women authors who are included in the avant-garde operates on different premises; it cannot be assimilated to the son's aesthetic revolution. (Stephan 1987, 117)

Excluded from the all-male cast of this oedipal drama, Fleißer's critical *Volksstücke,* with their small-town setting, regional dialect, and a cast of brutal, unenlightened characters, signaled the playwright's distance from the urban theater scene. Fleißer's plays used Ingolstadt as a condensed model of material and ideological mechanisms that—as *Deepseafish* dem-onstrates—urban capitalism had by no means replaced. Brecht's produc-tion, however, reinforced a reading of Ingolstadt as the epitome of "petit-bourgeois narrowness and stupidity, [and] bigoted mores" and offered it up as a target of ridicule for a "superior" Berlin audience (Brecht quoted in Stephan 1987, 126). It was the condescending portrayal of their town as a petit-bourgeois zoo to which the Ingolstadt city fathers objected in Pioneers. Fleißer's critique of the patriarchy and attention to women's issues, which had produced the critical Volksstück, enabled the critical conflation of gender with provincialism and contributed to "woman's exclusion from the intellectual and artistic discourse of the men, and her relegation to the periphery" (Stephan 1987, 116). Fleißer's work was caught between these charged categories, and her biography bore the brunt of the energies vested in them.

Fleißer's Volksstücke pivoted around the hotly contested term of the Volk [the people], which was bifurcated by the urban-regional dichotomy and which registered the ideological split that ran through the public arena and Fleißer's personal life. During the Weimar Republic, Volk and Volkstümlichkeit [populism] acquired two widely divergent meanings as they were claimed by opposing ideological camps. The Nazis appropriated the term Volkstümlichkeit as an aesthetic criterion evoking mythical authenticity and an essentialist racist and nationalist concept of the Volk as Aryan Germans. The Marxists, whose notion of Volk was synonymous with the working class, developed a Volkstheater designed to raise the proletariat's class consciousness and support the emergence of a vanguard party. As such, it valorized the industrialized urban centers, an environment it privileged over the ideological "backwardness" in the provinces.

Fleißer's popular idiom fell outside the purported dichotomy between the city as the site of radical politics and avant-garde literature and the provinces as the locus of social and political stagnation. It equally eschewed the fascist evaluation of this polarity that denounced metropolitan life as a Babylon, corrupt and degrading, and viewed the countryside as a well of wholesome communality with nature, the residence of innocent people untouched by ideology—an attitude that spawned the Blut und Boden literature of the Third Reich. Fleißer's Ingolstadt represented a regionalism that prohibited any nostalgia for a better past, as the Nazis propagated it. Ironically, her work was shunned in postwar West German theater because it was associated with fascist Volkstheater, prolonging the twelve years of enforced silence even as it reversed the reasoning.

Whereas Fleißer's brutal revision of the pastoral drama prompted her persecution by Nazi authorities on political grounds, her socialist allies objected to it because they deemed her dramaturgy incapable of actively promoting antifascism. From the epic theater's point of view, Fleißer's closed systems, in which the possibility of social change appears only in its negation, appeared "apolitical." Although her drama, as well as Brecht's, abandoned Aristotelian principles and fostered audience opposition to oppressive systems—be they class or gender—each differed considerably in the methods they deployed to reach their goals. In her self-deprecating essay, "Women's Dramatic Sensibility," written in 1930, Fleißer remarks on the lack of a "singular, clearly-drawn [*sic*] line" in women's plays (Fleißer 1986, 16). Rather than striving for a "well-balanced structure" culminating in a cathartic moment, women's writing follows, instead, the dynamic of "condensation" and "accumulation," withholding the emotional release Aristotelian rules demanded. Fleißer notes: "[T]he unification of the scenes... only occurs in the subconscious through the mounting pressure of the atmosphere" (Fleißer 1986, 16). The dramaturgical principle she describes in reference to writing applies as well to the reception process. Here is where she differed markedly from Brecht's dialectic theater, which addressed the spectator's *analytical* faculties and advocated critical distance to complex social mechanisms in order to instigate change. Fleißer's plays, in contrast, rely on audience empathy with the protagonists' rising anxiety and frustration to methodically build *emotional* pressure. Mirroring the entrapment of her heroines in patriarchal Ingolstadt, Fleißer's plays, unlike Brecht's, lack a metalevel from which to reflect on women's oppression. They do not allow for a removed vantage point from which to formulate a counterdiscourse. Nevertheless, Donna Hoffmeister argues, such a dramaturgy contains a critical, feminist potential: It evokes a powerful, emotional *and political* response by provoking the spectator to ask "the largest possible questions about the historical and ongoing damage to women" (Hoffmeister 1983, 406).

As *Pioneers* demonstrates, Brecht understood the gender dynamic that Fleißer portrayed to be a mere metaphor for the property relations between the classes. The Marxist avant-garde remained blind to the differences between the two and failed to see that its own solutions to capitalist oppression built gender bias right into epic dramaturgy. Fleißer's lack of a clearly drawn party line was perceived as a shortcoming by her associates who viewed the theater as a weapon in class struggle, proposing an alliance between avant-garde drama and a vanguard party. The epic theater's dialectic, which guides the spectator toward a synthesis in terms of revolutionary attitudes and actions outside the theater, assumed a counterhegemonic social space sustained by a vital, political movement—a space not accessible to an isolated writer's dramatizing women's oppression and unsustained by a feminist agenda or organization.

In their refusal to facilitate the resolution of contradictions shown on stage, Fleißer's critical *Volksstücke* lacked the key ingredient of political theater as Brecht defined it. In an article written in 1938, entitled "The Popular and the Realistic," Brecht explained: "'Popular' means . . . representing the most progressive section of the people in such a way that it can take over the leadership . . . [and] handing on the achievements of the section now leading to the section of the people that is struggling for the lead" (Brecht 1964, 108). *Purgatory* does not offer a spectatorial position from which the play's protagonists could appear as "progressive," much less empower Olga and Roelle to challenge or change the ideological fabric of Ingolstadt. In their inability to "educate" the audience toward a proletarian (or feminist) revolution, Fleißer's texts register their distance from a social movement like the one that supports the Brechtian project.

Fleißer's attention to subjective processes in her work aligned her with expressionism, a style that emerged in German art, literature, and theater around 1905 and was waning by 1923, the time Willett pinpoints as the beginning of New Objectivism. Both artistic movements attacked bourgeois aestheticism and exploded conventional forms. However, New Objectivist theater, the prominent proponents of which were Brecht and Piscator, rejected expressionism because, they argued, the diffusely anarchic political agency it constructed was too easily appropriated by a fascist rhetoric.[10] Expressionism centered around a deeply asocial subjectivity that promised to tear apart the social fabric. This will to violent change was exemplified by the recurring patricide motif that pits rebelling sons against overbearing, authoritarian fathers. Expressionism's mystical iconography and dream structure appealed to the emotions, scorning reason and the intellect, faculties that were associated with the "fathers'" petty bourgeois, capitalist mentality. In contradistinction to expressionism, Brecht's plays and theoretical articles, Piscator's experiments, and Jessner's innovative stage practices proposed a "scientific dramaturgy" and espoused a presentational mode that abandoned emotion and empathy in favor of distance and analysis (Rühle 1967, 1:27).

Fleißer's subjective, nonlinear dramaturgy, which she attributed to "women's dramatic sensibility," situated her in close proximity to expressionist theater, although that style proved problematic for a playwright concerned with women's oppression. Oskar Kokoschka's play *Murderer the Woman's Hope,* which typifies the expressionist discourse on gender, pits its messianic hero against a Lilith-like female antagonist, and ties agency to virility (Sokel 1963). The subjectivity that rends the social fabric purports to proceed from a space outside ideology; its mythical (Germanic) and archetypal (male, Aryan) representation, however, reveals its contiguity to nationalist, misogynist, and racist projects. Fleißer's essay "Is Rebellion Sin?" which she burned at the behest of Feuchtwanger because he thought it expressionist and outmoded, might have illuminated the dilemma expressionism presented for a woman writer. As it is, the destruction of that piece paradoxically enacted the masochism of Fleißer's embrace of New Objectivism's radical politics. By acquiring a new voice that promised liberation, she confirmed her own personal submission and political-artistic marginalization.

Fleißer's position between the antagonistic schools of expressionism and New Objectivism is not merely a case of stylistic ambiguity; it had material consequences, which bring to the foreground the ownership of artistic discourses by an elite of male critics and theater practitioners. While to some extent her deviation from dominant models provided the rationale for forty years of exclusion from theater history (which was to last until the late 1960s), the legendary scandal that alienated her from the Brecht circle as well as from her Bavarian hometown is tied to her gender more than to any other perceived transgression. After the opening of her first play, *Purgatory,* liberals applauded her as a new, original talent, only to suspect: "Fleißer is talented and naturalistic—if she exists . . . and if she is not a pseudonym for Brecht" (Rühle 1973, 37). Franz Servaes' review of *Pioneers* typifies the reactions of many conservative critics:

> This was the last thing we needed! What German woman of radical observation has ever before combined sexual explicitness with the denigration of national traits to a lovely bouquet? We finally found her in Marieluise Fleißer from Ingolstadt in Bavaria! No value or

custom is holy to this corrupt womanly spirit. She pours her ma-
nure into everything, deluding herself into thinking that she serves
intellectual liberation. Where the lowliest man would still feel a
trace of shame and respect, there is now a woman who sheds the
last regard for moral propriety! (Rühle 1973, 77)

The critics' defamation of Fleißer, and her banishment from Berlin,
which preceded her actual "inner emigration" in 1935, configured her
artistic deviation as a gender transgression compounded with more formal considerations. Finally, her recuperation in connection with the male
Volksstück authors of the 1960s is tied to the metaphorical "taming" of
that "corrupt womanly spirit." Only after Fleißer, who incidentally
never had children, could be safely contained in a reproductive metaphor—she was frequently referred to as the "mother" of Kroetz, Sperr,
and Fassbinder—did she become acceptable to the theatrical institution
that presented her with a "renaissance" in the 1960s.

The Deepseafish

The genre through which Fleißer articulated the difficulties she encountered in the metropolitan environment of Berlin was the realistic domestic drama. In many ways, *Deepseafish* is a sequel to *Purgatory,* in that it
picks up many of the themes Fleißer had set up in the earlier play: it
investigates the possibility of resistance for a woman who is situated
outside the prevailing social order—but here, the protagonist is a mature
woman who identifies as an artist. Again, the woman is placed between
two men—but this time, both of them are designated as outcasts. As
before, these men represent opposing ideological positions—however,
their differences are informed by urban politics, specifically the split
between ultraright and communist factions. *Deepseafish*'s most
significant break with previous models and solutions lies in its ending:
for the first and only time in Fleißer's oeuvre, the female protagonist
extricates herself from her sexual and emotional dependency on male
mentors and asserts the possibility of independence. The play constructs
a narrative of emancipation from dominant gender ideology that leads
Gesine, Fleißer's most autobiographical heroine, to refute the efforts of
the Group 28 headed by Chief Tütü (Brecht) and leave her destructive
relationship with Laurenz, a character based on Draws-Tychsen,
Fleißer's fiancé from 1929 to 1935.

Deepseafish opens with a domestic quarrel between the two main characters, Laurenz and Gesine, which shows him asserting his financial and psychological dominance over her, while she struggles in vain to stand up to him and his fits of temper. Their battle is embedded in the larger rivalry between competing literary camps. Gesine, a well-known and fairly successful writer, has severed her personal ties to the influential Tütü. As a result of that break, which is exacerbated by her engagement to Tütü's political enemy, she has difficulty getting published and supporting both herself and Laurenz, who shamelessly exploits her. Laurenz's connections in the publishing business are similarly jeopardized by their romance. Hütchen, the editor of a newspaper formerly supporting the journalist's work and political views, refuses to continue printing either Laurenz's articles or those of Gesine because Gesine's previous work has rendered her suspect. A public reading by Gesine, which Laurenz has organized, is sabotaged when unknown men release white mice in the auditorium and the event ends in chaos. Laurenz's friends, who report the incident to him, further inform him that the scandal had been set up. The event recalls Fleißer's personal trauma when they mention that audience members had been instructed to bring their house keys with them in order to whistle their disapproval. It later turns out that the Tütü organization had paid members of Laurenz's own circle of friends to deliver the mice.

Shortly after, Tütü invites Laurenz to his headquarters, and offers to launch his writing career with the resources of Group 28, which Laurenz calls a "literary factory" (Fleißer 1972, 1:344). "I prefer to call it a collective," replies Tütü, but the euphemism fails to appeal to his opponent who prefers the loneliness of the maverick to any popularity an organized group could offer.

The last act illustrates the increasing peril in which Gesine finds herself after the Party has come to power. She is harrassed in the street as well as at home, since Laurenz is unwilling to extend his support to her now that she is no longer the breadwinner. When he asks her to write what the Nazi newspaper would print, Gesine realizes that he demands her artistic annihilation in order to secure his own autonomy. He explains his outlook to her: "I will never amount to anything with them. I will never join the Party. But that will have consequences. I will never have much to live on. I cannot pull someone along who doesn't have anything herself" (355). At this, she decides to leave him.

Whereas in *Purgatory* no new system of values has come to replace the crumbling premodern structure, *Deepseafish* shows both the quasi-feudal practice of heterosexuality by Gesine and Laurenz and the modern transformation of gender roles in Tütü's literary "collective." Gesine is not only caught between the two warring camps but also marginalized and exploited within both. The play is further cleaved by the end of the Weimar Republic and Hitler's assumption of power, which effects a radical shift of power in the intimate relations between Laurenz and Gesine. The play stresses the intertwining of the political and the personal, the social and the sexual. While the public sphere in *Purgatory* was predominantly defined through the discourse of religion, *Deepseafish* portrays the literary marketplace and urban politics as the public arenas in which the woman writer must compete and survive.

Olga's dream that self-realization might be possible far away from Ingolstadt is shown to be a delusion in *Deepseafish*. While the young girl is at least permitted freedom of movement within the city walls, the downwardly mobile Gesine is imprisoned in a succession of furnished rooms. The only times she leaves the house, she is accompanied by her fiancé's friends who also bring her back. The successful writer seems to be under surveillance by Laurenz's associates who jealously guard her against the influence of Tütü's organization. Moreover, neighbors in her apartment building complain about the noise and comment condescendingly on the company she keeps. She is harrassed by a landlady who confiscates the key to her closet in order to bully her into paying rent. In addition, Gesine is harangued by a Nazi in the street. Life in a metropolis awards the woman writer neither privacy nor anonymity but rather multiplies the agencies of control and observation.

The concurrence of Romantic and modern modes of urban literary production offer Gesine two alternative identities as a woman artist, both of which she rejects. Neither allows her to pursue her own aspirations or reap the reward of her own work; both cast her as property and helpmate of a male artist. It is no coincidence, therefore, that the third act of *Deepseafish*, which dramatizes these alternatives, is the only one from which Gesine is absent. The confrontation between Tütü and Laurenz highlights the differences between the Romantic notion of the artist as an autonomous individual and (misrecognized) genius and the modern literary worker as a manipulator of public opinions and emotions. The antagonism between the two men is conceptualized primarily in terms of gender identities and behaviors; Laurenz's subjugation of one woman is contrasted with Tütü's quasi-industrial exploitation of his "Squadron

B." Apart from the number of women involved, the attitudes of both men are remarkably similar.

Where Laurenz orders Gesine to surrender ("You shall no longer be yourself. I want to absorb you," [294]) until she has nothing left to give, Tütü proceeds according to the same principle but on a larger scale: "They are used up doing our preparatory work as volunteers, without pay. Of course, this only works for a limited time. Then they revolt and leave us soon after" (343). While Laurenz's rhetoric of love as a never-ending emotional bond obscures his material interest in Gesine, Tütü mystifies the commercial usefulness of Squadron B as an "educational experience" for them (343). However, as soon as Gesine becomes unable to support Laurenz and his family, she becomes a liability to him. Tütü, in contrast, frankly acknowledges the exchangeability and expendability of Squadron B individuals.

The resemblance between the two men even extends to their temperaments. Both terrorize the women around them with random and violent fits of rage that reinforce their helpmates' subservience and the wish to always anticipate the men's every mood, constantly placating them in an effort to avoid their wrath. The men's sadism and unpredictability cast women as masochists. Rather than just suffering Laurenz's anger, Gesine is also fascinated with it. It proves to her his strength, which she needs as reassurance against a hostile world.

> LAURENZ: I am more than you.
> GESINE: That's why I suffer through the craziest moments. That's the only reason. Because I want to believe it.
>
> (300)

In a society that measures men by their capacity to subjugate women, women will condone their violence against them and interpret their own suffering as proof of their femininity and a source of vicarious self-worth (Kord 1989, 64).

Fleißer's comparison of Brecht and Draws-Tychsen in terms of gendered behavior cuts across the political oppositions that haunted her life and shaped the reception of her work. Their similarly misogynist behavior toward their female "collaborators" eschews the ideological rifts between fascism and socialism, feudalism and modernity. For Fleißer, as for Gesine, the urban avant-garde proved to be an "educational experi-

ence," as Tütü puts it. Unlike their male counterparts, the rebels and
artists who gain self-realization, independence, and even a position of
superiority outside the bourgeois order, Fleißer's female outcasts find
only variations on the patriarchal theme even when they leave the narrow confines of the petit-bourgeois family. In fact, the purgatorial relationship of the heterosexual couple may be preferable to the large-scale,
depersonalized exploitation to which the modern woman artist must
submit. "The Fall from Grace—leaving the bourgeois order—can lead
to freedom only for the men, for women it leads into a new subordination," Eva Pfister notes (Pfister 1981, 42). The freedom they are seeking
"has something murderous about it," as the heroine of "Avantgarde"
reports (Fleißer 1972, 3:147). Confronted with the choice of submitting
to an oppressive bourgeois order or to their equally misogynist male
allies, they risk losing themselves and their own aspirations. "[W]omen
either abandon their male allies and try to regain admission into society,
or they are subsumed by their fellow outcasts to the point of non-
existence," concludes Susanne Kord in a perceptive essay on Fleißer's
early dramas (Kord 1989, 59). Even in her most fervent wish to escape
from Ingolstadt, Olga cannot imagine leaving alone—"I am looking for
some who'll emigrate to America with me" (Fleißer 1992, 67)—and
decides instead to repent and return to her father's home.

The only instance of a woman's refusal to be further victimized by
her mate occurs in *Deepseafish*. Whereas Olga's isolated perspective in
which the critical *Volksstück* scenario casts her serves to throw the traditional "just" order into doubt but locks the woman into perpetual torment, *Deepseafish* broadens the scope of its patriarchal critique as well
as assuming a more aggressive tone. Women's exploitation in the literary
marketplace adds another layer to their subjugation in the home, but the
juxtaposition of two modes of misogyny also opens up a critical space
from which Gesine can eventually exit the system. *Purgatory*'s seamless
discursive universe has given way to one that is rent by internal tensions
and thus is inherently unstable. In that way, *Deepseafish* is able to challenge the determinism of the earlier plays and reclaim some measure of
agency for its protagonist. Significantly, Gesine's decision to "never let
[herself] be eaten up again" (356) and leave Laurenz only became possible
in Fleißer's revision of the play in the early 1970s at a time when she
herself had finally attained freedom from male interference and domination.

Critical Reception: The Men

The intepretation of Fleißer's oeuvre, which failed to appear at the time, concurred with a renewed interest of the New Left in the Frankfurt School analysis of German fascism. The Frankfurt School's attention to psychosocial dynamics such as the role of the "authoritarian personality" revised orthodox Marxist theories on German fascism that had formerly been focused on economic and military apparatuses and the political elite. The Frankfurt School approach had produced the notion of fascism as an exaggerated form of capitalism, which dominated postwar leftist representations of the Third Reich. It had also exempted the lower classes from a critical interrogation of the reasons for Hitler's popularity and power. The population, and particularly the Communist party, were viewed as victims of fascism. Examining fascism on an everyday, domestic level challenged the black-and-white schema of guilt versus innocence that made postwar efforts to cope with the Nazi past so difficult. By addressing questions of complicity and resistance, it implicated Germans of all social classes, including those formerly exempt from responsibility. In the 1960s, Fleißer's focus on microsocial, subjective, and local practices began to be seen as central to a critical project interested in the investigation of psychological mechanisms and their function to replicate dominant ideology in terms of emotions, behaviors, fantasies, and intimate relations formerly considered unimportant to a political critique.

"My instinct was not political," Fleißer wrote in reference to *Pioneers,* illustrating her acceptance of Brecht's definition of the term *political.* Franz Xaver Kroetz, Martin Sperr, and Rainer Werner Fassbinder, less deferential than Fleißer, whom they regarded as their model, rejected Brecht's transparent language that provides the illusion of the working class's mastery of dominant discourse from which it is in fact excluded:

> Because Brecht's figures are so articulate, his plays can show the way toward a positive utopia, toward revolution. If the workers at Siemens had the verbal competence of Brecht's workers, we would have a revolutionary situation. It is Fleißer's honesty that leaves her characters without language or perspective. . . . (Kroetz quoted in Rühle 1973, 381)

The critique of language that influenced the thinking of the New Left led these playwrights toward Fleißer and Horváth, and toward a reformulation of the notion of political theater. The neo-Marxist critique, exemplified by the Frankfurt School thinkers, retheorized the relation of material base to ideological superstructure. The notion of the base as the site of historical agency gave way to a mutually interactive model and shifted critical attention toward the function of language and art located in the superstructure. Precisely in response to fascism and its wide support among the *Volk,* neo-Marxism abandoned the utopian hope of the proletariat as the subject of history and displaced revolutionary agency onto the realm of art. Theodor W. Adorno's notion of the "autonomous work of art" accorded revolutionary agency to the intellectual activities of the artist and the aesthetic theorist. In 1971, Kroetz wrote: "Can Fleißer's plays be called socialist then? Yes, since nothing but capitalism is responsible for the monopolization of language for the purpose of exploitation" (Rühle 1973, 384). Ironically, the absorption of revolutionary agency by the student movement replicated previous ideological constellations. The movement's subsequent dogmatization and alignment with the German Communist Party (KPD) produced a functionalist approach to art that equalled a return to Brechtian orthodoxy in the theater. Kroetz's writing reflects this development after his joining the KPD in 1972; his initial rejection of Brecht's transparent language gave way to a "constructive" model of drama that offers a positive utopia in the representation of *Erkenntnis* [enlightenment], and the endowment of the proletarian subject with agency and the ability to effect social change.

Critical Reception: The Women

Purgatory's view of the world as a place without mercy or final absolution of sins, stands in contradiction to a socially engaged criticism that assumes the possibility of change. "I lay bare injuries that should be healed," Fleißer said in an address to a dramaturgical conference, but continued: "I have no real hope of healing them" (Fleißer quoted in McGowan 1987, 19). Thus, her vision of social change is mediated by her reluctance to represent that utopian possibility and by her perceived powerlessness.

The mimetic weight of the critical *Volksstück* imprisons the subject in oppressive conditions, whose accurate, "objective" description precludes the utopian possibility of change and liberation. Unlike Brecht's enlightened dramas, which make material relations completely accessible to the analytic force of the intellect, Fleißer's *Purgatory* contains a grotesque, quasi-expressionist residue in the mysterious figures of Gervasius and Protasius as allegories of persecution. These characters embody the terror of church and community when Fleißer represents them as atavistic, immutable powers. The imagination, struggling to grasp oppressive mechanisms, fails to render the universe utterly intelligible from a vantage point outside ideology; instead, it is structured and dominated by the same ideological mechanisms it seeks to demystify. The text thus registers the proximity of its author to the material. Feminist criticism in particular has called attention to the entanglement of the subjective and the objective, of fact and fiction, in Fleißer's writing.

In the 1970s, concurrent with the growing women's movement, feminists turned their attention to Fleißer's writing and life. A number of biographies and monographs appeared that combined textual with biographical analysis, since the line between autobiography and fiction in Fleißer's work was perceived as tenuous. Feminist critics, in evaluating Fleißer's oeuvre as a whole, pointed out the emancipatory move of her texts. While noting the representation of the women characters as weak, passive, and, especially in the early pieces, victimized, Angelika Führich remarked on the progressive liberation and autonomy of the female figures throughout Fleißer's work that mirrored her development: "She literally attained autonomy as a woman and as a dramatist, through/in her writing" (Führich 1992, 124).

In the 1960s, having survived her marriage while slowly gaining public recognition of her work, Fleißer started to revise her oeuvre. She eventually abandoned the "truthful" representation of her experience and followed instead the "escape routes into the mind" (Fleißer quoted in Pfister 1981, 22). The distance allowed her to wrench her texts from their self-destructive, autobiographical proximity. In 1970, she rewrote the ending of *Deepseafish,* that record of her failure to free herself from victimization by abusive partners, and closed the play with its heroine's departure. Only this abandonment of autobiographical accuracy permitted her to carve out an autonomous subject position endowed with self-determination and the power to change.

Susan Cocalis evaluates Fleißer's work from a feminist perspective and concludes: "In her two plays *Purgatory in Ingolstadt* and *Pioneers in*

Ingolstadt, she offers neither a feminist alternative to a patriarchal world, nor any utopian illusions" (Cocalis 1979, 210). As Cocalis points out, Fleißer's refusal to represent a feminist utopia resists the male tradition of metaphorizing woman as "savior" to a corrupt capitalist, imperialist (and so on), world after excluding real women from actively participating in it. Cocalis critiques the very notion of utopia as gendered, and calls attention to its ultimately conservative function:

> Those dramatists pit "the feminine," i.e. receptiveness, sensitivity and non-violence, against a dehumanized male world, i.e. the world of achievement, competition, and toughness, and represent it as a desirable utopia. At the same time they leave the patriarchal system at the base of this utopia uncontested. (Cocalis 1979, 209)

From this perspective, Fleißer's prioritization of gender as a system of oppression appears the more radical because of her preference of realist accuracy over utopian delusions. Cocalis's effort to recuperate Fleißer for a women's dramatic history in spite of its lack of a positive perspective operates against the prerogative of feminist scholarship and playwriting in the 1970s and early 1980s to provide positive representations of an autonomous female subject. Contemporary feminist criticism has come to recognize the necessity of a wide range of strategies in women's writing. Within this diverse discursive field, materialist analyses of oppression that deny positive solutions are no longer prone to the accusation of defeatism but take their place as one valid analytical method among many.

Fleißer's milieu-studies have produced a useful model for the investigation and representation of class and gender relations in closed systems. By carving out a place within and against dramatic models of her time that were dominated by the achievements of male playwrights, Fleißer paved the way for a feminist use of the *Volksstück* that serves as a point of departure for contemporary women's theater. Recent feminist drama, such as *The Little Red-Hot Man,* can now situate itself within a female tradition that has appropriated the *Volksstück* as a vehicle for the analysis of male-female relations.

Kerstin Specht: *The Little Red-Hot Man*

The Little Red-Hot Man is the second play by Kerstin Specht, a young author from southwest Germany. Specht, who holds an academic degree in Germanics, theology, and philosophy, worked as an actor and director before she began writing plays for the theater in 1988. Her biography shows some remarkable similarities to Fleißer's: Specht grew up in Kronach, a small town in the same region described in *Red-Hot Man;* she moved to Schwabing to study at Munich University, and spent some time in Berlin, where she participated in a one-year playwriting project sponsored by the city. The play was received very favorably and was produced at three theaters in 1991, once under Specht's direction. After her quick intitial success, Specht has withdrawn to write again, trying to avoid the commercial pressure of an institution intent on creating stars.

Her three plays, as well as the short films she has made, are set in the border region between the two Germanies, whose populations are characterized by downward mobility, religious fervor, and the liminal existence between competing systems. In Specht's fictional no-man's-land adjoining the GDR, the Nazi past lingers on, since geographic isolation and economic stagnation have produced cultural stasis as well. The mentality of the border dwellers is determined by the tangible reality of the German division and the social relations it has produced. The hatred between neighbors, who watch each other through binoculars, and the fear of observation replicate the surveillance systems installed along the mine strip.

In this landscape, Specht places her outsiders: the bearded bride called Wilgefort [Wantoleave] who leaves her wedding to stride toward the horizon; the lonely woman in the monologue-piece *Amiwiesn,* who wanders through the fields while cursing her provincial life; and the Philippine mail-order bride Lila in the play of the same title.

Red-Hot Man dissects the relationships in a family comprising three generations: grandmother, mother, and a young son on the threshold of adolescence. The son's sexual needs, the mother's overprotective control and hatred of outsiders, and the grandmother's dependency on her grandson for affection together produce a suffocating atmosphere that continually erupts in violence and ends in the murder of the son's girl-friend Anke, which at least temporarily restores the family's equilibrium.

The play consists of thirty-three very short scenes whose condensed language and composition illuminate the family dynamic in a series of tableaux. The trio is welded together by the mother's and grandmother's fixation on the son, whose maturation presages his leaving the family unit and who consequently must be bribed into staying. As a young male, he is asked to compensate for the women's experience of deprivation and failure. "You'd always bite me to the blood when I was nursing you. I nursed you with my blood," the mother impresses on him, in order to solicit his gratitude (Specht 1992, 78). It is the boy's awakening sexuality and his imminent entry into the system of production that drive the plot, fanning the women's efforts to secure their hold over him by infantilizing him. Their fawning over him recalls Roelle's overprotective mother in *Purgatory*. In addition, the Mother's rejection of men her own age—her dead husband and Berthold who pursues her—underlines the fact that the only power available to women in relationships with men is the necessarily transitory one of the parent. After seeing the son masturbate in the kitchen, the mother ties him to a chair in an impossible bid for domination because this act only fuels his desire to escape.

The patriarchal system in which the triangle is embedded not only stresses material gender differences such as the women's economic despondency and the boy's professional aspirations but drives a wedge between the mother and the grandmother. Each perceives the other as her rival in competing for the son's attention and affection, thus contributing to an atmosphere of hate, jealousy, and contempt. They reproduce the sexism and ageism of the culture at large within the walls of their home when the mother turns herself into a sexual object for the son: "Your mother's legs are still pretty. Look" (92). In contrast, the old woman has to buy the son's attention with money, food, and finally her last piece of jewelry.

Each woman is regarded as "damaged goods" by the community: the mother as a "loose" woman with a "bad mouth," and the grandmother because of her age. In their competition for the son, each turns the community verdict against her rival, forfeiting solidarity between them as well as alternatives to the dominant definitions of femininity contingent on propriety and usefulness. Entering adulthood and masculinity, the son is interpellated into a gender system characterized by male domination and female subservience. It is no surprise, then, when he brutalizes Anke, concluding that sexuality is only possible in sadomasochistic relations:

> SON: That's the thing women notice, because that's what they want. To be forced. That shows a man is really interested. The only way.

ANKE: Don't say such things.
    You don't mean them.
SON: I'm a cynic, and I'll grow up to be a gynecologist. To look
    into black holes.

(104)

The invalid grandmother, whose lonely monologues in her bed make
her the central figure of the play, embodies the detritus of a patriarchal
system that determines their value on the basis of their domestic services,
sexual or otherwise, to men. She can no longer ante up in the competition for the Son's love. Ageism is revealed as integral to an economy
that accords value only in relation to usefulness.

    The border situation functions as a metaphor for the dynamic
within the household and that between the family and the local community. The border fence signifies the proximity to a perceived enemy who
in fact resides within the very walls of the house. The stage directions
preceding the play illustrate the metaphorical character of the border:

    The play is set in the Frankenwald Forest.
    The Frankenwald is on the border.
    The border cuts through the forest,
    through the brook, through a kitchen. (75)

The best-guarded border in Europe comes to stand for the wall between
both men and women and the generations. The fence, always in sight,
signals insurmountable differences as well as the yearning to overcome
them. Within the world of this play, each act of reaching out is interpreted as an attack illustrated by the story of the son's father who had
crossed the border. Unable to touch, yet unable to escape each other,
men and women are locked into a sadomasochistic cycle of destruction.

    While Ingolstadt was representative of many cities lagging behind
capitalist development, the Frankenwald setting calls attention to the
economic effects of the German division in the belt of artificially induced
poverty running along the border. Thus, the provincialism of the Frankenwald is the result of a reverse process in capitalism, which has discarded a formerly prosperous but inconveniently located region by cut-
ting it off from the country's infrastructure. The analogy of economic
conditions and sexual difference, which the image of the border high-

lights, reveals gender relations as historically constructed and as a result of government planning.

The "bestiality" of social relations under these conditions is forced to the foreground by animal imagery. Reading an old newspaper, the grandmother recognizes herself in the violence and suffering of zoo animals. The image of the monkey's hurling itself against its cage bars and lapping up its own vomit, which the mother relates, illustrates with brutal clarity the social conditions in which the characters find themselves and from which they are unable to escape. *The Little Red-Hot Man* offers no hope for a better future, but forces the spectator to endure the perpetual recycling of the familiar. The precision and violence of its images, however, convey a view of social mechanisms that is so horrific it demands social change in the very absence of hope.

Erika Mann as Clown in the *Pfeffermühle*

Chapter 2

The Cabaret: Erika Mann and the Peppermill

In January 1933, Erika Mann and her brother Klaus leased the Bonbonnière, a tiny Munich nightclub with a rich history of political cabaret, in order to revive this art form and use it as a vehicle against the Nazis' cultural *Gleichschaltung* [synchronization].[1] The Peppermill offered Mann the possibility of political agitation that was prohibited by Nazi laws. In March, soon after the elections that instated Nazi rule in Germany, the Peppermill troupe fled across the Swiss border, and embarked on a four-year journey through Europe. Touring the bars in Switzerland, Czechoslovakia, Belgium, and the Netherlands from 1933 to 1937, Mann and her troupe warned against political developments in Germany with biting mirth, always on the run from officials in their host countries who often accommodated fascist laws and views.

The biographies of artists who fled the Nazi regime frequently chart journeys into isolation, alienation, and despair—in some cases even suicide. Theater artists were among the hardest hit. Many actors, playwrights, and directors were deprived not only of their language and their artistic community but also of their audience. Erika Mann's cabaret troupe is an interesting exception to the equation of exile with disempowerment. In fact, the company was deemed the "most effective and successful theatrical enterprise of the emigration" (Klaus Mann), not because it managed to avoid the vicissitudes of transience and persecution but because it turned them into their cause. Moreover, the troupe deployed a politics of humor that reconciled the constraints of censorship and the audiences' desire for entertainment with the company's goal to educate and agitate. The Peppermill, whose work has only recently been documented, produced a brand of activist art that was both commercially viable and politically interventive.

From its inception, the troupe and its program was determined by an adverse political context of open threat and censorship, which produced a performance style guided by a "strategy of covertness" (Keiser-Hayne 1990, 60). Censorship was practiced not only by the German police but also by Germany's European neighbors, despite their ostensibly neutral status. A work permit was often made contingent upon the emigrants' abstaining from criticizing their country of origin. The cabaret programs record Mann's radicalization and convey a growing sense of alarm. The texts often perform a precarious balancing act between the desire to name names and alert the public in various neighboring countries to the situation in Germany and the need to avoid censorship, which prohibited precisely that.

The Peppermill confronted its liberal audiences with fascism's impingement on civil liberties and asserted the superiority of reason over chaos, thus promising the ultimate victory of humanism over the Nazis' "evil will." The troupe's belief in the moral superiority of enlightened reason yielded effective rallying calls for an antifascist opposition. The exiles asserted that willpower can work miracles; if the victimized German people refused to comply, they implied, the system would crumble. They empowered the spectator by breaking the paralyzing spell of an all-powerful regime. Moreover, the pieces served as a counterweight to the dominant definition of exile as lack and loss by implicitly affirming emigration as a radical choice. Ultimately, the Peppermill's political appeal resided in the admission that consciousness-raising alone cannot effect change. Mann's sketches and songs posited that an understanding of oppression was not enough in the face of totalitarian control; activism must follow.

The antifascist critique of the Peppermill, a predominantly female and largely homosexual company, also intervened in hegemonic constructions of gender and sexuality. Mann, the first female conférencier of the German cabaret, flaunted her lesbian sexuality by wearing drag. Therese Giehse, one of the foremost German actresses of the legitimate stage at the time, developed physical comedy as a style that could challenge the classical, ill-fated heroine through popular theater without falling into the sexually objectifying conventions of that tradition. Lotte Goslar and Cilli Wang, performers who practiced *Grotesktanz* [grotesque dance], which had emerged in Berlin in the interwar years, likewise transgressed the codes of feminine propriety through their parodies of the vamp and the femme fatale, stock figures of the traditional cabaret. The grotesque dancers developed a physical vocabulary of satire and irony, addressing and unraveling female stereotypes through humor.

The discussion of Mann's troupe and their work considers their performances in relation to the social issues they address. The specific strategies they developed to empower emigrant communities, solicit alliances, and evade prosecution are situated within the aesthetic traditions of the cabaret, a format that proved congenial to the Peppermill's project in some ways but challenging in others. Finally, the cabaret provides a critical space from which to question elitist assumptions within traditional theater history.

Erika Mann described herself as a "militant liberal" and as a "conservative with a social conscience" (Keiser-Heyne 1990, 12). She was the eldest child of Nobel laureate Thomas Mann, whose epic novels such as *Buddenbrooks* and *The Magic Mountain* epitomize bourgeois realism. In contrast, her uncle Heinrich Mann had socialist leanings; although long estranged from his brother's family, he nevertheless exerted a strong influence on the politically outspoken Erika and Klaus.[2]

After her graduation from high school, Erika trained as an actor in Berlin and worked at several theaters in northern Germany. Two of the plays in which she appeared were authored by her younger brother Klaus. His piece *Anja and Esther* was one of the first depictions of a lesbian relationship on the German stage, and his dramatization of Jean Cocteau's novel *Les enfants terribles* created a theatrical scandal (Klaus Mann 1989). In the late 1920s, Erika, a multitalented young woman, began to write in different genres, publishing travelogues, books and plays for children, and a comedy, as well as working as a journalist.

In 1932, Erika Mann first became a player on the political stage. She spoke at a meeting of the International Women's League for Peace and Disarmament, an event of far-reaching consequences, not only in terms of her personal process of politicization but also because her speech made her the target of a smear campaign in the Nazi media. Mann's activities were suspect to her right-wing adversaries not only because she came from a family of highly visible liberal intellectuals; she and Klaus were homosexual, which made them particularly vulnerable to Nazi attacks.

Although she agreed to a marriage with the homosexual director Gustaf Gründgens, Erika continued to openly perform her lesbian sexuality by wearing drag.

Perhaps because of their liberal upbringing, the Mann's for a long time underrated the danger and the power of the Nazis. Klaus Mann conceded:

> Undoubtedly—I was against Hitler . . . [but] apparently, our hatred becomes active only when we sense a certain affinity with our adversary. One doesn't fight—at least not with all one's might—that for which one feels only contempt. Is it worth it, to deploy logic against obvious nonsense and glaring idiocy? One lets it go with a disgusted shrug. (11)

This condescending attitude may explain in part the lack of activism on the part of many bourgeois intellectuals in the face of Germany's massive slide to the Right after 1929. Erika's speech aligned her with Heinrich and Klaus Mann, who had warned against National Socialism earlier on. The Peppermill, founded out of protest against fascism, was her next step toward active opposition—only twenty-nine days before Hitler was named chancellor. Many Peppermill texts register the guilt of their authors at their belated reaction to the political enemy. During February 1933, however, the Nazi presence could hardly be ignored any longer because they held their campaign meetings in the Hofbräuhaus, back to back with the Bonbonnière where the Peppermill presented their second program. Erika Mann remembered: "Hitler spoke, we played against him, and Herr Frick (Reichs-Minister of the Interior) . . . sat next door in our Peppermill and wrote 'black lists,' we saw him scribbling away intently" (Keiser-Hayne 1990, 47).

Even in the face of the Nazi threat to intellectuals, which in May 1933 first culminated in book burnings all over Germany, Thomas Mann believed in the possibility of neutrality and refused to take a stance against the Hitler regime. In contrast to him, his brother Heinrich, a pacifist and antinationalist, was one of the first writers to be excluded from the German academy of arts, and one of the first emigrants. In the following years, Germany's foremost literary family had its citizenship revoked. The Mann's fled across the Swiss border shortly after the elections that instated Nazi rule in Germany. Klaus Mann went to Paris. The Peppermill, too, was forced into exile.

The twenty-seven-year old Erika demonstrated considerable organizational talent during the next four years. Other women had headed cabaret troupes before her, most notably Trude Hesterberg, Valeska Gert, and Rosa Valetti; but none under circumstances as precarious and perilous as the Peppermill's. Mann also proved herself a clever and prolific writer, supplying the cabaret with innumerable songs and sketches, many of which are now lost. In addition, as conférencier (a position that combined the function of a master of ceremonies with that of a political commentator) she served as mediator between performers and sometimes disruptive audience members. After the Peppermill disbanded in 1937, Mann toured the United States as "the most popular female lecturer" (in her own words). She spoke on issues such as "Women in the Third Reich" and the "collective guilt" of the German people, arguing for their moral and ideological "re-education." She participated in the first mass demonstrations against Hitler in this country and viewed her work as a political journalist as a "continuation of the Peppermill's work with different means" (Keiser-Hayne 1990, 135).

Mann embraced the United States as her second home; during the early 1950s, however, her antifascist activism rendered her suspect to McCarthy and the House Committee on Un-American Activities, which spread rumors about her being a Stalinist agent.[3] Disappointed, she embarked on her second emigration, and persuaded her family to return to Switzerland, where she spent the rest of her life mostly editing and administrating her famous relatives' work. Like many other emigrants, including those who had most vehemently and courageously opposed fascism, she realized that West Germany preferred to forget its Nazi past (Frisch 1988). Ironically, the Peppermill had made theater history in Switzerland, where it had spawned an indigenous tradition of political cabaret. It was revered by Dutch critics and audiences for whom the German occupation, and resistance against it, constituted an important chapter in their country's recent history. Likewise, the Peppermill's performances in Czechoslovakia, sponsored by the embattled Social Democrats there, were held dear as part of an oppositional culture not ready to give in to the nationalist rhetoric deployed by the ethnic German minority, the Sudetendeutsche, which had enabled the country's annexation by the expanding Third Reich. Only West Germany remained willfully oblivious to much of the literature created during the emigration. In 1947, Klaus Mann—who had edited two emigrant journals—recognized that the end of the war did not mean the end of exile, noting the lack of publications by emigrant authors, including himself.[4] He committed suicide two years later, in the year that the two German states were founded. His work became widely known and available only in the 1960s, as part of the belated popular and critical attention to exile literature. Erika, who in 1963 had begun preparations for a television documentary on the Peppermill, changed her mind about the project because she did not believe in the possibility of communication between the Germans of the Adenauer era and herself. She remained alienated from her former home country, which she believed had not changed all that much after the war: "The main reason for my saying No to the above project: the nasty neo-Nazism—which in truth is just the old one—over there," she wrote in 1966, the year West Germans voted for Kiesinger, a chancellor known to have been a National Socialist party member and opportunist (Keiser-Hayne 1990, 138).

Mann died in 1969, long before her work with the Peppermill, which she herself regarded as the most significant among her many accomplishments, could be reclaimed as a contribution to exile art, political cabaret, antifascist activism, and women's performance traditions. Helga Keiser-Hayne's extensive documentation and critical commentary, published in 1990—much later than the work of Erika's male relatives—takes an important step in that direction. One of the main obstacles to that historiographical project is the way in which a multifaceted personality and artist had become a "pale shadow executing the wills and editing the posthumous works of [her] beloved dead" (Keiser-Hayne 1990, 137). Mann's many gifts with which she had earned her livelihood as an actor, an award-winning race car driver, a writer, and a lecturer disappeared from the records of German history, not only because she was overshadowed by the literary giants in her family but also because that history still bears the imprint of postwar Germans' effort to contain the Third Reich by representing it as an ideological aberration. The work of her troupe, which Erika Mann had feared was outdated and irrelevant, resurfaced at precisely the moment when the end of the forty-year-long division of Germany prompted a resurgence of those discourses that the Peppermill had addressed. In the same year that Keiser-Hayne's book appeared, the young playwright Elfriede Müller published her drama *Goldener Oktober* [Golden October] which deals with the rise of nationalism, racism, and sexual exploitation in the wake of German reunification. Set in a Berlin cabaret, the play denounces that medium as a cultural site where those forces are staged most vehemently and damagingly. I would hope that the examination of Erika Mann's Peppermill offers a way of reinterpreting and revitalizing the cabaret tradition from a perspective of feminist intervention and resistance.

The Peppermill

The Peppermill opened in Munich, during the last days of the Weimar Republic. Despite the lively cabaret tradition of the Bavarian capital, Erika and Klaus Mann perceived the lack of a politically outspoken troupe that, while accommodating their financial needs, would offer political entertainment to the public in response to the increasing threat of German fascism and nationalism. The Peppermill only produced two programs while still in Munich; in March, the core members of the troupe, including the pianist-composer Magnus Henning, actor Therese Giehse, who also served as the company's director, her colleague Sybille Schloß, and dancer Lotte Goslar, moved to Zurich.

Even when the Peppermill had a "home," first the Bonbonnière, followed by the club hall in the hotel Zum Hirschen in Zurich, which temporarily housed the troupe, the cabaret relied on stage properties and costumes rather than elaborate set pieces in order to indicate the setting of their songs and sketches. The troupe's ambitions ran toward political effectiveness rather than artistic innovation. The simple backdrops they used were made of painted cloth, which could be rolled up and carried easily. When the troupe no longer had a permanent base and their sets and costumes had to fit into the trunk of Mann's old Ford, their economical use of material enhanced their mobility.

The texts from the Peppermill's first program show that initially their emphasis lay on entertainment that was spiced with topical allusions and satirical remarks. The troupe's politics were benignly liberal rather than radical or militant—an early reviewer remarked that their name "promised hotter dishes than were actually served" (Keiser-Hayne 1990, 32). Even Mann herself conceded that their first program lacked in bite, which might have been due to the troupe's inexperience and to the fact that some of the songs and sketches had been purchased.

Their second program, more aggressive than the first, consisted of their own material with few exceptions. Erika had written the bulk of the texts herself and had collaborated with Klaus on a few. The program was divided into two sections, a principle that the company maintained from then on. The first part of the evening consisted of a loose sequence of satirical numbers, humorous pieces, and topical comments. The second part was a revue unified by a topic or a setting. In one case the Peppermill chose bureaucratic pedantry as their leitmotif; in another, to which I will return, they created a revue of fairy tale spoofs.

With the songs "Beauty Queen" and "The Cook," the Peppermill's second program exemplified the emerging political stance of the troupe as well as their tone. The first song, which deals with a man who wants to have his nose changed, is ostensibly a critique of plastic surgery but can also be read as an attack on anti-Semitism. "The Cook," performed by film actor Max Schreck, was fairly blunt in its portrayal of Hitler as a diabolical dictator-cook who forces his rotten food down the diners' throats.

Erika Mann's decision to move her company to Switzerland was prompted by her wish to perform in German but not limit herself to emigrant audiences. Since the Peppermill defined its task as outreach to those who knew little about the situation in Germany, neither Paris with its large emigrant population nor Vienna with its numerous political cabarets offered what Mann was looking for. While initially envisioning a new permanent home for the cabaret in Zurich, difficulties with the censoring agency and the presence of German and Swiss nationalists in the audience began to affect the troupe's work. In the fall of 1934, mounting political pressure repeatedly led to rows and protests against the company. Erika Mann decided to take the Peppermill on the road. During 1935 and part of 1936, the troupe toured Europe and returned to Switzerland only once. This was the Peppermill's busiest and most difficult period; in fifteen months, it gave eighty-five performances. Despite its being in high demand, it often barely managed financially because its expenses tended to consume much of the earnings.

The Peppermill's first program in its new Swiss home was received with much critical and popular attention. Zurich, where the Cabaret Voltaire had housed the nascent Dada movement during World War I, lacked an indigenous tradition of political cabaret. In introducing itself, the troupe took the audience on a tour of the cabaret's stock figures and conventions while also pointing out its distance to the form. Giehse sang her song "The Entertainer," which ironically undercuts both the escapism of the genre and the gender roles fixed in the authoritarian hierarchy of director and performer. Her "heart of gold, head of tin" do not permit her to mention pain or trouble in her song, and her director—"such a strong man"—would not allow her to do so in any case (Keiser-Hayne

1990, 27). The "Poet" realizes that the ideals of peace and justice are mere fairy tale memories in a topsy-turvy world where evil prevails over good but ends with the appeal to rectify the moral order. The "Hunger Artist" and the "Magician" aimed more overtly at Hitler's Germany: The Hunger Artist is out of business, because everyone is starving and his art has become commonplace; the Magician mixes together black (the color of the nationalists), gray (the color of soldiers' uniforms), and red (socialism), creating a poisonous brown potion (the color of Nazi uniforms). But the brown phenomenon, he says, is only a cheap trick; the promise of economic recovery is just as false as the tinsel on the jackets of Nazi officers and must be exposed as the work of a malicious magician.

The reception in the press reflected a diverse political culture. While the bourgeois papers praised Erika Mann's literary talent, cultured elegance, and moderate politics, leftist publications reproached the cabaret for its lack of a class-conscious, proletarian agenda.[5] Both social democrats and communists found the Peppermill too palatable to the petite bourgeoisie, and not militant enough. One reviewer remarked that the troupe did not offer *Pfeffer* [pepper], but *Pfeffernüsse* [ginger nuts], the famous delicacy that the citizens of Lübeck (Thomas Mann's hometown) nibble during literary conversations (Keiser-Hayne 1990, 60). The harshest criticism, however, came from the nationalist Right, backed by continual protests on the part of Nazi Germany's ambassadors and representatives. These voices, together with Switzerland's ambiguous asylum legislation, turned that country into a difficult and volatile environment for the emigrants.

Although traditionally a haven for political refugees, Switzerland in the 1930s was marked by economic troubles, high unemployment, an increasing susceptibility to nationalist and anticommunist rhetoric, and rising xenophobia. Moreover, the Swiss government, like many other European states, shunned frictions with powerful Nazi Germany. It is no secret that Switzerland, while officially neutral, covertly collaborated with its German neighbor by extraditing wanted persons (Mittenzwei 1981). Many exiles were *staatenlos* [without citizenship], which legally placed them in an uncertain position. To openly agitate against Germany jeopardized any emigrant because the immigration police made residency and work permits contingent on compliance with the government's rule that "all applicants will be granted political asylum provided their quiet behavior proves them worthy of it. They will not be granted asylum if they continue their attacks on other countries' existence and legitimacy from our territory" (quoted in Keiser-Hayne 1990, 50). As a troupe of foreigners and declared antifascists, the Peppermill was under constant observation by the immigration police. In view of these circumstances, the cabaret pursued a strategy of covertness. Erika Mann explained: "Indirectness was our motto. We never mentioned names—not even that of our rotten country. We operated with the parable, with allusions and fairytales, unmistakable but innocent—on the surface" (Giehse 1973, 55).

Nevertheless, the Peppermill became more aggressive in its treatment of issues such as unemployment, poverty, and the political passivity of the petite bourgeoisie. Giehse presented some of the cabaret's more radical material, such as the songs "Frau X.," "The Nurse," and "Stupidity." Giehse's performances, which balanced between broad comedy and dead seriousness, became the Peppermill's trademarks. Frau X., the matron running the average corner store, typifies the fatalism of the "common people" who accept economic crisis and war like bad weather. Giehse's style of delivery, which had audiences roaring with laughter for the first three stanzas and chilled by the last, brought home the culpability of such complacence. Her Nurse, embodiment of the "gentle but strict" caretaker, gradually transforms herself into the monstrous helpmate of a dictator-doctor.

Giehse's Stupidity was the third in her fascist bestiarium. As an allegory of the Third Reich, clad in the costume of Germania and in a militaristic pose, she personified the liberal equation of National Socialism with ignorance, which can be cured by a dose of enlightened reason. Once recognized, Stupidity loses her power:

You call me by my name?
Me, such a worthy dame?
Now nasty Reason shines her light
and drives me from my home, the night.
I do not understand . . . how come?
My goodness, was I dumb!

(Keiser-Hayne 1990, 77)

The battle of light versus darkness in these songs echoes the iconography of Nazi art and theater, but reverses its fascist meanings. The ideology that chose the Indian sun wheel, the swastika, as its emblem and that

Therese Giehse: *Die Dummheit,* **courtesy Erika Mann Archive in the City Library of Munich**

signified the "reawakening" of the German spirit through torch marches was characterized as unjust, deadly, and evil. The song "The Cold" epitomized the darkness versus light imagery deployed by the Peppermill and roused the audience with the demand to "get involved and fight." (Mann 1992, 227–28) Since the darkness of ignorance can be remedied by the light of knowledge, the Peppermill endeavored to educate its spectators and pique their conscience. However, insight was always tied to action; Frau X. is contemptible precisely because she

knows but does nothing. A large proportion of the cabaret's songs and
sketches culminated in an appeal to activism. The piece "Children of the
Ruling Class" asked:

> What was it you studied, tell me what you thought?
> What have you been reading, tell me what you did?
> What have been your actions, had you premonitions?
> What have you encouraged, did you give your labor?
>
> (Keiser-Hayne 1990, 72)

By centering their politics on action rather than knowledge alone, the
Peppermill exceeded the appeasing liberalism of the bourgeois stage as a
"moral institution." Erika Mann reported later that this strategy had
proved effective. Dutch and Czech emigrants whom she met in London
told her that it was the Peppermill that had persuaded them to go into
exile, even though their media had well acquainted them with Hitler's
political agenda. "'The horror *you* showed us led us to leave our country.
The Peppermill has saved a few people's lives. That's worth a lot.'"
(Keiser-Hayne 1990, 141)

In October 1934, the troupe presented its third program in exile.
The revue part was entitled "Fairy Tales," which subverted themes and
characters from folklore by revealing their apologetic and quietistic mor-
als. The title figures of "The Witch" and "Lucky Hans" are exposed as
passive and complicitous with their own oppression and that of others
(Mann 1992, 222–26). The fairy tale program illustrated the problem of
co-opting popular culture with which the Peppermill had to contend and
which played itself out around the notion of the *Volk* as the addressee
of competing ideologies.[6] In her opening remarks, Mann pointed out
that reactionary forces have used popular mythology to support their
"romantic-chaotic vision" (Keiser-Hayne 1990, 102). The genre is
shown to foster an unquestioning belief in superstitious traditions and
fate, an attitude that is inappropriate for the politically mature citizen
that the Peppermill envisioned. The humor of these pieces resides in their
parody of the fairy tale conventions, simultaneously inviting and denying spectatorial pleasure. That literary form and its theatrical presentation—the repetitive rhyme pattern, the regular recurrence of the refrain
and its resonances with children's chants—provides the illusion of a
wholesome world that caters to nostalgic and escapist desires. In pieces
like "Lucky Hans," however, this tradition is turned on its head, because

the narrative moves swiftly and inevitably toward violence and doom instead of the expected happy ending, throwing poetic justice into question. While "Lucky Hans" juxtaposes myth and reportage throughout the song, many pieces rely on a single punch line in which a disturbing reality suddenly erupts into the stage world. "The Witch" illustrates this technique. The witch's harmless announcement to "chat a while" chills the unsuspecting spectator, because the character's new-found comfort after a lifetime of torment and persecution turns out to rest on the fact that the Jews have taken over her scapegoat function. The black humor results in the sudden collapse of the assumption that "all's well that ends well." Unfortunately, this technique made it easy for the censors to cut the one stanza, or the single punchline on which the political effect of the songs relied, so that the troupe would have to discard the entire piece. Often, however, the Peppermill would not comply with the censor's orders, even though police spies sat in on the performances.

Both pieces exemplify the Peppermill's liberal humanist politics, its strengths and its shortcomings. Their belief in the healing powers of enlightened reason yielded effective rallying calls for an antifascist opposition; from their distance, however unsafe, the exiles asserted that willpower can work miracles. If Hans refused to be content, they implied, the system would crumble.

Similarly to Lucky Hans, the witch is represented as the victim of an oppressive system. Like Hans, the witch is not excused from all responsibility in this dynamic, because she "rests her hands in her lap," i.e., denounces all resistance or active opposition. Out of idleness, she prefers her victim role to standing up against her tormentors; she blows herself a kiss. In view of the fate of witches and Jews, the Peppermill's indictment of the victim, no matter how empowering it was at that historical moment, reveals the troupe's limitations because its interpretation of the majority's support for Hitler as ignorance failed to account for the population's emotional investment in a totalitarian regime.

Rather than offering a sophisticated analysis or aetiology of German fascism, the Peppermill appealed to the courage of its spectators to dare disagreement, to speak up, to forge alliances among antifascists. "The Witch" can be read as such an appeal for political coalitions. It exemplifies a progressive politics according to which each member of a society is responsible for the civil rights of all. By underlining the arbitrariness of persecution, the piece highlights the structural function of the scapegoat and disturbs the sense of safety among those who might feel that

the persecution of others does not concern them. In the context of totalitarian oppression, one person's peace of mind rests on another's murder;
there is no such thing as innocence.

In October 1936, Erika Mann made arrangements for the troupe to
transfer to New York, but apparently the cabaret did not translate well
into another language and cultural context. In 1937, after a two-week
sojourn at the New School of Social Research in New York, the Peppermill finally disbanded. During its four years of existence, the troupe had
staged 1,034 performances, involving about forty actors, musicians, and
dancers.

The Cabaret: Ambiguous Traditions

The Peppermill was very much an actor's forum, designed to allow the
most advantageous display of its members' talents and skills. The
troupe's size ranged between nine and ten members, including the two
pianists. Many of the troupe's participants had successful careers in
mainstream theater, such as Mann, Giehse, and Sybille Schloß. The
dancer Lotte Goslar, like pianist Magnus Henning, had appeared in the
famous Kabarett der Komiker. In order to evaluate the artistic accomplishments of Mann, Goslar, Giehse, and Schloß, and understand them
as *feminist* diversions, it is first necessary to sketch out more fully the
conventions of the cabaret against which they operated.

Mann struggled against the restrictions of the medium whose historical alliance with nightclub and music-hall entertainment abounding
with sexist jokes and strip shows impeded the political work of a predominantly female and largely homosexual company. While Mann and
her troupe never portrayed women as sexualized objects—a routine practice in the cabaret—reviewers continued to remark on the performers'
gender identity.[7] Moreover, the often uncritical humor characterizing
the cabaret had to be put to a subversive use in order to be politically
effective. In addition, the cabaret had historically thrived on, and fostered, a political-artistic subculture with frequently exclusionary traits,
a tendency that opposed the Peppermill's declared goal to do effective
outreach and address a wide range of audiences in their host countries.

The Peppermill is indebted to the tradition of the political cabaret,
which blossomed in Germany during the first three decades of the century. Historians and critics of the cabaret generally distinguish the political cabaret from the literary-artistic cabaret. Klaus Budzinski locates the

latter in the beginning years of that art form (1881–1918), while the former mainly coincides with the Weimar period (Budzinski 1982). Munich and Berlin each developed their own, very different cabarets. The Berlin cabaret, such as von Wolzogen's Überbrettl and Reinhardt's Schall und Rauch, had literary roots; likewise, Tilke's Der Hungrige Pegasus with its more bohemian atmosphere and clientele, became a home to the artistic vanguard as well as political agitators.[8] In Munich's thriving artistic community at the turn of the century, the cabaret grew out of the local tradition of the carnival, which imbued the new form with its exultant, mocking humor. The first and foremost cabaret troupe of the time, the Eleven Executioners, grew directly out of a carnival march that demonstrated against police interference with, and censorship of, the arts. Although they only performed for three years, the Eleven Executioners, who performed at the Bonbonnière where the Peppermill played many years later, had a lasting impact on the cabaret in their mixture of avant-garde art and political satire.

The cabaret often served as a forum for writers and performers who otherwise practiced the more "serious" arts as poets, musicians, and dancers. The intimacy of the cramped spaces filled with enthusiastic spectators was conducive to a closer rapport between artist and audiences than the formal setting that the city and state theaters, or the pages of a literary magazine, could offer. Erika Mann, initially at home on the legitimate stage as a professional actor, left the theater because the cabaret offered her the opportunity for political activism. Likewise, Giehse recognized the cabaret as a way to escape from "theater without urgency or necessity" (Keiser-Hayne 1990, 14).

The cabaret's suspension between artistic experimentation, political agitation, and mass entertainment created a unique site of cultural production, especially for women. Excluded from the male-dominated discourses of high art—whether mainstream or avant-garde—it allowed them to enter the arts as active participants through the back door, from below, as it were. In unprecedented numbers, women conquered the stage as chansonnieres, dancers, and artistic directors. They made their names not as interpreters of men's work but by virtue of their own creations. This was especially true for the dancers, who, around the turn of the century, had left the rigid discipline of the ballet under the control of an invariably male choreographer in order to shape a new genre of solo dancing. Dancers like Valeska Gert and Lotte Goslar estranged conventional images of femininity—epitomized not only by Isadora Duncan

but also by the expressionist dancer Mary Wigman—through the satirical vocabulary of the *Grotesktanz* (Manning and Benson, 1986). Moreover, principals like Valetti, Hesterberg, Gert, and later Mann, achieved
a large measure of artistic and financial independence as entrepreneurs.
The entertainment industry offered women the opportunity to become
authors and owners of their texts in ways that were all but impossible
in the institutions of high culture.

Nevertheless, the cabaret posed as many problems for women artists as it offered them opportunities. The end of censorship in 1918, and
the luxury industry that burgeoned during the period of inflation (1918–
23), heralded the era of the Girl. The term *Girl* entered the German
language at that time, denoting a specific female type characterized by
the commodification of previously emancipatory impulses. Gisela von
Wysocki speaks of the "domestication of woman as the 'type' of man's
equal, liberated partner."[9] American-style revues, like the ones depicted
in the films *The Blue Angel* and *Cabaret,* titillated its middle-class audiences with a femininity that was alluring precisely because it transgressed
conventional gender roles. Marlene Dietrich, Claire Waldoff, and Erika
Mann—artists who flaunted their deviance and performed in male
drag—were regarded as sexually alluring, which points to the dynamic
of co-optation at the center of cultural production in the modern age.
As a cultural form that defined itself by its sting, the socially critical
cabaret, positioned on the historical faultline between bourgeois art and
the modern entertainment industry, struggled against market mechanisms that turned any gesture of defiance or rebellion into a pose. Thus,
the flapper who appeared on the cabaret stage, in popular songs, and on
the movie screen, was no proof of women's liberation or equality in and
of herself; neither should that figure, however, be altogether dismissed
as mere commodity. Rather, it highlights the problematic position of
women in popular culture. The cabaret was one battleground on which
gender and sexual identities were continually presented, appropriated,
challenged, and negotiated.

According to several critics, Trude Hesterberg's Wilde Bühne [Wild
Stage] was one of the most ambitious and successful enterprises during
the Weimar Republic (Lareau 1991, 477; Appignanesi 1977, 139). In
1921, Hesterberg turned the basement under the centrally located Theater des Westens into a club that seated 175 and featured a small stage.
As was the custom, the place was leased to a manager who persuaded a
brewery to furnish and finance the cabaret. After reviewing the pro-

gram, the brewery supplied tables, chairs, and kitchen equipment in exchange for a guaranteed amount of alcohol sales (Budzinski 1982, 102). Thus, literary cabarets like Hesterberg's had to compete with other commercial enterprises, from large-scale revues to strip joints. Rising inflation in the postwar years, and the necessity to spend money as rapidly as possible before it lost even more value, resulted in the proliferation of nightclub entertainment catering mostly to the newly rich (Lareau 1991, 474). At the same time, a range of politically outspoken and artistically innovative cabarets addressed both the widening gap between the classes and the economic hardship caused by the inflation. In 1922, Berlin counted thirty-eight cabarets.[10] Many of the medium's greatest talents performed at the Wild Stage, from Walter Mehring and Kurt Tucholsky to Max Hermann-Neiße.[11] Here, Bertolt Brecht made his first and only appearance on a Berlin cabaret stage. Among Hesterberg's female artists were Rosa Valetti, the expressionist actor who ran her own cabaret, the Größenwahn [Megalomania]; the butch balladeer Kate Kühl; Gussy Holl, who often performed in drag and was regarded a star; Blandine Ebinger, who typified the "poor girl"; the pencil-thin Margo Lion, who specialized in grotesque parodies of high-society women; and Annemarie Hase, a "madcap, singing comedienne" with a rasping voice.[12] The shows at the Wild Stage, which changed weekly, comprised socially critical songs and sketches about the urban underworld, a sizeable portion of eroticism, and burlesque humor. Neither Hesterberg's Wild Stage nor Valetti's various ventures survived the inflation, and the club closed in 1924.

Weimar cabaret constituted an alternative to the classical and the modern theater, both of which subscribed to a notion of high art that cast the spectator in the role of student or believer who should learn his or her lesson in respectful darkness and silent awe. Filled with smoke, light, and laughter, the Weimar cabaret replaced an aesthetic of obedience and empathy with an interactive notion of performance in a space where spectators were as aware of each other as they were of the performers. The cabaret offered a new model of "culinary theater," where the audience would appreciate the virtuosity of the performers as they would relish the taste of a good cigar.[13] The use of epic dance, "gestic music," and the revue format of loosely connected pieces contributed to the erosion of empathy as the base of theatrical communication.[14] The cabaret can be seen as an antitheater of sorts, one reveling in a stance of mockery and disrespect.

The Peppermill combined a critique of the legitimate theater's authoritarianism (which aligned it with the political cabaret of the time) with a critique of many of the popular, folk, and mass entertainment forms that the cabaret fostered, thus placing itself at a distance from both discourses. The figures and plots of the fairy tale, the dance revue, the popular song, the folk comedy, and cabaret history itself were held up to scrutiny as to their ideological alliances. The relationship between cast and audience came to stand in for social relations at large, calling for an emancipation of the spectator from the role of passive consumer-subject toward becoming an interlocutor or even director. Thus, the troupe addressed social relations through theatrical tropes. By asking its audiences to resist the familiar, sexist stock characters, the Peppermill debunked outdated, patriarchal identities and relations. The spectator was cast as conscientious objector to oppressive performance traditions as well as hegemonic ideologies.

The dance number and the chanson were the centerpieces of the cabaret, and women dominated both genres. Each exhibits the pull of popular traditions in conjunction with market forces toward the performer's commodification and sexualization as well as marking an important site of feminist intervention. The styles of *Ausdruckstanz* [dance of expression] and *Grotesktanz* developed expressive and epic modes of movement and choreography to combat the cold classicism of the ballet as well as the solicitous lasciviousness of the leg-swinging, befeathered, or nude revue girl. By estranging stereotypes and creating new physical vocabularies of sexual expression, both styles have become the foundation for the contemporary form of *Tanztheater* [dance theater] that is practiced in Germany and that, in that country, is the only art in which female artists play a leading role today (Manning and Benson 1986, 45). The chanson, usually written by a man and interpreted by a woman, was similarly weighed down by the history of sexism engrained in cabaret traditions and organizational setups. The Poor Girl and Whore songs popular throughout Weimar cabaret epitomized the sentimental, voyeuristic, and prurient appeal of the fare many cabaret performers were expected to offer. To some extent, Blandine Ebinger recuperated the Poor Girl for her socially critical songs, and Hesterberg undercut the conventions of the Whore song by casting against type.[15] The Poor Girl songs presented by the Peppermill's Sybille Schloß appealed to the audience's compassion for victims of the Nazi regime, while the figure of the whore rarely appeared at all on the Peppermill stage. Lotte Goslar's pieces "The Racey Wench" and "The Vamp" satirized sexual stereotypes through dance, exiting the narrative pull of the chanson that moved along a trajectory of moral condemnation. The operation of the Peppermill as a collective sustained its members' feminist departures from patriarchal traditions and concomitant hierarchical structures.[16]

Like *Ausdruckstanz*, which was practiced by Rudolf Laban, Mary Wigman, and Gret Palucca during the 1920s, *Grotesktanz* rejected the Victorian images of women that were staged by the classical ballet, and presented its audiences with a range of alternatives to the figures of virgin and whore. The burgeoning life-reform movement of the early twentieth century, centering on gymnastics, nudism, and attention to spiritual well-being, along with the more relaxed fit of women's clothes, also helped reshape popular notions of femininity in regard to physical appearance and movement. According to dance historian Susan Manning, *Ausdruckstanz* was located at the cusp of physical culture and avant-garde art, populism, and elitism (Manning 1993). The motor of that form was the dancer's spontaneous and authentic expression of an inner self, creating a choreography of "emotional kinesthetic-honesty" (Goldberg 1989, 104).

While Wigman's choreographies retreated into esoteric aloofness and an asexual androgyny, dancers like Anita Berber pushed at the limits of sexual expression and developed a new physical vocabulary of eroticism and ecstasy.[17] Like Berber, the practitioners of *Grotesktanz*, Valeska Gert, Lotte Goslar, and Cilli Wang, rejected the construction of an almost divine femininity and the celebration of cross-generational bonding in the dances of Wigman and her all-female company, which presaged the gender segregation enforced by the Nazi regime.[18] Gert, whom cabaret historian Appignanesi calls "the inventor of the social-critical dance pantomime" (147), developed an epic dance style that "mocked and commented upon the forms she used" (Manning 1986, 38). In pieces like "Das Mädchen aus dem Mumienkeller" [The Girl from the Dungeon], or "Canaille" [Whore], Gert parodied gender stereotypes from cabaret history. Her stylized movements signified the social meanings of a prostituted body while her deadpan expression signaled her ironic distance from such meanings. By demystifing stereotypes through humor, Gert created a dancer's version of physical comedy. The *Weltbühne's* critic Peter Panter wrote: "Her deeper significance lies in her humor. . . . True humor is productive, in motion, free, excessive, pulling its subjects along. Her laughter is often loud, sometimes shrill."[19]

In the same vein, the Peppermill's Lotte Goslar developed a vocabulary of satire and parody, which complemented the troupe's stylistic
range extending from the poetic to the burlesque.[20] Her figures, such as
the "Poet," the man-eating "Vamp," the "Hero" (a coward in under-
pants), and the "Unwirsch" and its counterpart, the "Wirsch" [Gruntle
and Disgruntle], dismantled social types and gender roles. Although it
is difficult to reconstruct her pieces with but a few photographs and
descriptions, particularly in regard to the music, "The Vamp: The Cruel
Woman" exemplifies Goslar's feminist subversion of that popular figure.
The dance parodies the convention of the demonic nymphomaniac that
the Eleven Executioners' Marya Delvard had made infamous. Goslar
wears the tight black dress of the stage vamp, and her eyes are heavily
painted. Her lipstick emphasizes the pouting cherry mouth familiar from
the movie stars of the time. With rigid body and large, stylized gestures,
Goslar first bites into a little man-puppet, then rips out one of his limbs,
and finally discards him. She closes her performance with Delvard's
famous pose of the hand floating under her chin, which Toulouse-
Lautrec portrayed in his drawing of the artist, staring directly into the
audience. Her straight look across the "man's" corpse offers her performance up for inspection and ridicule, while dissociating herself from it.
Her exaggerated movements and stark appearance, contrasted with the
small size of the puppet, invoke the castration anxieties associated with
the vamp but demonstrate their fictional quality unsustained by an
"authentic" femininity. Her grotesque make-up and dishevelled, short
hair undercut the fetishization of her black-sheathed body and replace
seduction with clowning.

Gert and Goslar, who, in contrast to Wigman and Palucca, both
emigrated to the United States in 1933, refrained from their colleagues'
feminist choreographies, which were all too easily co-opted by Nazi
culture. While *Ausdruckstanz* turned to myth, subjectivism, and ecstasy,
Grotesktanz centered on a vocabulary of social meanings, dissecting
popular stereotypes through irony and a strident wit.

The contemporary *Tanztheater* that emerged in West Germany in
the early 1970s through the work of Pina Bausch, Reinhild Hoffman,
and Susanne Linke has its roots in the political dance experiments of the
1920s (Manning and Benson 1986, 44). It fuses epic and expressive elements into a repertory of images whose motor is the "rage of a woman,"
which otherwise remains unheard and unseen on the stage of classical
or postmodern dance.[21]

Lotte Goslar, courtesy Erika Mann Archive in the City Library of Munich

The chanson was a genre that had its roots in the French cabaret of the late nineteenth century; since the legendary Yvette Guilbert, its practitioners have been regarded as performers in their own right rather than mere interpreters of a musical score. Sometimes called *diseuses,* from the French word *to speak,* these women's delivery was expressive rather than conventionally melodious. Claire Waldoff, one of the famous cabaret

Lotte Goslar: *Vamp,* courtesy Erika Mann Archive in the City Library of Munich

singers of the 1920s, imbued the chanson with the local flavor of Berlin
street kids and belted out her nonsensical, silly, and audacious songs in
dialect. Some of the passages were yelled rather than sung, which lent
her interpretation a tough, sometimes raunchy note. She performed in a
boy's suit with knickerbockers and a man's cap, which several times
prompted trouble with the police, since women at that time were not
permitted to wear men's clothes after 11 P.M. A medical student from
Bavaria as well as a well-read intellectual, Waldoff created the distinctive
persona of a disrespectful, loud-mouthed Berlin underdog; and in the
early thirties, Berliners gleefully sang her spoof on Hitler's minister
Hermann Goering. Waldoff's spunky songs, such as "Oh My, Men Are
So Dumb," along with her butch appearance defied the heterosexist
assumptions of the genre in a city with a rich lesbian subculture.[22]

Waldoff, Annemarie Hase, and Therese Giehse diverged from the
model-thin stereotype of the chansonniere; the comic effect of their performances derived in part from the juxtaposition of their physical appearance with the gender conventions against which they played.
Giehse's performance of "I Want" is a send-up of the lascivious chansonniere with come-hither eyes who sensuously seduces her audience. In the
manner of the stage vamp, she breathes:

Because I want it, I fascinate
Because I want it, you're riveted
Because I want it, I am desired
Because I want it, I am admired.

(Keiser-Hayne 1990, 96)

The second part of the song, however, interprets her "I want" politically:

I had an idea
behind my curls up here (please don't laugh now)
How would it be
if someone—just for fun—
started wanting something good?
. . . .
I want justice
and a new era
and peace everywhere

(Keiser-Hayne 1990, 97)

The political appeal was thus tied to a send-up of the sexy-but-dumb cliché that provided the foil for Giehse's comic subversion.

The pale, fragile Blandine Ebinger represented another type: her Poor Girl songs recalled the consumptive wraiths often portrayed by graphic artists Käthe Kollwitz and Heinrich Zille. Her songs were milieu studies describing the poverty, sickness, and homelessness in the Berlin slums. Ebinger's virtuoso performance turned a sentimental convention designed to titillate into social criticism and incited the compassion of bourgeois audiences used to voyeuristic thrills. Her sad, pallid face, slight body, and thin, lisping voice, and the dialect she used combined into chilling portraits and reminded audiences of the "shadow children" whose labor had made the affluence and glamour of the Roaring Twenties possible, even though they were excluded from enjoying its fruits.[23] Each chanson, according to Hermann-Neiße, "compressed social truth and protest into mini-dramas more effective than long-winded stage plays" (Hermann-Neiße 1988, 51).

Sybille Schloß played off the same convention as Ebinger. Of similar build and appearance, the actor, trained at Max Reinhardt's school

Sybille Schloß: *Kinderlied*, courtesy Erika Mann Archive in the City Library of Munich

in Berlin, brought to the Peppermill stage the naive perspective of a child, through whose eyes the horror of persecution and the pain of exile appeared all the more vivid. Where Ebinger had illustrated the devastating effect of urban capitalism on its weakest members, Schloß trained her critique on the Nazi regime as the system responsible for her Poor Girl's fear and sorrow. Dressed in a pinafore and torn stockings, Schloß performed her "Children's Song," a medley of German songs and nursery rhymes, edited and altered so as to illuminate the life of a homeless emigrant. The girl uses the familiar melodies and images connoting the carelessness, safety, and happiness of childhood to describe her poverty, hunger, loneliness, and finally the murder of her companion. Rather than proving the never-changing wholesomeness of childhood, as Erika Mann's introduction of Schloß's performance slyly announced, the Poor Girl, on the contrary, confronted spectators with the unremitting horror of life under fascism. Her child's voice, unmitigated by a political critique, spoke to the adults' conscience and responsibility and implicitly asked them to restore what had been destroyed.

Epic acting, which Bertolt Brecht later theorized in such works as *The Short Organum for the Theatre,* was a presentational style created by great comic actors like Therese Giehse, Karl Valentin, and Liesl Karlstadt, who enlivened the Munich cabaret scene during the 1910s and 1920s (see Case 1981). Physical comedy, with its focus on social types rather than on complex individuals, its visualizations of power dynamics through blocking, and its vocabulary of intensified and exaggerated movement, provided Giehse, who was trained in the line of business of the "comic old woman" at one of the best naturalist acting schools in Germany, with the tools to put that demeaning stock character to a productive, critical use. Initially an acclaimed performer in the folk-comedy tradition, Giehse's skill turned that genre itself into an object of glee. In fact, her first appearances at the Peppermill, squeezed into her busy schedule as a famous actor, exemplify her straddling of mainstage and fringe. Her career as a whole evidences an increasing distance between the stock type with which she began and her political work as an artist who persistently investigated the social motivation and historical determination of characters and actions in an effort to expose behavior as changeable convention.

Likewise, the sketch *Stimmungsbild* [Vienna Atmosphere], set on a beer-hall stage, demonstrates the gradual defamiliarization of theatrical types—the Viennese coachman, the cobbler's apprentice, and the washerwoman played by Giehse—under pressure from a grisly economic-political reality. The sketch begins with the sound of shots ringing outside, underlining the rising militancy preceding the Austrian referendum to join Germany. The gunfire also literalizes the forces bearing on the performance (both the one in the beer-hall and the one by the Peppermill),[24] which is illustrated by the responses of the three tourists—a German couple and an American woman. The German woman cheerfully interprets the sound as fireworks, while the American remains oblivious to the rising heat in the Vienna atmosphere: "I think, it's the most romantic place, I ever saw [*more shooting*] and so peaceful!"[25] The

German man bullies the performers to begin: "Don't stand around like still-lives, that's going to change soon enough." His command resonates within German–Austrian relations, culminating in the 1938 annexation. The play within the play presents the stock figures which in music, film, and theater have come to embody Austria. Giehse, in quaint Viennese costume but with dark circles around her eyes, sings:

> I am a washerwoman, come have a look at me
> I am a classic figure, from head to fleshy knee,
> So clean and quaint, so humorous, in a dirndl and with curls
> This is how God has made me, a classic Vienna girl.
>
> (Keiser-Hayne 1990, 100)

The clichés depicted in these lines start to crack, however, when reality seeps into the stage idyll. Property seizures, the silencing of dissenters, the fascist infiltration of government posts, economic crisis, and hunger effect the crumbling of the "classical figures," punctuated by a refrain spoken by the guests whose invariable response is:

> AMERICAN WOMAN: Well, I think, it's marvellous.
> GERMAN MAN: Could be a bit more snappy.
> GERMAN WOMAN: It's in the blood. . . .
>
> (Keiser-Hayne 1990, 100)

The disintegration of Austria's national identity in the international arena, under threat from the German neighbor and regarded with indifference by America, is here presented as a theatrical performance. Political pressures make it impossible for the actors to continue "in character." Rather, the stock figure becomes an object of scrutiny held up to the audience:

> COACHMAN: The world loves our capers
> On film, on stage, on paper.
> If it keeps laughing, I'm afraid,
> And won't watch out—it'll be too late.
>
> (Keiser-Hayne 1990, 101)

The sketch ends with a waltz that the characters dance, each by herself, again accompanied by gunfire.

The stock figures' effort to entertain is likened to the European countries' stance toward Nazi Germany. The characters' quaintness and humor have become a pose that not only is inappropriate and difficult to maintain but has turned into a liability. Just as the three figures pay with their physical well-being for the spectators' approval, Austrian independence is threatened by that country's concern for a positive public image and good neighborly relations. Moreover, the piece executes a shift in the power balance between stage and auditorium: The spectators are revealed as directors in this interactive, international theater. With *Vienna Atmosphere,* the Peppermill warned its Swiss host against a show of good faith put on for the benefit of Germany. Phrased in the language of theater and spectatorial agency, the troupe emphasized the audience's power to command, change, or stop an offensive performance, whether on the theatrical or the political stage.

The appeal to refuse stock figures and plots as an act of social responsibility and political commitment forms the base of the Peppermill's activist cabaret. Mann's texts and Giehse's performances often linked the critique of theatrical conventions with that of gender roles, as in the early song "The Entertainer." Giehse's great talent lay in the simultaneous depiction of these roles' emotional appeal and social reprehensibility. The dialectic move between a psychologically persuasive performance and its defamiliarization through comic exaggeration opened up a gap in which a political analysis could be articulated. Erika Mann described the typically contradictory effect of Giehse's acting:

> [T]hose who witnessed her performances at that time—and that's an empirical fact—can still feel the goosebumps running down their backs. They remember: she incited horror and laughter simultaneously, anger *and* pity. (Mann quoted in Giehse 1973, 56)

Positioned between empathy and distance, pity and anger, the spectator could see around the roles held up for her inspection, recognize her own investment in them, and learn to refuse them.

Therese Giehse's acting career provides a link between the epic performance techniques she helped to shape during the Weimar Republic, the socialist stage practices of the Berliner Ensemble headed by Brecht and Weigel during the 1950s, and the West German renaissance of political theater in the 1960s. Giehse, who was throughout her life a prolific actor, always sought employment at theaters respected for their social and political commitment. Klaus Mann dedicated his novel *Mephisto* to her, a highly symbolic gesture attesting to her political integrity as an emigrant during a time when artistic success in Germany was contingent on party membership.[26]

As a great naturalistic actor, Giehse played many roles in Gerhart Hauptmann's plays, and later inspired Friedrich Dürrenmatt to write roles for her.[27] She worked with both Piscator and Brecht, and became most famous for two of the roles in Brecht's plays *The Mother* (an adaptation of Maxim Gorki's *Wassa Schelesnowa*) and *Mother Courage*. Giehse performed the title role of Mother Courage between 1941, when the Schauspielhaus Zürich first produced the play, and 1961. While Brecht's wife, Helene Weigel, was similarly applauded for her interpretation of Courage, many critics thought Giehse to be the definitive Wassa Schelesnowa.

Like Fleißer, whom she met in 1950, Giehse associated with the young men who tried to revolutionize the theater during the late 1960s. In 1970, the Schaubühne in (West) Berlin, a collective uniting West Germany's most creative, radical, and socially committed theater workers, produced Brecht's *The Mother,* in which Giehse played the title role. Her acting style, defined by the political theater of the 1930s, and her involvement with many of the socialist experiments of that time inspired a new generation of actors and directors who rediscovered and claimed the tradition of Weimar theater as part of the project to revitalize the drama as an arena for political intervention and subversive practices.

In the absence of feminist theater in Germany, Giehse had to struggle against typecasting throughout her career. Although many critics noted her intelligent and unconventional portrayal of female characters, she was continually associated with mother figures. Despite her many depictions of independent, intellectual, and multifaceted female characters, from the lesbian Countess Geschwitz in Wedekind's *Lulu* in 1928 and the school director in Christa Winsloe's lesbian drama *Mädchen in Uniform* [Girls in Uniform] (on stage as well as in film) to Dr. von Zahnd in Dürrenmatt's *The Physicians,* Giehse is most often remembered for her proletarian mothers in Brecht's plays.

Under different historical circumstances, Giehse might have been recognized as one of the originators of a materialist feminist stage practice. As it is, a feminist school of acting, utilizing many of Giehse's techniques, emerged in Britain during the 1970s in the work of troupes like the Monstrous Regiment, inspired by playwrights such as Caryl

Churchill and Pam Gems who in turn had been influenced by Brecht's work.[28] It is ironic that an epic feminist acting style, first created by a woman for the cabaret stage, should be attributed to a male theorist and writer whose greatest heroines continued to be defined by their reproductive function.

For a politically engaged theater artist in exile, the popular form of the cabaret offered advantages the institutional theater lacked. The legitimate theater's costly production apparatus and its dependence on large, regular audiences rendered it stationary. For that reason, the study of exile art and literature has so far neglected the drama. Those theater artists who emigrated had to adapt to their new environments. Only a few of them were so lucky as to perform in their native language as did the cast members at the Zurich Schauspielhaus where Giehse worked after the Peppermill disbanded. Everything that distinguished the cabaret from the legitimate stage and excluded it from the status of high art turned into its greatest assets during the emigration: its mobility in terms of sets, costumes and props; its flexibility in terms of cast and program; and its topicality. The Peppermill turned the transience of the exiles to its advantage by capitalizing on the talents and skills of a mixed company of dancers, singers, actors, and acrobats in constant fluctuation.

While the Peppermill as the most successful emigrant enterprise occupies a prominent place within genre studies of the cabaret, it has to a great extent been disregarded by historical and critical discourses on the theater, which exemplifies the discipline's low regard for popular and alternative performance practices. Lareau's study of cabaret in the Weimar Republic, which appeared in a theater journal, amounts to a wholesale dismissal of the genre: "The German cabaret of the early twentieth century was at heart always aware of the ambivalence and co-optation of its own rebellion against modern culture," he concludes (Lareau 1991, 490). The many enterprises that "failed" in their effort to reconcile high art and popular culture are judged by artistic standards and political effectiveness, both of which were compromised by commercial concerns. Unlike the legitimate stage—or the few literary cabarets that Lareau exempts from condemnation—the cabaret did not see itself as a moral institution where spectators, described as "pleasure-seeking," prejudiced, and narrow-minded, should be edified. Duplicating the bourgeois condescension of the early cabaret-owners Bierbaum and Wolzogen, Lareau denigrates the taste of the "masses" as low and implies that artistic value grows in proportion to its distance from the sphere of commerce. This concept of art not only rests on a modernist notion of autonomy with its low regard for popular forms but exhibits a masculinist bias, since high and low art, the "pure" and the commercial, were also gendered categories, excluding women from the former and relegating them to the latter.

Feminists, cultural critics, and performance historians are now questioning the equivocation of theater history with the history of the institution and call attention to the elitist assumptions that operate in the term *Kleinkunst* [small art] which theater historians have reserved for the cabaret. The cabaret's hybrid forms, blatant commercialism, and open agitation have long served to maintain the fiction of the legitimate theater's aesthetic purity, untainted by financial considerations or political agendas. That fiction, which sustains the notion of "high art," obscured the implication of the stage in the market mechanisms governing cultural production in the modern age, which the cabaret unabashedly acted out. The Peppermill, a vehicle for many German theater artists of integrity at a time when the practice of "high art" was predicated on a fascist government's approval, throws those value-laden distinctions into question and prompts a reconsideration of cabaret artists as masters of the brief, concentrated form, rather than connoting "inferior" theater.

Self-portrait of Else Lasker-Schüler, courtesy Bildarchiv Preußischer Kulturbesitz

Chapter 3

Queers, Tramps, and Savages: Else Lasker-Schüler

In 1869, Else Lasker-Schüler, alias Tino of Baghdad, alias the Prince of Thebes, alias the Malik, alias Joseph of Egypt, was born in Elberfeld/ Westphalia, an industrial small town in western Germany. The atmosphere of social, artistic, and spiritual ferment in turn-of-the-century Berlin, where she moved with her first husband, provided the setting for her emergence as a bohemian artist. Just as her work bridged many artistic media and genres, it spanned numerous styles. Her contemporaries were particularly confounded by her highly theatrical sense of identity, which informed both her dramas and her everyday life. Tino of Baghdad and the Prince of Thebes are two of Lasker-Schüler's favorite poetic personae through which she claimed her marginalized position as a poor, bohemian, Jewish woman with proud defiance and humor. Her politics, which one can perhaps best understand through the recently activated notion of "queer," complicated her religious, national, sexual, and political allegiances in that she persistently refused a hegemonic position. Lasker-Schüler, who according to her friend Hilde Domin was "one of the most eccentric people of the eccentric decade of the 1920s in Weimar Germany" (Domin 1982, 147) spoke from the margins, eccentric, of every discourse and social group she associated with, a condition that metaphorically exiled her long before Nazi agencies actually repossessed her passport and revoked her citizenship. Like Erika Mann, Else Lasker-Schüler left Germany shortly after Hitler's accession to power in 1933; unlike Mann, however, the poet could lay no claim to representing the "other Germany," the tradition of German idealism and humanism. Neither was she, who called herself a "savage Jew," embraced by Jewish communities in her host countries Switzerland and Palestine. Her theater, always highly personal, records the fragmentation of identities under pressure from historical forces and diverges from the contemporary social and political drama in its highly subjectivist and spiritual movement through the lyric toward the unification of differences and redemption of the abject.

The work of this artist, which spans three-and-a-half decades at the beginning of this century, is astonishingly congenial to a postmodern sensibility. Her dramatic oeuvre, from her early play *Die Wupper* ([The Wupper River], 1909) to her last piece *IandI* (1941), comprises a wide range of styles and dramatic traditions, which sets her apart from the artistic and critical avant-garde of her time. Her last play is especially demanding and assumes a great deal of cultural literacy in its rapid code-switching between the master texts of German high culture, Jewish mythology, and pop iconography. Lasker-Schüler's oeuvre crosses many literary and nonliterary forms and genres. One of her collections bears the subtitle *Essays and Other Stories,* indicating her refusal to distinguish between fiction and nonfiction. She also illustrated several of her books with drawings. The artist wove together her writing and her life, fictionalizing her personality and transforming her own biography into legend. Her role-playing in the streets and coffeehouses of Berlin, Zurich, and Jerusalem prefigures contemporary women's performance art, matching it in wit, outrageousness, and courage. The page and the street became performance sites for her subjectivity, an aesthetic she captured in the metaphor of the "heartstage."

Lasker-Schüler, who is better known as a poet than as a playwright, is often dismissed as a political artist because her visions of unity between Christians and Jews seemed out of place at a time when Germany was cleaved by anti-Semitism. Moreover, her performances of biblical and "oriental" figures have been seen as whimsical and unworthy of serious critical attention. The following discussion of Lasker-Schüler's work revises her traditional reception as a harmless eccentric in an effort to investigate the operations that all but erased her from the map of German theater history. The examination of this artist's performance and dramatic texts is attentive to her production of marginalized subject positions, to their containment and oppression, as well as to the way she resists and exceeds those mechanisms.

The Performances: Camp, Grotesque, and Fantasy

The relationship between biography and fiction in Else Lasker-Schüler's art has frequently puzzled critics who responded to the poet's intensely personal work with a psychologizing and moralistic approach that often replicated contemporary evaluations of her texts and performances as a symptom of "brain-softening."[1] Such an approach neglects their critical aspect, and reinscribes women's exclusion from sociopolitical intervention. In order to reevaluate the entanglement of, and tension between, art and life in the work of this artist, a brief biographical overview is necessary.

Lasker-Schüler's parents and ancestors were emancipated, assimilated Jews. The young girl was raised in the cultured surroundings of an upper-middle-class German family in the Bismarck era, writing poetry, encouraged by her mother, and listening to her family's staged readings of the German classics. Early on, she learned about the biblical stories and figures, of which one in particular caught her attention: the legend of Joseph, the reader of dreams who was betrayed and sold by his brothers only to win the love of the Pharaoh in the faraway land of Egypt. Throughout her life, she would identify with this figure and weave it into many of her literary and dramatic incarnations. Her childhood was not untroubled. Family legends of anti-Semitic persecution despite, or perhaps because of, the growing integration of the Jewish communities into their German-Christian environment at the expense of their own cultural specificity, combined with her own experience of being ostracized by her schoolmates, later informed much of her writing, especially her second drama, *Arthur Aronymus and His Forefathers* (1932). In that play, the young boy Arthur Aronymus, Else's father, is loved both by Christians and by Jews and triggers a jealous confrontation between both factions that threatens to culminate in a pogrom. At the intervention of a bishop, it ends with a Seder banquet on the eve of Passover, uniting the warring parties in a shared celebration. It is noteworthy, however, that the utopian ending is preceded by a mutual recognition of differences, thereby refuting assimilation as a path toward peace and cultural coexistence.

Both Lasker-Schüler's family background and her marriage to Berthold Lasker, a medical doctor, bespeak a comfortable middle-class existence. In 1894, the couple moved to Berlin. Lasker-Schüler rented a small studio in order to write poetry, practice art photography, and draw. Her art exhibits a highly visual sense: Not only did her poetry revolve around expressive images, but facsimiles of her writing also show the intertwining of graphic and linguistic elements when she adorned pages with portraits and decorated words with moons, suns, and stars—the emblems of her personal mythology.

Her emerging artistic identity was influenced to a large degree by the "New Community" founded by the brothers Hart and headed by the poet Peter Hille, which she joined in the late 1890s. The commune espoused neo-Romantic ideas and an art nouveau style; it strove for spiritual renewal by reorienting itself toward nature, and signaled its rejection of bourgeois morality through a dress code that echoed the loose-fitting garments and "natural" hairstyles of the youth movement. Like many groups within the so-called Life Reform movement searching for a nonalienated existence, the New Community comprised both men and women, thereby endeavoring to break down the segregation of the sexes in order to combat the bourgeois double standard and achieve a closer relationship between men and women. The New Community differed from other groups in one important respect, however: Whereas the youth movement tended more and more toward asexuality as a prerequisite for coed comradeship, the New Community embraced a highly eroticized style of communication and art. Its members adored Hille as the Great Bacchus who would tell them the stories of his many lovers, and his disciples strove to emulate him. The flaunting of sexual promiscuity (whether actual or rhetorical) was at odds with the hegemonic discourse on sexuality, which was dominated by fears of infection and degeneration not just on the individual but on the national level.[2] Moreover, the cultural sites of bohemian art (and the New Community understood itself as such) were demonized: The bars, coffeehouses, nightclubs, variety theaters, and cabarets that Lasker-Schüler celebrates in her collection Gesichte ([Visions/Faces], 1913) were identified with sexual contagion and racial contamination and contributed to the invocation of Berlin as the "Great Whore Babylon" (Linse 1985, 251).

Lasker-Schüler's exit from bourgeois society, which she formalized in her divorce in 1903, was tied to her rejection of conventional gender roles and to an ecstatic, hedonistic sexuality. In 1899, already separated from her husband, she gave birth to a son whose parentage she never revealed, attributing fatherhood to various exotic and probably imaginary personages. She invented her first persona, the princess Tino of Baghdad, who marks Lasker-Schüler's break with Wilhelminian femininity.[3] According to her own account, Peter Hille gave her that name when she left her middle-class existence behind, and Tino became the first of the extended fantasies that the artist staged not only in her own appearance and fiction but in which she also involved everybody around her by assigning them imaginary offices and posts in her magic realm. Tino loves savagely and with abandonment, scorning the property relations of bourgeois marriage, and unleashes lust, jealousy, and hatred. This is the work for which Lasker-Schüler first became famous, the songs of love and passion that dominate her early books *Styx* (1902), *The Seventh Day* (1905), and *The Nights of Tino of Baghdad* (1907). Her fictionalized and real love affairs became more notorious as she grew older and the age difference between herself and the objects of her lust increased.

After her divorce from Lasker, she soon married the musician, writer, and critic Georg Levin, whom she renamed Herwarth Walden. The two became central figures of the Berlin Bohème.[4] As the editor of the expressionist journal *Der Sturm,* which also sponsored many seminal exhibitions of modern artists, and as founder of the Verein für Kunst [Artists' Club], Walden became a comrade-in-arms to Lasker-Schüler, who was admired by the avant-garde of her time, even though she was frequently criticized and derided by the popular press. Her epistolary novels *Mein Herz* ([My Heart], 1912) and *Der Prinz von Theben* ([The Prince of Thebes], 1914), and her essay collection *Visions/Faces* are monuments to the bohemian life, full of quirky portraits of fellow artists and their intrigues set in the coffeehouses, bars, cabarets, and circuses of Berlin, vacillating between passionate adoration, irony, humor, and silliness. *My Heart* traces the end of her marriage to Walden, who left her in 1910 for a younger woman, and her transformation into Jussuf the Prince of Thebes, another incarnation of Joseph the exiled artist-visionary and unrequited lover of his people.

After the divorce, Lasker-Schüler never had a permanent home again, living in sublet rooms, attics, and hotels, sometimes sleeping on park benches. Her poverty and fragile health, together with her son's sickliness, overshadowed the following decades. Only in the final years of her exile in Jerusalem did she enjoy a modest degree of financial security. At intervals, her friends would make concerted efforts to collect donations for her benefit. In spite of her productivity she barely managed to get by, a situation that may have been exacerbated by her frequent change of publishers. In 1925, she published a long and enraged polemic against her publishers in which she called attention to the poverty and exploitation of her colleagues and demanded a trade union for artists (Lasker-Schüler 1962, 2:505–55). Her article prompted a scandal but failed to remedy the situation against which she protested.

In Lasker-Schüler's career, the highest and the lowest point of her success lay close together. In 1932, she was awarded the prestigious Kleist prize; a year later, she was beaten up by Nazi thugs and fled to Zurich in a panic. After her son's death, and separated from her circle of friends, her years in Switzerland, interrupted by two brief journeys to Palestine, were especially difficult. She had to beg in order to support herself since she was officially forbidden to exercise her profession as a poet, i.e., she was not allowed to publish or perform. She was denied reentry to Switzerland after a third excursion to Jerusalem in 1939, and Jerusalem became her third home. There, the seventy-year-old woman once more undertook the task of building a literary-artistic community. In 1941, after finishing her drama *IandI,* she founded the club Der Kraal, where artists and scholars gathered to exchange ideas and present their work. In 1945, Else Lasker-Schüler died.

From the late twenties on, her work demonstrated a shift toward spiritual questions and concerns, which is less prevalent in her earlier writing. Under pressure from an increasingly anti-Semitic environment and political rhetoric, the poet articulated the aspect of her identity that became most vulnerable, with the gesture of passionate and unreserved abandonment that Tino and Jussuf had already performed.

Her biographer Jakob Hessing contends that she was at odds with the assimilationist philosophies espoused by her family as well as by her husbands. Lasker and Walden, who were at opposite ends of the political spectrum—one conservative, one radical—both viewed integration as the goal for German Jews (Hessing 1985, especially chapter 2). While Lasker, a middle-class professional, believed in the promise of the Enlightenment—which in theory envisioned a human brotherhood across religious lines and in practice sustained the gradual sacrifice of Jewish customs, history, and rites—Walden, the expressionist, likewise renounced his Jewish upbringing and faith for a socialist utopia. Hessing suggests that Lasker-Schüler refuted assimilationism and advocated a return to the roots of Judaism, tending instead toward a separatism akin to Zionism. Other biographers and critics point to the artist's hatred of all religious orthodoxy, including the Jewish one. Her relationship to Martin Buber, a key figure in Jewish culture and politics in the first decades of the century, remained troubled from their first encounter in the New Community to their renewed acquaintance in the Jerusalem of the 1930s and 1940s. This scholar, who popularized Chassidic legends and thereby bridged the chasm between eastern and western European Jews, became instrumental in the Jewish renaissance that culminated in Zionism. Whereas Buber devoted his life to the study of Jewish history and mythology as part of an organized movement, Lasker-Schüler found no solace in Chassidism. Her notion of the "savage Jew" who wears the bloody coat of Joseph illustrates the distance between herself and her community which she also captured in her famous poem *Mein Volk* ([My People], 1905).[5]

Her anthology *Hebrew Ballads* (1913), which many critics regard as her most brilliant achievement, together with *Arthur Aronymus* (1932) and her novel *Hebrew Country* (1937), illuminate the poet's relationship toward her faith and ethnicity. Although she was proud of her background, she remained unaligned with any cultural or political faction within Judaism. Instead, she recreated Jewish spirituality and legend within her own imagination. One can read her *Hebrew Ballads* that praise figures from the Old Testament as her way to inscribe herself in Jewish mythology in a manner that closes the distance between herself and her people. Whether as Joseph, David, Sulamith, or Abigail, these characters speak with the fervor and passion of savage Jews. It is noteworthy that this stance is attributed to members of other religions as well in Lasker-Schüler's later work. In the story *Der Scheik,* the protagonist and most sympathetic character is a Muslim whose love for a Jew crosses the gulf between the religions (Lasker-Schüler 1962, 2:95–98). Her yearning for reconciliation extended not only to her own relationship vis-à-vis Judaism but to all divisions between world religions. *Hebrew Country,* which recounts the coming together of Jews and Arabs in Palestine, has been viewed as her most fervently utopian and most naive book; likewise, *Arthur Aronymous,* offered as a gesture of reconciliation and appeal for tolerance on the eve of fascism, was derided as out of step with a polarized culture and growing political militancy.

Lasker-Schüler's biography charts her move toward the cultural margins—as a Jew in an increasingly anti-Semitic Germany at odds with the Jewish communities she encountered in exile; as a poor person in a class society; as a bohemian in an art market dominated by middle-class values and institutions; as a twice-divorced, cross-dressing lover of young men in a heterosexist and ageist culture; and as a politically un-aligned social critic. In this context, her creation of regal roles for herself has often been interpreted as escapism, or even as a symptom of her delusions of grandeur. Sigrid Bauschinger compares her costumes to the whimsical garments of other bohemians, which emphasize their differ-ence from ordinary mortals (see Bauschinger 1980, 122). Yet the article against artists' exploitation by their publishers demonstrates that she neither lacked a rational understanding of oppression nor the courage to voice her criticism. One of her contemporaries wrote that "in its special province, the pamphlet engage[d] in the larger battle of the socially disenfranchised, in a forceful and effective way, because supported by precise and unequivocal facts" (Hermann-Neiße quoted in Hedgepeth 1967, 131). Critics frequently view Lasker-Schüler's construction of a private mythology as evidence of her ignorance concerning social and political issues, rather than as a dialectical relationship between a fantastic subjectivity and the material world. The poet used her personal life as material and model to address, and change, reality. In a letter to Martin Buber, she wrote: "That I only speak of myself comes from a great commitment to justice and conscientiousness, not from vanity. Because my self is all I can know and tell" (Lasker-Schüler 1969, 1:117). Her body registered and performed the factors that marginalized her (class, ethnicity, gender), but the persona of the oriental prince forestalled their mimetically accurate reinscription in favor of aggressively utopian coun-terimages to an oppressive reality.

Else Lasker-Schüler played many roles during her life, turning her-self into a work of art in such colorful guises as Princess Tino or Prince Jussuf of Thebes, pauper, dreamer, poet, and fervent lover. She elabo-rated on this figure in her storybook *The Prince of Thebes*. In her exten-sive correspondence, including her epistolary novels *My Heart* and *The Malik* (1919), she calls herself Jussuf, or Prince, describing her imaginary kingdom and inventing roles and offices for her friends within it. They in turn addressed her by that name and title.

Lasker-Schüler casts herself in the complex role of the sovereign who is poor in material possessions yet rich in his art and in his passions. He generously expends his gifts, his poems and songs, a gesture that is captured in her drawing of the prince carrying his tiny city on his out-stretched hand. The inhabitants of his kingdom are artists like him, mostly orientalized versions of the author's friends. But Jussuf is also an outcast, set apart from his people by the greatness of his talents and his love. The Jussuf figure, in its emphasis on artifice and fantasy, challenged the essentialism lodged in the oriental image. As one much-reproduced photo demonstrates, Lasker-Schüler began to appear in the costume of Jussuf as early as 1909 (Case 1992, 132). Gottfried Benn's description of the artist's costume, properties, and gestures both illuminates the dramatization of her persona as well as records the reaction of her audience:

> Neither then nor later could one walk in the streets with her without everyone stopping and following her with their eyes: extravagantly wide skirts or pants, impossible dresses, her neck and arms laden with conspicuous, fake jewelry, necklaces, earrings, cheap fake rings on her fingers, and since she was incessantly pushing her hair out of her face, these, one must say: servant girl's rings, were constantly at the center of attention. (Benn in Domin 1982, 150)

Lasker-Schüler awarded honors and medals to the coinhabitants of her imaginary kingdoms, exaggerating and inverting the paraphernalia of the militaristic Wilhelminian state in a carnivalesque spectacle. The profusion of regal and exotic adornments she chose for her mise-en-scène of the Other, her properties, and her costumes display their cheapness and "fakeness," which lent her performance an ironic, parodistic quality. The campy display of ornamentation, read against the fact that she was sleeping on park benches, mocked and subverted the sign system of social hierarchies through what Case calls "a strategy of appearances" (Case 1988–89, 70). She marked her own exclusion from the imperial codes of reward and recognition, from what Russo calls a position of "debasement" (Russo 1986, 218). In contrast to many of her fellow bohemians, who celebrated a playful eccentricity that remained unattached to a social position or critique, Lasker-Schüler's grotesque charades addressed and disturbed the semiotics of material oppression, a subversive tactic utterly missing from Marinetti's antics or Joachim Ringelnatz's fantasy adventures.

Jussuf, the pauper-prince of Thebes, clearly denounces the politics of Jewish assimilationism. He flaunted the ethnic-racial Other in images of oriental splendor, a provocation to German anti-Semites as well as Jews who wished to downplay German-Jewish differences. Her biblical figures evoke the essentialism—and perceived threat—of Chassidism, with its poor Eastern European origins, and the Zionist movement, which celebrated Jewish culture and religious traditions. Her performance of the Other as artifice operated against the life-threatening essentialism of ethnic difference, to which German Zionists responded with separatism and eventual emigration in the course of the Weimar Republic. Rather than locking a Semitic identity into racial exoticism, her oriental costume marked that identity as fictional, as fantasy. Her Jussuf, a savage Jew, remained unaligned with any organized faction in the Jewish community.

Like the three tramps in her play *Wupper* (she identified explicitly with Amadeus), Lasker-Schüler's drag performance transgressed gender boundaries, claiming both male and female roles interchangeably.[6] Moreover, her cross-dressing announced her desire to others—women and men.[7] At a time when both homophobes and activists for homosexual rights claimed that homosexuality was genetic, the fluidity of her desire challenged the stable roles and hierarchies of gender and sexuality and chose a strategy of confrontation over assimilation or apology. She flaunted taboo practices such as promiscuous and intergenerational sex, which, if they are not erased from the critical records, still hold the power to prompt outrage and censorship.[8] In the context of homophobic retribution against sexual misfits, it is noteworthy that the male persona Lasker-Schüler impersonated most frequently—Joseph of Egypt/Prince Jussuf—appears in her poetry and fiction in homosexual relationships, signaling a recoding and displacement of the explicitly lesbian imagery from some early poems into male homosexual constellations.[9]

She rejected the conventional bipolar construction of gender, as well as the bourgeois valorization of monogamy over promiscuity. In a letter to a friend, she wrote:

> If you would rather call me Princess, you should. But once you know me better, you will recognize that I am Jussuf in reality. . . . Once I met a Hadrian, who thought my Princedom was pure,—I do not like that attention to Difference. Also, I love the boys, Prince, and, secretly, some of the whores among them; perhaps I myself am a prostitute/prince of joy, a rose-prince of Thebes—. (Lasker-Schüler 1969, 1:139)

She refuted and mocked the bourgeois catalog of values at the basis of the opposition marriage/prostitution. Her description of herself as both promiscuous and "pure," compounded in the subversive image of the "prostitute prince," holds out the reconciliation of this oxymoron as a fantasy and a promise.

Lasker-Schüler's performances map a heterogeneous and mobile subject that shifts positions in relation to changing ideological contexts. It actively engages with the performance space, imbricating the subjective with the social. The mutual construction of these two categories is captured in the metaphor of the "heartstage."[10] That central image compounds her movement between the poles of subjectivity, located in the heart, and the public stage as the production site of the social subject.

The notion of the heartstage operated against the principle of aesthetic distance and objectivist accuracy formulated by naturalism and, later, New Objectivism. Lasker-Schüler's subjective images and ideosyncratic language ran counter to the efforts of many of her contemporaries, from Brahm to Brecht, to grasp a complex social reality through a scientist mode of description and predicate knowledge on a cool, removed gaze. Yet her work cannot be grouped with expressionism either, which embedded violence and misogyny at the core of an antisocial subjectivity. Even the protosocialist expressionist plays asserted the emotions, drives, and archetypes over rationality in a celebratory narrative of destruction. They configured social change as patricide, inscribing violence and the exclusion of women in the dramatic structure.

Lasker-Schüler's texts insist on the proximity between the subjective and the social, rather than privileging one over the other in an antagonistic scenario. She transformed her body into a stage on which social differences played themselves out. Her biography supplied the material for the drama of oppression and opposition that she performed in the streets of Berlin, Zurich, and Jerusalem, which called forth the aggressive and punitive mechanisms securing the social codes she challenged. Her flesh in turn registered the effects of anti-Semitism, misogyny, and heterosexism, which she acted out and solicited in the form of public spectacle,[11] from the hostile stare of her spectators, to the humiliation of public ridicule, to the beatings she took from Nazi thugs.

The Plays: The Fracturing of Identities

The characters Lasker-Schüler created in her plays illustrate her sense of social roles as performance. Her dramatic figures in *Wupper* and *IandI* can be read as inscriptions of the author's experience of distance and alienation from dominant discourses. Written more than thirty years apart, the two plays problematize different sets of discourses and the genres in which they have traditionally been articulated. *Wupper,* written in 1907 at a time when Lasker-Schüler lived at the center of the Berlin Bohème, played out differences of class and sexuality and the subversion of bourgeois moral codes. The transgressive sexuality that punctuates the drama effects the disintegration of its structure that was built around class differences. In contrast, the exile play *IandI* addressed the tensions created by conflicting national and cultural allegiances that cleave the author's heart in half. In negotiating this split, Lasker-Schüler repositioned herself as an exiled German Jew vis-à-vis her ethnic-cultural heritages.

Wupper, at first glance, is structured like the socially critical dramas familiar from naturalist playwrights such as Gerhart Hauptmann or Max Sudermann. It alternates between the workers' quarters, home of the families Pius, Wallbrecker, and Puderbach, and the villa of the rich Sonntags. However, the upstairs-downstairs schema begins to blur in a web of sexual entanglement and intrigue, spun by the central, witch-like character of Mother Pius, and crisscrossing the class divisions. Despite continued economic antagonisms—at one point, the workers organize a strike because their wages have been lowered—the classes are shown to share bourgeois notions of gender and sexuality, which are characterized by unequal, and at times sadomasochistic, relations among men and women, prostitution, pedophilia, and pornography. Parodying the realist convention of the revealing letter, a nude photograph of the adolescent Martha Sonntag changes hands several times, soliciting the desire, fear, or greed of the respective beholders.

The three tramps, the androgynous Gläserner Amadeus, the exhibitionist Pendelfrederich, and the transvestite Lange Anna, disrupt the sexual order based on neatly distinguished gender difference, "correct" object choices, and genital sexuality.[12] These sexual nomads rove the no-wo/man's-land between the frontiers of gender that are fixed in family structures. In contrast to both workers and owners, the outcasts are outside the sphere of production and reproduction. Where rich and poor alike are preoccupied with material possessions and the procuring or guarding of social privilege, the tramps are useless in any utilitarian sense and openly profess their disinterest in "getting rich" (Lasker-Schüler 1962, 2:988). Their impaired, grotesque bodies are endowed with poetic gifts and supernatural faculties, they are clairvoyants, dreamreaders, and prophets.

These "unsavoury" characters (in one critic's words), rather than epitomizing the "sordid aspects of daily reality" that naturalist drama likes to depict, open a window to a different order of sexuality and spirituality, gradually dissolving the familiar social fabric (Tyson 1985, 146). They make their entrance when Grandfather Wallbrecker has gone to bed, and the adolescent Lieschen sleepwalks in the light of the full moon. Here the drama shifts to another register, signaling its first departure from naturalism and its scientific mode of description and analysis and setting in motion sexual and spiritual forces otherwise suppressed.

The contrast between two spiritual modes is enacted in a confrontation between Carl Pius and Lange Anna. Pius, whose wish to become a pastor signals not only his desire for upward mobility but also a piety devoid of spirituality, brutally attacks the transvestite after admonishing the three to "get work and stop that nonsense" (Lasker-Schüler 1969, 2:987). Their sexuality transgresses the heterosexual organization of desire designed to reproduce the extant order and the power inequities engraved in it. The three queers, whose performance is marked by autoerotic display, nonprocreative spectacle, and a seemingly asexual androgyny, provoke the wrath of a character who is himself oppressed in terms of class but hopes to improve his social station at the expense of spiritual integrity.

The tramps not only represent counterimages to the prevailing sexual order, but offer the utopian possibility of reconciling oppositions. Pendelfrederich's open exhibition of his penis inverts and challenges the repressed sexuality of bourgeois and workers alike, which remains hidden and erupts only occasionally.[13] Lange Anna's transgendered voice and costume calls into question the supposedly natural conflation of anatomical and acquired gender. The androgynous poet Amadeus with the cracked glass heart throws the genital organization of sexual desire into doubt, and with it the classic division between eroticism and rationality, passion and intellect. The merry-go-round on the fairground in the third act, which ties all characters and plot strands together, becomes the metaphor for this world in which opposites unite and antagonisms are put in spin.

Rather than portraying social milieux, the play captures a series of atmospheric impressions. In a letter to artistic director Leopold Jeßner, who oversaw the 1927 production of *Wupper,* Lasker-Schüler called the piece an "urban ballad with fuming smoke-stacks and signposts," and stressed as its central impulse "the poem, the lyric, that which floats, the moon in the blue or black cloud of the play" (Lasker-Schüler 1962, 2:658). The Wupper river's red water signifies the fluidity and dispersion of human passions, as well as signaling industrial pollution, thus bridging the realistic and the fantastic. Set in perpetual twilight and underscoring its illicit encounters with the screams of mating cats and maudlin tunes, the play revels in the decomposition of the bourgeois sexual order. The mysterious murmurings of the three tramps serves as a refrain of sorts, punctuating this ballad of urban perversity. The crumbling of the naturalist drama, which can no longer maintain its traditional five-act structure,[14] can be attributed to the impact of the subjectivist lyric on the social milieu. Read in this light, the "pessimism" of the play, which many critics garner from the various gruesome endings most characters meet, can be reinterpreted as the effect of queer agency on the bourgeois order. After all, the tramps have the last word, after the "normal" characters have been killed, blackmailed into marriage, put away in a home for juvenile delinquents, or have submitted to alcoholism. From a certain perspective, the meltdown of the orderly world of naturalism appears promising, even utopian, rather than sad or tragic.

Accordingly, *Wupper* presents its social criticism in the vernacular of "low" comedy, occasionally emphasized by regional dialect (in which the entire play was originally written). Lasker-Schüler's bohemian love of mass and popular culture is well known. She cherished the motifs and spaces of popular art forms, such as the carnival, the circus, the cabaret, and especially the movie theater.[15] In *Wupper,* the central act of the play is literally set on a fairground, replete with sideshows, escaped zoo animals, a hurdy-gurdy, and a life-sized merry-go-round whose pairs of wooden animals—leopard next to lamb, and tiger next to deer—mirror the unequal couples that are swirled around in it. *IandI* uses film clips in its montage of scenes, and the rapid changes of focus within acts can be compared to the editing of a movie. Lasker-Schüler abhorred the naturalist theater for which the *Wupper* was at times mistaken. She similarly loathed any kind of didacticism. In a brief essay entitled "The Theater," which she dedicated to director Max Reinhardt, she decried the objectivist transformation of the stage into "a lecture hall for medicine or any other scientific discipline" (Lasker-Schüler 1992, 180). She loved the primary colors, the tinsel and glitter of the puppet show, and the variety theater. She admitted, "I'd rather miss the first act of a stage play than the pretty rider in her tasseled saddle" (Lasker-Schüler 1962, 2:207).

The reception history of *Wupper* illustrates how gender and the notion of dramatic style conspire to tie artistic value to formal prescriptions embedded in patriarchal institutions, thus excluding women from the theatrical apparatus and dominant theater histories. Published in 1909, the play was produced ten years later at Max Reinhardt's Deutsches Theater in Berlin with a boldly expressionist set and interpretation. In 1927, Jürgen Fehling's production at Leopold Jessner's Staatstheater in Berlin approached the piece as a *Volksstück,* and presented it in a naturalistic style. The variety of scenic interpretations corresponds to the range of critical evaluations from "outdated" to "precocious," from an assertion of its expressionist spirit to its allegedly naturalistic love of detail. In its obsession with aesthetic purity, genre criticism must necessarily fail because *Wupper* defies neat stylistic categories. The reception of Lasker-Schüler's play demonstrates, above all, how her transgression of dramatic prescriptions effectively excluded the author from a literary-critical "home." In 1927, Paul Fechter spoke of *Wupper* as "a peculiar mixture of Naturalism, literature and little scenic representations of a female impression of the world . . . with all its weaknesses, a very feminine comedy" (Fechter in Tyson 1985, 144). The site of inferiority to which Lasker-Schüler is exiled, is here revealed as her gender. Fechter equates it with inefficiency and weakness and defines a "feminine" aesthetic as a muddle of impressions instead of a worldview. Whether in terms of gender, subject, style, or politics, Lasker-Schüler fell through the critical apparatus. If she did not fit any of the established categories, her deviancy was attributed to her gender; and if she *did* fit, then in spite of it.[16]

During the years 1940–41, Else Lasker-Schüler wrote her last play *IandI* while she was in exile in Jerusalem. The play, which takes on the German topos of the entanglement of *Geist und Macht* [mind and might], through the classical story of Faust and Mephisto, was withheld from publication by the author's friends who viewed the text as "atypical" of her and suspected a deterioration of her brain rather than a politicization of her mind.[17] The play was not published until 1970 and had to wait until 1979 for its first German production. Some scholars, Sigrid Bauschinger among them, argue that the play is unfinished, and inferior to Lasker-Schüler's other work. Others point out that the author herself tried everything to have it published and therefore must have regarded it as complete.

IandI marks Lasker-Schüler's attempt to come to terms with her anger and bitterness at the loss of German culture from which she had been expelled, while also mourning the separation from her home. In her last play, Lasker-Schüler turned herself literally into a fictional character. The poet speaks prologue and epilogue, locating the play in the semihistorical, semifictional space of Jerusalem/hell. The cast includes characters from Goethe's *Faust,* people from the author's own acquaintance like director Max Reinhardt and critic Gershom Swet; historical personages like Adolf Hitler, his entourage, and the Nazi army; figures from American popular culture like the Ritz Brothers; and figures from the Old Testament like King David, King Salomon, and the god Baal. The stage on which these representatives of various cultures interact and on which the author's multifragmented identity plays itself out is literally her heart. Her project is the performance of a Jewish-German subject in crisis.

The plot is simple: An illustrious production crew oversees the public rehearsal of a play attended by real and mythical inhabitants of Jerusalem. The play is called the third part of Goethe's Faust tragedy, dramatizing the interaction of the familiar pair Faust and Mephisto with the Nazi elite and their army. These two classical figures embody two aspects of German culture, the humanist intellectual and the antibourgeois. From their exile in hell they observe the atrocities committed by their countrymen. When they finally agree in their condemnation of fascist Germany, the Nazis die, and the pair ascends to heaven, closing the play within the play. The epilogue shows the death of the exiled author in a Jerusalem garden.

The play historicizes the metaphysical problem of the divided self in the European theater of war and posits that peace and salvation can only be attained through an unequivocal rejection of evil, personified by Hitler and his cohorts. In an ironic reversal of Goethe's drama it is Mephisto who leads the way to heaven while Faust must go through a series of tests and confrontations before he, too, recognizes that in the face of totalitarian brutality the liberal virtues of tolerance and compassion must be replaced with a more militant, oppositional stance. Goethe's seemingly "universal" questions are historically reframed in order to address nationalism and anti-Semitism through the Faust legend. In the course of this critical enterprise, the classical form is dismantled along with the humanist value system. *IandI* deploys many of the techniques of the epic theater; however, Lasker-Schüler's *démontage* of Faust examines the impact of ideology on the author's subjectivity, her cleaved heart, and challenges the seemingly natural and preordained order of events through lyrical rather than objectivist devices. In her last play, the author calls on her entire cultural-imaginary universe, her mythical Orient, biblical figures, and popular personages, in a concerted effort to change Faust's mind, the outcome of the tale, and history.

The Prologue opens with the poet on her way to a rehearsal of a play she has written, which takes place in a district of Jerusalem named Gehenna, or the Infernal Regions. In conversation with her companion, she outlines her flight from Nazi Berlin to her present residence. At the same time, she traces quite a different journey: that of a poet descending from the heavenly realm of art into the narrow, mundane world below. With this description, she offers her own ideas of socially committed theater, one that tells the truth through poetry, rather than objectively reporting facts. Moreover, she says, the domain of art is not altogether untainted by a painful reality. Her experience becomes the stuff of poetry, her blood is the ink with which she writes.

Act I further develops the historical moment in which *IandI* was written, introducing emigrant members of the production crew, such as director Max Reinhardt, who has come from the United States; and two of the actors are familiar from the Berlin stage. The poet's address to the audience, in the fashion of an epic narrator, locates the play within the play in war-torn Europe. When she announces that Satan has capitulated, the spectators interpret this to mean that Hitler has been vanquished and they turn in outrage to the newspaper editor Swet, who is also present and who denounces this report as a lie. Again, fiction competes with facts, the poet with the reporter, in the critical enterprise of telling the truth. The debate between the two continues in the sixth act.

The poet's splitting in two parts sets up the frame for the Faust topos of the twin souls within one chest, and the ensuing play is presented as both an enactment of, and a counterimage to, the painful reality of bifurcation. Whereas life has forced the poet in two halves, the heart-stage offers the possibility of imagining the healing of cultural, gendered, and national divisions. The mobilization of the imagination appears as a politically productive act, even though it fails to save the poet, who dies from exhaustion in poverty and on foreign soil.

The play vacillates between grief and bitterness against the Nazis and against the "noble German soul" embodied by the Faust character. Through Faust and Mephisto, Lasker-Schüler staged two conflicting parts of herself, whose relationship to each other and to their German heritage changes in the course of the drama. Mephisto is a rebel, an antibourgeois cynic and libertine who sneers at Faust's pedestrian, even philistine, way of life:

> The ordinary man must follow established rules.
> No matter how much he has to suffer, and he does,
> he does not veer from the familiar path
> nor venture into deeper darker ways[. . . .]
> But I blow my top when I get drunk and scorn the
> rules and regulations of society.
>
> (Lasker-Schüler 1992, 160, 161)

Mephisto's contempt for the mediocrity of bourgeois customs, however, aligns him with the Nazis, with whom he shares a common forebear. He invites the fascist elite to a banquet in order to close a business deal with them and speaks a toast to Hitler, whom he calls a "blood relation." As the play proceeds, Mephisto turns against the Nazis and sets a trap for Hitler's troops, preparing to defend the infernal regions against the German usurper. Faust, who is at first appalled at the Nazi officer's unmannerly conduct, their quarreling, drunken swearing, and open exhibition of greed, demands that Mephisto take on the "brownshirt troublemaker;" however, when the Nazi warriors meet their death at hell's gate, he pleads for mercy and claims that "only the one who loves can rise again!" (163). Ironically, it is Faust's capacity for love and compassion in the face of the Nazis' demise that identifies him with the fascist hordes that rule his "Fatherland." The sin of which this arch-German intellectual is guilty is his pity, which ultimately renders him incapable of distinguishing between good and evil.

In contrast, Mephisto condemns not only the fascists but also Faust's sentimental tolerance. In a dialogue on theological questions, he forces Faust to reveal his unquestioning belief in God's omniscience, which echoes the German people's passive acceptance of their authoritarian leader. Mephisto calls Faust a "little preacher" whose "answer would cause God—and I know Him well—great annoyance" (166). He implies that a state of grace is predicated on taking an active stance against evil rather than being predicated on pious faith in divine providence. He challenges Faust with the question "How then could such an evil horde overrun the rest of humankind?" (163) and condemns Hitler as "a false note of cowardice in humanity's harmony" (101). The ancient idol Baal and King David from the Old Testament join Mephisto in his argument that spiritual wholesomeness must be earned by good deeds and cannot be assumed. Faust and Mephisto, those two divided souls of German culture, are united only after Faust agrees that "the antichrist and anti-Semite must die an unredemptive death" (172). Only then can the pair be redeemed and ascend to heaven.

Faust's transformation from pious and uncritical lover of human-kind into a conscientious objector to Nazi ideology enabled the poet to differentiate between Germans and Nazis, allowing her to maintain the notion of a "home" untainted by fascism and anti-Semitism. Through Faust, Lasker-Schüler claims her roots in German culture, which she learned from her mother. But while claiming her German identity, she nevertheless critiques it. Faust's compassion, which he bestowes on Na-zis and tortured Jews alike, reveals his kindness as a sentimental pose, his indiscrimination as complicity. At the sight of the Nazi army drown-ing in the swamp, Faust responds with sympathy and melancholy. While feigning engagement, his reactions betray his distance from a world whose mechanism he wants to study, but which ultimately does not touch him. The juxtaposition of the chess game with the rhythmic stomping of the approaching Nazi army and of the quaint tune "Enjoy Life . . . " with the brutal song "Five Times 100,000 Devils" denounces Faust's stance of detachment as wilfull blindness. *IandI* as the self-pro-claimed third part of the Faust drama delivers a damning indictment of Germany's humanist tradition when it shows the scholar in complicity with the military dictator.

Faust functions as Lasker-Schüler's stand-in, allowing her to self-critically examine her own social role and commitment as an artist. The way that quotations from Lasker-Schüler's poetry are woven into his dialogue highlights the escapist tendency of verses such as this:

Come, draw closer, let us hide—
life lies in our hearts—
as if in coffins.

(145)

While the poem rings with deep feelings of sadness and loss, Mephisto's answer, "He doesn't hear you.... This Hell in which you find yourself is modernized and hardly God's domain" (145), rejects this tone as pseudoreligious, indulgent, and self-pitiful. If hell is man-made, Mephisto implies, Faust's melancholy is inappropriate; his wish to hide from the world is revealed as smug resignation and evasion of responsibility. The Faust figure illustrates how a context of oppression transforms anguish into escapism. Mephisto's interjections serve as a lens that distances and distorts the beauty of the poetry.

Mephisto's recitation of Lasker-Schüler's poems is not removed into a distance from which it can be questioned and ironized. The shifting position of the Mephisto figure from an individualist antibourgeois stance toward militant antifascism parallels Lasker-Schüler's journey from the Berlin Bohème to her exile in Switzerland and Palestine. Early on, Mephisto emerges as the hero of this drama, which revises his role as God's adversary and reveals him instead as a divine spokesman. Mephisto, a loutish but essentially beloved creature, resonates with the poet's favorite figure, the savage Jew, who sings his prayers alone, cast out from the community of believers, but faithful nonetheless.

Mephisto's savage voice may also be read as "queer" in a sexual sense, when one considers that Faust and Mephisto exemplify one of the male couples familiar from the author's work. Mephisto speaks to Faust of their first encounter in terms of courtship and constructs his relation to Gretchen as one of successful rivalry (161). In fact, Gretchen appears merely as his tool, a body he occupied and discarded in order to approach the beloved. The speech contains all the familiar tropes of a lover's discourse: the first encounter, the rivalry with a heterosexual partner, courtship and pursuit, rejection, and finally acceptance by the beloved. Lasker-Schüler ingeniously reconstructs the biblical story of the Fall from grace into a homosexual genesis in which the serpent seduces Adam. Mephisto initiates Faust into a rebellious existence scornful of "married bliss and the safety of the parental house and hearth," the cornerstones of bourgeois reproduction (162). Here, a radical class politics intersects with the discourse of desire in the figure of a queer subject, one that abandons the "slave galley" of institutionalized heterosexuality (162). As with David and Jonathan, or Joseph and Pharoah, these lovers are regal outcasts, set apart from the rest of humanity by virtue of their artistic gifts and spiritual purity, and by their scorn for "custom's comfort" (162). The trajectory of political radicalization and spiritual growth along which Mephisto guides Faust constitutes an itinerary of seduction toward a nonhegemonic, queerly empowered stance.

Through the changing relationship of Faust and Mephisto to the Nazis, Lasker-Schüler negotiates her own position vis-à-vis a heterogeneous German culture, articulating a pan-spiritual voice, as it were, which is marked as different from both Faust's submissive Christianity and the Nazis' worship of Hitler. That voice resonates with hedonist, atavistic idols such as Baal and Psyche, with the Jewish kings David and Solomon as well as Mephisto, all of which combine in a spiritual position marked as queer (rather than Jewish) in the sense of savage in Lasker-Schüler's personal vernacular. While at that historical moment the Nazi regime forced "Jewish" and "German" identities into opposition, the play challenges that bifurcation even as it represents it, for instance in the torturing of the Jew Grynspan during the banquet.[18] In a production by the Living Theatre directed by Judith Malina, herself an emigrant from Nazi Germany, Grynspan was played by the actor portraying King Solomon, which underlined the victimization of the "chosen people" in a transhistorical continuum culminating in the Holocaust. However, anti-Semitism is historicized as a component of the ideology of Aryan supremacy and expansionism rather than being naturalized. Moreover, anti-Semitism is condemned as antispiritual per se. In a reversal of Nazi rhetoric, Mephisto accuses Hitler of having "poisoned the vintage of our German blood" (172). The Nazi army's demise does not signify the victory of Jews over Germans (which is quickly put in perspective by the author's death) because the opposite of anti-Semitism is not Semitism but a spirituality that ignores institutionalized appellations and borders. Neither the victimization nor the victory of the Jews are allowed closure in this play, since both positions reproduce dominant, bipolar constructions of the Other. Its utopian moment resides in the unification of the divided self, and the overcoming of differences from the transreligious position of the sanctified savage.

Lasker-Schüler's critique of anti-Semitism is not bolstered by a sense of community or collective vindication. For her, the real Palestine was no more home than Switzerland or Germany had been. What she yearned for instead was the "Hebrew country" of her own imagination, peopled by savage Jews like her—a vision that met with much criticism and hostility on the part of Palestinians. The final act of *IandI* offers a chilling image of Lasker-Schüler's isolation and poverty in the figure of the scarecrow, who is portrayed as financially dependent on the Jewish bourgeoisie in Jerusalem, represented by the arrogant Gershom Swet, editor of the *Haarez*. The confrontation between Swet and the scarecrow in *IandI* attests to the poet's resentment of, and humiliation by, the established, affluent middle-classes. Ultimately, her yearning for unification overcomes the pain of division and separation: Her death is accompanied by diverse voices from Jewish culture and history and welds King David, Gershom Swet, and the scarecrow together into a loving chorus of mourners.

Lasker-Schüler offers a critique of her own work as a writer in the sixth act when the poet and the reporter return to their debate about socially critical theater, and the role of the artist in an oppressive society. They are joined by the scarecrow, who wears the tattered wig of the Goethe period and the rumpled clothes of the poor emigrant. As Case has pointed out in her introduction to the play, this pathetic figure, "the counterfeit of a higher being" (175), may be read as a representation of the German woman writer, the illicit voice whose authority and authorship has been suppressed and belittled for centuries.[19] This creature claims to have been a friend of Goethe and even to have written some of his poems, but in the literary salons of the cultured elite it had to answer to the names of its Jewish forefathers, Abraham, Isaac, Jacob, or Little Cohen, recalling the names Nazis stamped in Jewish passports.

The ensuing discussion about political art is thus framed by a literary history divided along the axes of gender and ethnicity. The rivalry between two notions of political theater, and their competing approaches to telling the truth, are staged in the prologue and acts 1 and 6 of *IandI*. The poet, who claims that she speaks the naked truth, whether in prose or in verse, is called a liar by the newspaper editor Swet, a believer in cold, hard facts. The poet counters that such reporting is "spiritless, lifeless" and contends that the truth can only be told on a "higher level" (177). To her mind, the stage offers the possibility of investigating questions and solutions on such an elevated plane as a fantastic, utopian laboratory, as it were.

As a dramatic representation and critique of National Socialism, Bauschinger compared *IandI* unfavorably to works such as Brecht's *Fear and Misery in the Third Reich,* and concedes only that the play takes on "politics in an apolitical fashion" (Bauschinger 1980, 290). Her insistence that the poet was incapable of a political critique becomes clearer when she explains, "political thinking must be realistic and cannot solve problems by sending political adversaries to Hell and have them drown in

streams of lava" (Bauschinger 1980, 290). By taking Brecht as the model
of political theater, Bauschinger sides with Swet, whose notion of reporting echoes Brecht's scientistic belief in "cold facts" and modern
technology that are brought to bear on classical theatrical figures and
plots in their effort to produce a different, objective truth. This approach
resulted in a high-tech style of presentation, in which the noise of electri-
cal and mechanical devices almost drowned out the human voices on
stage. The materialist critique itself turned into a heavy, slow-moving,
creaking and clanking machine.[20] The woman writer is barred access not
only from the discourse of high, classical literature but also from the
costly machinery the political avant-garde deploys to dismantle it. Lasker-Schüler invokes the issue of material privilege when the scarred,
hungry scarecrow in its faded rags offers the hat of colonialist Ohm
Krüger to the well-to-do editor. The humiliation caused by sorely
needed commissions, such as the scarecrow's article on horticulture, and
the (self-)censorship arising from financial dependency are underscored
throughout the play, for example when Max Reinhardt entreats the
playwright to cut a line criticizing academics, at the request of the theater's business manager (169).

Unlike Brecht's objectivist theater, the voice Lasker-Schüler deploys is highly personal, rife with biographical allusions, at times lyrical
but often speaking in the register of low comedy, even slapstick. No-
where is this mocking, campy voice used more effectively or humor-
ously than in the fifth act, when the half-deaf Martha serves as Goebbel's
mouthpiece and begs Mephisto to save the drowning Nazi soldiers.
However, she mishears Goebbel's words, twisting his pleas into comic
nonsense. The brief bit, barely a page long, captures the co-optation of
the classic figure by the Nazi demagogue who attempts to manipulate
Mephisto through the mouth of Martha; at the same time, the play
subverts the fascist appropriation of German humanism. When spoken
by an old woman, Goebbel's and Goethe's words are turned upside
down. Martha "mistakes" Hitler for a "mighty cock" who has laid an
egg. As in her own performances, Lasker-Schüler uses the strategy of
the counterfeit, the debased imitation, to mock the hallowed words of
the classic and the commands of the powerful alike. Like Martha, she
twists the master narratives out of their original allegiances through the
low humor of, say, a children's puppet show, or a vaudeville act—an
aesthetic that has been regarded as distasteful by some critics.[21] Martha
exits from that scene with the complaint that "no one cares about [her]

misery" (168); like the distorting mirror in a funhouse, she manages to warp the intimidating images of the masters into ludicrous counterfeits but cannot speak her own truth. Likewise, the poet's death in the sixth act seems to reinscribe the oppressive conditions that the play tackles: The isolation of the emigrant, handicapped by age and gender, excluded from German high culture and the Jewish mainstream alike, ostracized because of her poverty and her bohemian scorn for "custom's comfort," is confirmed by her death in the arms of a scarecrow.

Appropriately enough for this complex play that navigates between an oppressive reality and the vision of a spiritually healed world, Lasker-Schüler follows the death scene with an epilogue, delivered by the poet. In that final monologue, she once more summons all the tropes of salvation familiar from her oeuvre: a utopian world of artists, children, and players. In this final, lyrical moment, she stakes her entire personal universe on the transformative and redemptive power of art. According to a well-known anecdote, the poet conceived the play as a "literary assassination" of Hitler, since she could not kill him in the flesh (Klüsener 1980, 124). She, who once called herself "the fist that prays," turned her own subjectivity into an explosive device deployed in the name of a queer spirituality.[22]

Often judged apolitical, Else Lasker-Schüler fervently engaged herself for the cause of the poor and exploited without associating herself with an organization—whether as an author, an antimonarchist, or as a Jew. Nevertheless, she associated with political activists who accepted her in her own right.[23] Her aesthetics and politics are imprinted with a longing for reconciliation of differences between the religions, nationalities, and classes. Her belief in the ultimate dissolution of antagonisms also informs her sexual politics regarding traditional gender roles and heterosexist conventions. The motif of the self, suspended between and separated by social, cultural, and historical divisions, that runs through much of her work crystallizes in the title of her last play. *IandI* maps her positionality between social categories that had been historically constructed as contradictory and unbridgeable.

In her last play, Else Lasker-Schüler tackled the difficult issue of the ideological implication of poetry and the question whether the flight of her "starsparkling lip" must be denounced as escapism, even complicity (as in the case of Faust); or whether the poetic transformation of an oppressive material reality can be used as a counterhegemonic strategy. When the New York Living Theater performed *IandI* in (West) Berlin in the summer of 1990, Judith Malina, in an interview on opening night, called attention to the play's significance in the present historical moment. At a time when capitalism seems invincible and Coca-Cola marches triumphantly into the East, it is necessary to call attention to pockets of resistance and to alternative culture as it exists, for example, in Kreuzberg, the Berlin district where the theater is located. It is crucial to create (material and metaphorical) free spaces for the imagination at the very moment that the last great utopia, communism, has seemingly collapsed. In that sense, the production of fantasies resists and counteracts the homogenizing, unifying forces of capitalism with its mass-produced cultural images.

"I die of life—in art, I breathe again," Lasker-Schüler wrote in one of her poems (Lasker-Schüler 1962, 2:357). She turned her art into her weapon of defense, creating dense images of eroticism, pride, splendor, and divine grace that are never completely otherworldly but that continually refer back to a painfully contradicted and conflicted reality, a technique that represented the worlds of fantasy and misery in such a way as to highlight each other, often in an ironic fashion. "Fiction" and "reality" are arranged in a dialectic that does not dissolve into postmodern indeterminacy but remains grounded in the material world.

Else Lasker-Schüler's performances and plays juxtapose the naturalistic entrapment of the subject by social determinants with the destabilizing fiction of a "self" suspended between class, racial, ethnic, and sexual identities. They thus present a double perspective that is situated both within and outside dominant ideology and engages in the continuous enterprise of self-criticism and revision, resulting in a great deal of agency and mobility. Lasker-Schüler's forays into the cultural imaginary yield a pool of fantasies that subvert and resist the homogenization by totalitarian ideologies and their appropriation of revolutionary impulses.

PART 2

Inroads

The second section of this study charts the work of Gerlind Reins-hagen, Elfriede Jelinek, and Ginka Steinwachs, which exemplifies the incursions that contemporary women playwrights have made into the theatrical institution. Their accomplishments are reflected in production records and awards. In those terms, Gerlind Reinshagen is certainly the most successful of the writers under discussion, but recent years have seen the debuts of many promising, new playwrights. For instance, since I began writing this book in 1990, Kerstin Specht has garnered critical attention, Elfriede Müller's plays were published, the Austrian Marlene Streeruwitz has had four plays produced at major theaters within twelve months and was elected "playwright of the year" in 1992 by the journal *Theater heute,* and Elfriede Jelinek's plays, some of the most difficult texts for the German stage, were produced several times; that author is now widely regarded as one of the major voices in German-speaking literature and theater, and a number of anthologies critically address her work.

However, women's invasion of the theater follows a zigzag course, it doubles back on itself, reflecting the necessity for women playwrights to engage in a twofold battle. The large number of texts that problema-tize the legitimate stage and its function to (re)produce dominant ideol-ogy, brings to the foreground the contradictory relation of these authors to the institution in which they wish to participate but which they also wish to destroy. Many women playwrights, such as Jelinek, Steinwachs, Gisela von Wysocki, Marlene Streeruwitz, and Libuše Moníková, share the postmodern critique of cultural apparatuses or "technologies," which has been predominantly associated with the work of Heiner Müller and Thomas Bernhard. "I am no postmodernist," says Jelinek, because her texts are written from a position of political engagement different from, say, Bernhard's. "His identification is with the master, mine with the slave," she insists in an interview (Roeder 1989, 154). The dramas written by these authors offer resistance to the "theater as it is," motivated by their feminist politics.[1] Their plays, to some degree, supply the political conscience of postmodern theater,[2] a theater largely occupied with the deconstruction of the Western, male, humanist subject yet unwilling to stage anything but that subject-in-demise. They confront the classical traditions from the perspective of the Other. Their texts, which bore through the garbage heap of Western culture, revel in rage and destruction so that our "heads are cleared for something new and different," as Wysocki, a feminist scholar and critic as well as playwright, phrased it (Roeder 1989, 131).

Most significant, this section on contemporary women playwrights documents their efforts to clear a space in which a female subject can appear. For Reinshagen, she resides in the Not-yet, that domain of dreams, fantasies, and silent glances exchanged by the disenfranchised, the girls, madwomen, and abandoned secretaries. Jelinek denies the possibility of female autonomy, but constructs a spectatorial position that opens an oblique view into the wings of the representational apparatus. From that spot, the absence and invisibility of women as subject agents in dominant discourses becomes noticeable. Steinwachs, finally, flaunts her existence loudly, boldly, and larger than life, even though she marks her vision as a fantasy. While some critics would privilege the deconstructive dramaturgy developed by Jelinek, Steinwachs, Moníková, and Wysocki (to name but a few), I believe it is important to also consider those contemporary playwrights whose aesthetic registers the politics of identity, who insist on representing gender oppression and mark spaces partially outside patriarchal ideology, a technique sometimes charged with essentialism and therefore the reinscription of sexual difference and complementary gender roles. While I would agree with Sabine Wilke that most German feminist playwrights share a resistance to psychological realism (Wilke 1993, 201), I would not identify a feminist aesthetic with postmodernism, as her essay implies. A sizeable group of authors, including Reinshagen, Friederike Roth, Gundi Ellert, Monika Maron, and Gertrud Leutenegger, have deloped various subjectivist, often lyrical styles of representation, and compose their plays as musical scores, including poetic monologues and choric passages (especially in Reinshagen's later work) that convey a strong sense of rhythm and melody. Kerstin Specht's minimalist but densely imagistic language, particularly in the grandmother's monologues, as well as the poetic passages in Lasker-Schüler's *IandI* exemplify the use of the lyric as a dramatic mode in which the experience of oppression can be expressed with authority. The lyrical voice invites proximity rather than analytical, historical, or social distance—a move with radical possibilities, as I hope to show in my discussion of Reinshagen's *Sonntagskinder* [Sunday's Children]. Most importantly, the lyric marks the space of desire, which is always a desire for change, a subjective, utopian laboratory as it were. Although imprinted with the social condition it contests, it does not solely obey the rules of verisimilitude. The present expansion of capitalism as a system that neutralizes the radical potential of hopes, dreams, and wishes by directing them toward commodities calls for the use of the lyric rather than rendering it obsolete. The most recent piece by Reinshagen, always a sensitive chronicler of German history, bears the title *Drei Wünsche frei* ([Three Wishes to be Granted], 1992). The play records the desiccation of the imagination in its characters who have learned to stake their happiness on the acquisition of objects. Thus, the lyrical drama remains an important tool for feminists' confronting the changed ideological and social conditions in postwall Germany.

"Inroads" maps the historical emergence of feminism as a countercultural field of diverse material and aesthetic practices within which these authors' work resonates and which it supports. Their political allegiance registers in the presses and journals in which they choose to publish their texts, in the organizations in which they participate, in the dialogue with feminist critics in which they engage, and in their collaboration with feminist theater practitioners. In an economic, material sense, these networks of support stake out a territory for women in the literary marketplace. They also mark the culture at large, and women's counterculture in particular, as a heterogenous discursive terrain inhabited by a wide range of critical, resistant, and oppositional factions.

This notion of culture as diverse and contradictory calls attention to the changed conditions within the West German and Austrian political topography, and their place in the international arena since the end of World War II. While "Inroads" in many ways functions as a sequel to "Lines of Flight," in geographical and ideological terms it also signals a reversal. Whereas exile operated as the major trope in the first section, the democratic constitutions of the Federal Republic of Germany (FRG) and Austria prohibit the overt state control and censorship of the arts that drove Weimar women into flight. Moreover, emigration as a form of protest against a system that many continued to perceive as oppressive and fascist, became less and less of a politically viable option in the decades following the war. During the McCarthy-years, the United States became a less-than-hospitable place for leftist intellectuals and artists. FBI surveillance and harassment drove many German emigrants back to Europe. As for the East, only the most orthodox communists could ignore the implications and effects of Stalinism and the rigidly authoritarian administration of East-bloc countries even after Stalin's death. The regular expatriations of critics, among them many artists, drove home the fact that the East had as yet failed to deliver on its utopian promise of freedom and equality. Therefore, dissent and discontent had to be voiced and negotiated within the parameters of Austria and the FRG, within their democratic institutions however suspect and contested.

"Inroads," then, describes the direction of critical avenues of attack, and connotes the integrity and tenacity of these writers to persist in a critique that many of their fellow citizens interpreted as the airing of dirty laundry. The critical representation of their home countries, which includes the investigation of "real existing democracy" and the repressed Nazi history, functions both as a critique of hegemonic structures and as a self-critique that examines mechanisms of complicity. Reinshagen's plays, like many New Subjectivist texts, evidence a shift of focus to the private realm of personal relationships, and carve out revolutionary agency on the level of the individual's consciousness. The plays of the Austrian communist Elfriede Jelinek, seldom produced in that country, construct an unbroken narrative of fascism; her play *Clara S.* highlights the misogyny and authoritarianism of the discourse of music and its violent exclusion and deformation of women, a representation that hit dangerously close to home in Salzburg and Vienna, the music capitols of the Western world. Her play *Burgtheater,* which depicts the Nazi history of that institution, outraged many Austrian spectators who preferred to believe that high art is untainted by ideology.[3] More than most contemporary authors, Jelinek has been the target of hostility and defamation.

Furthermore, this section delineates the inroads feminism has made into extant critical theories and attendant aesthetic models, most notably Marxism, poststructuralism, and psychoanalysis. Reinshagen's work illustrates the theory and politics of socialist feminism and its interweaving of class and gender as the base of that critique. Jelinek's texts are informed by poststructuralism, and Steinwachs turns the Freudian narrative of sexuality around, propagating "theatorality" as the regression to the oral stage. Feminism raids and erodes other theoretical discourses at each intersection, much in the manner of Steinwachs's notorious "explora-terra-rist." The interventions in and subversions of critical theories that inform the experimental and formally innovative work of these authors demonstrate great intellectual versatility and sophistication, often bolstered by academic training. Many authors, including Reinshagen, Steinwachs, and Elfriede Müller, have published theoretical texts about the position of women in theater, examining the consequences of social exclusion on their writing.[4]

Finally, the title of this section announces women playwrights' exploration, deconstruction, and reclaiming of a plethora of aesthetic strategies and traditions from a feminist perspective. Both Jelinek and Steinwachs examine historical dramatic and other artistic forms for their ideological baggage. Whereas Jelinek focuses on dominant traditions, such as Romantic music and classical theater, Steinwachs rediscovers and claims marginal practices, from the puppet play to surrealism, which she puts to a subversive use. For that reason, she occupies the climactic moment in this narrative. Her celebration of a female, queer subject that joyfully skips across the discourses of "high" and "low" art, cavorting between slapstick and dense eroticism, who courageously dives into the abyss where she begins to write, holds out great promise for the feminist theater of the future.

In the following pages, I will briefly sketch the emergence of feminist theater in West Germany, in order to provide a more coherent analytical frame for the three authors discussed in the remaining chapters and to give the reader a sense of the numerous other contemporary authors not included in this portion of the book.

The difficulties that Fleißer and Mann encountered even after the regime that had forced them into exile and inner emigration had been destroyed illustrate the predicament of many antifascist artists after the war. In West Germany, soon settled in Western economic and military alliances engaged in the cold war against communism, the critical voices of German women playwrights, most of them still in exile, appeared ideologically suspect. Ilse Langner, several of whose plays had been staged during the Weimar Republic, addressed the need for and the difficulties of coming to terms with complicity and guilt and investigated the possibilities for a new beginning in her play *Heimkehr* [Homecoming], written in 1947. Her female perspective, her concern with gender issues, and her attention to women's role in the reconstruction rendered her play unacceptable to artistic directors and critics. In the Eastern sector, the theater's insistence on socialist realism prevented the consideration or production of Langner's drama with its mystical and surreal elements, its moaning ruins, and its army of undead war victims that haunt the animated body of the wounded city of Berlin. German audiences embraced Wolfgang Borchert's famous play *Draussen vor der Tür* ([The Outsider] 1946) that similarly engaged the dual dilemmas of moral responsibility and the pain of dealing with a nightmarish past, because he presented these concerns from the perspective of the male home-comer/veteran and the all-male world of soldiers (see Stürzer 1993, 233). Erwin Piscator, in exile at the New School for Social Research, chose Langner's *Homecoming* for a production in New York, but was prevented from realizing his plan when he was accused of "un-American activities" and decided to leave the United States. After his return to Germany, he was unable to find a theater interested in a production of Langner's play. Convinced of its merits, however, Piscator produced it as a radio play that was broadcast in 1953. As late as 1962, when he became artistic director of the West Berlin Volksbühne, he considered staging *Homecoming*. The documentary theater of the 1960s, rediscovered by a new generation of political theater artists, remained an all-male domain.[5] Langner's play *Cornelia Kungström* (1955), which addressed the problem of the moral and ethical accountability of scientists in the nuclear age through the figure of its heroine, a chemist, was dismissed by critics who chided the author for leaving the province of poetry and tackling the drama. In contrast, Dürrenmatt's play *The Physicists* (1962), which engaged similar questions, was soon accorded the status of a classic. Perhaps the insistence on gender issues in the work of Langner and others prompted the renewed exclusion of women from the stage at a time when West Germany renegotiated the role of men and women and encouraged women's return to the home to make place for the men returning from the POW camps. Langner's strong *Trümmerfrauen* [rubble women] and competent scientists suited the state's gender agenda as little as did the author's persistence on the dramatic form.

The work of other women artists, who never returned from exile, was ignored by postwar West German theater, among them the Jewish writers Nelly Sachs and Hilde Rubinstein, who had emigrated to Sweden.[6] Their geographical distance from their home country exacerbated the difficulties they had in having their plays produced. In contrast to Fleißer's oeuvre, which was revived decades later, the plays by Gmeyner and Winsloe were rarely performed and were declared dated, though a 1949 production of *Girls in Uniform* in Buenos Aires demonstrated the topicality of Winsloe's indictment of authoritarianism (Stürzer 1993, 234–35).

The situation of women playwrights in the German Democratic Republic (GDR) differed somewhat from that of their Western colleagues in the postwar years. The egalitarian gender politics of the nascent socialist state, which aimed at women's integration in the workforce, and the propagation of this program in the theater, provided women dramatists the opportunity to publicly address questions, problems, and concerns pertaining to the relationship between men and women. Some wrote plays that dramatized the difficulties of implementing equality not only in public but also in the private sphere of the home (Sieg 1993).

In West Germany, the relationship between the male-dominated state theater and feminist artists remained tense. In 1974, Ursula Krechel's *Erika* and Reinshagen's one-woman play *Himmel und Erde* [Heaven and Earth] were produced, which showed women grating against patriarchal structures and constraints and their inability to attain a self-defined female identity. While the West German women's movement, which grew into a full-fledged, political counterculture during the decade of the 1970s, spawned a plethora of artists who found images for feminist struggles and utopias, the theater proved a bastion impervious to women and one that many feminists, working toward an "autonomous" women's culture and scorning patriarchal institutions, regarded as a waste of revolutionary energy. The anthology *Frauen-Theater* (Papula and Kentrup 1982), a collection of three feminist plays that includes documentation of their production process, provides a good indication of the various cultural contexts for the emergence of feminist performance in the state theater, in the fringe or "free" theater scene, and in socialist agitprop, respectively. In the case of the Hannover troupe Schedderhecks, the text that documents the company's work process takes up an almost equal number of pages as the play itself, underscoring their belief in feminist theater as consciousness-raising. Their reflections on obstacles posed by the hierarchical structures that framed dramatic creation—namely the distance between player and observer/director and the power differences inscribed in the process of decision making—and the difficulties in finding alternatives are rendered in dialogue form. It illustrates their conviction that their own development as artists and women is as important as their communication with spectators and readers.

Furthermore, what is noteworthy about early feminist theater is its use of physical comedy. The first play in the anthology (which was performed only once in 1978) was arranged as a revue, linking individual numbers through "disruptor-clowns," who sing out scene captions or briefly comment on the action. These figures provide not only comic relief but illustrate the actors' effort at reaching for a movement vocabulary that challenges the manner in which the female body is performed on the traditional stage. The Schedderhecks' play echoes the itinerant players who roamed Germany before Hanswurst was sacrificed to a national, bourgeois theater in the eighteenth century, but also the street balladeers who entertained their poor, urban audiences as recently as the 1920s.

Feminist uses of physical comedy and other popular forms continue to constitute important strategies for a stage practice aiming to decenter the language-heavy tradition of the German *Sprechtheater*. Heidi von Plato's report on ANNA KONDA in *Divided Home/Land* illuminates the influence of *Tanztheater* on feminist stage practice, and suggests a way in which the lyrical dramas by authors like Reinshagen might be imagined in production. Plato's piece highlights the importance of improvisation for the invention of images; it acknowledges a commitment to alternative production processes; and it exhibits a sophisticated understanding of the relation between spoken text, choreographed movement, and gestural styles. In 1990, Barbara Bilabel made use of such richly metaphoric stage language for her production of Jelinek's *Illness or Modern Women*, a text that does not ask to be acted out in the tradition of Stanislavsky's method of psychological realism, but in which the speech act itself is underscored and exaggerated as an oppressive process. Upon entering the theater, spectators were greeted by two actresses in clinging black dresses and brightly colored headpieces of flower petals. They held glasses from which they sipped milk, giggling and toasting each other as if standing at a cocktail party. They kept refilling their glasses by pumping milk through a rubber contraption affixed to their breasts. This image captured the discursive compound of woman, nature, and technology that Jelinek addresses in *Illness* without acting out or illustrating a character or a subtext. The repetitive loop of the actors' actions highlighted the contradiction at the heart of bourgeois femininity as a performance of artificial naturalness.

The work of ANNA KONDA, reportedly the first feminist theater troupe in Germany, indicates that feminist theater appeared much later and took much different forms than did feminist theater in the United States (see Canning 1991). Likewise, feminist scholars showed interest in the theater only in the 1980s. In 1984, Yvonne Spielmann published preliminary thoughts on a feminist theater aesthetic, and pointed to the lack of communication between feminists (who ignore the theater, or scorn the institution) and theater artists (who cannot afford to identify with feminist politics). The organization Frauen im Theater (FiT, women in theater), founded in 1983, set out to bridge this rift. In addition, FiT aimed at supporting and sponsoring women playwrights and women's theater groups, and broke through the isolation of women in the theatrical institution. Moreover, FiT established an archive and published annual reports to facilitate the exchange of information among feminist theater scholars (Ahrens 1992). A report published in 1985, which analyzed the situation of women in German theater, stated that the number of women in the artistic and administrative hierarchy of the state theater decreased with rising authority and power: While many dramaturgical assistants were women, only a few were chief dramaturges. The same was true for the relation of assistant directors and directors (Schregel/Erdmann 1985, 28). Even today, few women are directors or dramaturges, although their numbers are on the rise. Of those, hardly any claim to be feminists. Exceptions are Ulrike Ottinger, a director and filmmaker who has staged several of Jelinek's plays, and Lore Stefanek, who has produced a number of Reinshagen's texts. Barbara Bilabel and Mechthild Erpenbeck sometimes direct plays by women or take feminist approaches to a production.

The reunification of Germany, in conjunction with the large migratory movements from the impoverished eastern European countries, has thrown the notion of national identity into renewed focus. A racially and culturally homogenous Germany is once more being contested; the idea of a multicultural Germany is still a threatening idea to many. Conservative West German critics like Karl-Heinz Bohrer have issued a call for the autonomy of cultural discourses unhampered by social and political concerns, and the 1993 Theatertreffen in Berlin, an annual festival, seems to indicate that some of the western state theaters have heeded this call.[7] At the same time, a notion of socially engaged drama persists in the stage practice of East German theaters as well as in many of the recent plays by feminists.

The rise of racist and xenophobic violence and the tightening of Germany's asylum law in 1993, at the same time that the German supreme court exhorts women to return to their primary responsibility as homemakers and restricts their reproductive rights, calls attention to the intersection of oppressions. As yet, German theater has developed few dramaturgical models equipped to address racism; Specht's *Lila*, a play about a mail-order bride, uses the conventions of the critical *Volksstück* to dramatize the jealousy and hate with which the German villagers react to the foreigner.[8] Although Specht's endeavor to critically account for race and gender is important, it is questionable whether the *Volksstück* form, even though it works through subjective and internalized practices of oppression, can adequately account for differences among immigrants rather than reinscribing in its scenario the distance between an allegedly homogenous social body and the alien particle to which it reacts.

Jelinek's play *Totenauberg* (1991) links the resurgence of racist, specifically anti-Semitic, violence to the fascist past that has been repressed by West Germany's facile identification with Western, antitotalitarian nations and discourses, and which reemerges once the cold-war antagonism between capitalist and communist Germany is cancelled. The play closes with the frightening image of mass destruction, which it holds out as a warning. However, Jelinek's deconstructive dramaturgy of acceleration and excess is unable to represent anything but the discourses that result in annihiliation (Sieg 1993).

In view of the growing urgency to challenge racist and misogynist constructions of German identity, it becomes all the more important to attend to the voices of those now living as "foreigners" in Germany, even though many of them are third-generation migrants from southern European countries whose grandparents had come to Germany during the 1960s, a time of economic growth when the country needed foreign labor. Emine Sevgi Özdamar's plays *Karagöz in Alamania* and *Keloglan in Alamania* (1982) use elements from Turkish theatrical history such as the shadow puppet figure Karagöz. That stock type, a folk hero traditionally pitted against an educated, upper-class adversary, embodies the plight of the Turkish migrant in Alamania [Germany], accompanied here by his friend, the donkey Semsettin, and his wife Ümmü. The problems caused by the migrants' dependency on the good will of bureaucrats and employers, the pain of families divided by immigration laws, the threat of deportation, and the domestic isolation of the Turkish women are presented in episodic form that interweaves violent and comic elements. Some scenes, for instance, are dramatizations of racist jokes circulating in Germany. When it was presented on the stage of a state theater, it confronted its German audiences with their worst prejudices and stereotypes, presented them with the experiences of the Turkish migrants offered in the language and storytelling traditions of that culture, and embedded those experiences in the economic relations between Turkey and Germany.

Each of the following three chapters will provide a more fully developed context for the discussion of contemporary women playwrights, situating the work of Reinshagen, Jelinek, and Steinwachs in relation to the socially critical theater of the New Left, the Austrian avant-garde and its experiments with popular culture, and the discourses of French and German feminisms, respectively. I hope that this approach, which historicizes the diverse theoretical strategies deployed by these feminist texts, is able to complement, if not eschew, the tendency to catalog and reify a "female" or "feminist aesthetic." In her introduction to *The Divided Home/Land,* Sue-Ellen Case examines the risks of importing critical practices from one ideological context (that of Brecht in East Germany) to another, suppressing the historical meanings and resonances of a particular set of techniques devised within and against a very specific discursive constellation and turning them into a style, a stable, universalizing aesthetic that can be absorbed, tokenized, and neutralized within the discourses it set out to challenge. This is not to say that feminist strategies developed by German theater artists cannot be transported to another culture or historical moment; on the contrary, I would hope that the political tactics and critical vocabulary that these texts have to offer will inform feminist practice in the United States as well. To my mind, however, these texts, which centrally revolve around the role of history as the base of national, gender, and sexual identities and which suggest new, exciting ways to contest the dominant, legitimating uses of history, also call attention to their own contingency on ideological formations and the necessity to continually invent moves that contest and challenge oppressive systems in their endlessly diverse and tiresomely similar manifestations.

Chapter 4

Utopian Subjectivism:
Gerlind Reinshagen

Born in 1926, Gerlind Reinshagen stands out among contemporary German women playwrights because she started writing before and independently from the emerging women's movement. Although working concurrently with Marieluise Fleißer and her contemporary Ilse Langner, Reinshagen belongs to a different generation. She was the first woman author whose career began after World War II. Reinshagen's oeuvre crosses genres, which is unusual in the United States but common practice among German women playwrights.[1] She had made a name for herself as a novelist, poet, and author of radio plays long before she started creating plays for the theater.[2]

Reinshagen's plays were produced at major theaters in the German speaking regions, such as the Theater am Turm (Frankfurt), the Württembergisches Staatstheater, the Schauspielhaus Bochum, and the Schauspielhaus Zurich. Her production record makes her one of the more successful German playwrights.[3] Claus Peymann, one of the most influential directors in the German theater, has directed most of her plays. Two of her pieces, *Heaven and Earth* and *Sunday's Children,* were turned into films. Her texts met with much critical acclaim and won her numerous prestigious awards.[4]

She brought new forms and subject matter to the stage; the office setting in *Doppelkopf* ([Double Head], 1967) and *Eisenherz* [Ironheart] introduced the workplace to the theater. The experimental collage *Leben und Tod der Marilyn Monroe* [The Life and Death of Marilyn Monroe], written and produced in 1971, examined the phenomenon of the female star as a construction of the popular media. Both *Heaven and Earth* and *The She-Clown* are virtually one-woman shows that provide insights

into their characters' fantasy life. Her play *Die Feuerblume* [The Fire
Flower] addresses ecological issues and abandons individualized characters in favor of collective choruses and choreographies.

Although rejecting the feminist label, Reinshagen was one of the
first women playwrights to actively engage with and support the organization Women in Theater (FiT). She participated in their events and
discussions, making her experience available to other women in the
theatrical institution (see Ahrens 1992). As a political playwright, Reinshagen's work has persistently engaged with women's concerns before
feminism started addressing aesthetic issues in the midseventies.[5] Her
"German trilogy," which comprises *Sunday's Children, Frühlingsfest*
[Spring Party], and *Tanz, Marie!* [Dance, Marie!], demonstrates her
approach to topical debates from a gendered perspective, locating issues
of nationality and identity among women in the domestic realm. Indebted to Marxist theory, Reinshagen insists on the utopian possibility
of an autonomous female subject propelled by a history and experience
of oppression and the need to struggle.

Her play *The She-Clown,* written in 1985, thematized the experience
and position of women in the classical theater, pitting the actor-writer's
fantasy of self-expression against an institution that has traditionally
constructed representations of women as heroines while barring them
from participating in the cultural production of images. The central
character, Dora, experiences a crisis both as an actor and as a woman,
because, in a double sense, she can no longer play her assigned role.
She-Clown examined the conditions and possibilities of women in representation and raised the question of a feminist aesthetic, an issue that
was hotly debated among German feminists at that time. In regard to
Dora's efforts to break through social-theatrical prescriptions, the final
image of the acrobat clown suggests two avenues out of her dilemma:
to refute gender as a bipolar structure by claiming the position of the
androgyn; and to leave the text-dominated theater for nonverbal performance traditions. The play leaves the problem of oppressive social and
theatrical roles in suspension.

Reinshagen's plays span a wide range of topics from fascism, to
women in representation, to ecology. They cover an array of styles from
Sunday's Children's realism to the epic style of *Double Head* and *Marilyn,*
the fantastic subjectivism of *She-Clown* and *Dance, Marie!,* and the
strongly formalized choral dramaturgy of *Fire Flower.* Her work also
offers a multitude of dramatic forms from the monologue to the collec-

tive choreography. In view of this diversity and versatility, no one text could be representative of Reinshagen's oeuvre. *Sunday's Children* and *Ironheart* seem the most intriguing choices for the purpose of introducing an American readership to that author's work. The former is one of her most acclaimed plays, and was, at the time, regarded as an important contribution to contemporary debates around Germany's fascist past and its bearing on present figurations of German identity. *Ironheart* seemed an appropriate choice, because it makes available a socialist feminist critique, which in the United States has frequently been imported from Britain. It examines the sexual politics of the workplace, addressing differences among women while underscoring the necessity of gender solidarity. *Ironheart* raises the issue of political agency in the subjective and interpersonal realm, which replaced the notion of "concrete utopia" with a "negative dialectic."

Sunday's Children

Sunday's Children, written in 1977, addresses the question of what it means to be a German, a question that in Germany has long hinged on the historicization of the Third Reich. In the 1960s, the Left began to advocate confronting the past in order to come to terms with it. The theater contributed to this task with the form of the docudrama, which suggested intellectual strategies of coping with collective guilt. Reinshagen shares in the project of facing the past; like other leftists, she perceives a continuity between fascism and the supposedly liberal democracy in West Germany, which she exposes in order to open it to public debate. However, she differs in her approach, which advocates proximity and identification, rather than distance and abstraction. Her investigation of fascism on the subjective level of everyday life, with a focus on women, was able to rearticulate the terms of national identity as complex and differentiated rather than remaining locked in the dualism of oppressor and oppressed, perpetrator and victim. This approach, indebted to the feminist politics of identity, coincided with feminist revisions of dominant history and its representation of women under fascism. Thus, the play provided a public forum for discussing Germany's fascist past that operated against monolithic notions of the Nazi or the woman.

The debates around a Marxist aesthetic—particularly the deployment of objectivist versus subjectivist strategies, historiographical discourse and its concern with national identity, and feminist identity politics as a strategy to claim agency for a heterogeneous subject position—constitute the discursive matrix for reading *Sunday's Children,* the first play in Reinshagen's German trilogy.

The play traces the development of Elsie, a fourteen-year-old girl, from the beginning until the end of the war. In thirty-two short scenes, Reinshagen pastes together a collage of Nazi Germany, locating it simultaneously in the marketplace of an "average" German town and in the livingroom of the Wöllmer family. Designed as a "shelter" against the brutal world of men, the Wöllmers's home, however, does not remain outside the war but is intricately connected with it. The *Lebensraum* [living room],[6] a territory under female sovereignty that women believed would protect them against male machinations in the outside world, is literally undermined by the Nazi war machinery and permeated with violence.

During the course of the play, several characters die or suffer severe mutilations; Elsie's father is killed on the front, and the young Nolle is wounded and confined to a wheelchair. Lona, the Wöllmers's servant and Elsie's friend, dies during an air raid. The apprentice Metzenthin commits suicide, and the teacher Konradi, together with his lover Inka, is assassinated by the secret police. Elsie changes from a carefree, sensitive child full of imagination and a great love of storytelling, to a neurotic, almost autistic young woman whose desperate outcry against the adults' denial of the past is quickly stifled by her mother, who prefers to forget the horrors of the war. Elsie is the only character who perceives clearly the moral implications of the other characters' dangerous "amnesia," their willful ignorance of the crimes committed in their name during the Nazi regime. The play ends with the wedding of Elsie's mother to Rodewald, the director of a school. The traditional "happy ending" of the bourgeois realist play, with its promise of a prosperous future, appears as a monstrosity in the context of the postwar economy. The wedding marks a transition from war to peace that emphasizes that no real break has occurred. The ethical blinders that protected the adults from collective knowledge and therefore shared guilt are shown to have become second nature.

Scene six shows a party at the Wöllmers's house with the guests illustrating a range of political positions vis-à-vis the regime. Herr Wöllmer represents the bourgeois aesthete and cynic, who rejects the idea of joining the army because of its unappealing uniforms; director Rodewald illustrates the apologetic stance of the educated middle-class citizen who has internalized the Nazis' anti-intellectualism and who masochistically embraces their valorization of the "man of action"; General Belius, who, in this gathering, wields the most power because of his association with the military, ironically remains silent. The women, Frau Wöllmer and Frau Belius, do not join in the men's political debate. However, Frau Belius' enthusiastic intonation of a war-song disturbs the neat separation between participation and innocence. Frau Belius acts as her husband's ideological equivalent; at the same time that he commands military operations, she orchestrates the social relations among the civilians.[7]

While traditional historiography maintains that women's space remained "innocent" of ideology, Reinshagen denies the possibility of a female sphere untouched by the state. Frau Belius does not spout Party slogans; nevertheless she is instrumentalized by the fascist system. While her body becomes a breeding device for the Nazi war machine, her voice becomes the organ for state ideology. Reinshagen underscores the irony of women's support of a system that lauds them as mothers while killing their children, and sharpens this contradiction in the image of Frau Belius, who proudly wears her *Mutterkreuz* [medal for child-bearing] to her son's funeral.

The juxtaposition of public and private, male and female, highlights structural similarities between the two spheres, representing the home as the counterpart of the Nazi war machine. Women's belief in a female *Lebensraum* did not exempt them from responsibility for the atrocities committed in their name; nor could their subordination be blamed on male legislation alone. The fiction of a female sphere free from state interference appealed to many women, including many feminists at that time, who willingly relinquished political influence in exchange for what they perceived as relative autonomy.

While the older women's hope to profit from the fascist glorification of the home was contradicted by state regulation of the so-called private sphere, the young girls who were attracted to Nazi ideology were similarly confronted with a paradox. As the case of the young Inka demonstrates, the redefinition of femininity promised a degree of independence and a feeling of self-worth that many girls embraced, yet may have been misunderstood as an end in itself.[8] Inka enjoys jogging at night and takes pride in her body. Like many other members of the League of German Girls (BDM) she fits the Nazi ideal of womanhood by sharing the concern for health and hygiene.[9] These girls' education toward a new femi-

ninity served to synchronize every individual with state policies governing reproduction. Inka's training is not an end in itself but serves the sole
purpose of making her into a physically worthy companion to a racially
fit male. When Inka is shot in flight with Konradi, she pays with her life
for accepting the terms of a contract that allows her to be her lover's
equal only in death.

Conversely, Elsie's aunt Tilda, who places a bouquet of flowers at
an execution site to honor the victims of the Nazi secret police and
express her sympathy with them, signals resistance against a regime that
violently suppressed dissent and placed great emphasis on public signs
of affirmation. At a time when the refusal of the "Hitler salute" resulted
in arrest, Tilda's small act of kindness defies a system of control sustained by the individual's terror, fear, and distrust. Elsie's mother,
shocked at her sister's indiscretion, knocks the bouquet out of her hands:
"Tilda! Are you completely crazy? After all, these are traitors" (Reinshagen 1986, 329). Internalized mechanisms of ideological control complement actual surveillance by state agencies. Tilda's act throws into
relief the gray area of individual courage and risk taking that lies between
survival and moral integrity. Her bouquet breaks the assumption of
public consent and ideological unity among all Germans, encouraging
others to signal their dissent as well. Her sister's outrage, however,
cannot be condemned as mere cowardice, because Tilda's defiance en-
dangers not just herself but her entire family.

Reinshagen's investigation of the individual's possibilities for resistance operates against dominant historical accounts that, after the war,
transformed all Nazis into monsters, and all others into "silent resisters."
The Nazi girl Inka offers her sandwich to a hungry Polish prisoner of
war despite official proscriptions to interact with foreigners.

Reinshagen's shift of focus to the individual's subjectivity and the
interpersonal relations in the domestic sphere contributes to a
redefinition of *resistance* in the context of totalitarian control. Historiographical accounts of the Third Reich have traditionally focused on
mainstream opposition, which, according to Claudia Koonz, "came only
late, and was born of disillusionment with Hitler, not opposition to his
goals."[10] The frequent invocation of the passive, cowardly German people who did nothing to oppose Hitler does not take into account the
extent of control, surveillance, and punishment.[11] While some would
broaden the notion of resistance to comprise lack of cooperation, individual efforts to dampen morale, or the voicing of dissent in secret,[12] the

masses of Germans, who after the war described themselves as having been in "silent opposition," underscore the problematic implications of such subtle definitions. Reinshagen highlights the liabilities and complexities involved in Tilda's choice of moral integrity and Frau Wöllmer's decision to conform but provides no simple solutions.

Reinshagen's representation of the various degrees of women's implication in fascist practices subverts traditional historians' evaluation of women's position under the Nazi regime, which had yielded two very contradictory theories: While some maintained that the Third Reich's sexism had resulted in women's powerlessness and therefore lack of guilt, some claimed the opposite—that women were to blame for the advent of fascism.[13] This black-and-white picture of women in the Third Reich was shared by historians across ideological divisions. Both approaches replicate the Nazis' biologism by representing women as a unified, homogeneous group. Whether women were viewed as guilty or innocent, this generalized distinction elided any differences among women; moreover, blaming mass murder on women begged the question of their participation in a state that was characterized by strict gender segregation and in which women were virtually excluded from politics. Koonz points out:

> The chain of command from chancellery to crematorium remained entirely within men's domain; women took no part in planning the "final solution"; and, except for a few thousand prison matrons and camp guards, women did not participate in murder. (Koonz 1987, 387)

Women's lack of political power, however, cannot mean that they were not responsible for war and genocide but indicates that the question of involvement and liability has to be posed in different terms. Reinshagen focuses on the politics of indifference, shifting the attention from the liar and murderer to the one who "refuses to bear witness" (Koonz 1987, 387). To know is to be liable is to be guilty—Heydrich's statement about the populace's involvement in the Jewish genocide is echoed by Frau Wöllmer, the average citizen who supposedly knew nothing.[14] To maintain a stance of innocence, she must force herself and her children to remain blind and deaf to their surroundings: "One doesn't have to know everything . . . ," she whines (Reinshagen 1986, 330).

The same mechanism operates in Metzenthin's denouncement of

Konradi as "insane" and dangerous, leading to his and Inka's murder by the secret police. Metzenthin, a working-class apprentice, had kept a critical distance from Nazi politics and organizations, which makes him seek out Konradi, a teacher who had returned from the front wounded, disillusioned, and bitter. Konradi calls his attention to a subterranean military complex, showing him that the very ground he stands on is hollow. Metzenthin shrinks back from the implication of this knowledge, realizing that nonparticipation does not protect him from being implicated in a war machinery that is not far away but literally surrounding him. Ironically it is Metzenthin, the non-Nazi, who denounces Konradi to the police. His cooperation highlights the psychological mechanisms that operated across party lines and that produced the denial of knowledge, and the silence that mark the adults' stance of "the averted gaze."

Reinshagen's focus on the home, on women and children, consciously refrains from representing what dominant history has transformed into statistics: the war, the battles, the Party machinery. Her reduction of fascist everyday life to the "recognizable" dimension of the kitchen disturbs, through its proximity, a reception of the Hitler regime that allows distance through abstraction. The examination of Nazi ideology as the instrumentalization of the subjective and the quotidian turns her attention to small details, gestures, and procedures. Reinshagen's representation of the authoritarian structures operating in the bourgeois domestic sphere highlight women's participation in a totalitarian system whose greatest crime, as she defines it, was its everyday pragmatism and indifference that suffocated any oppositional project or fantasy (Jäger 1977, 45).

The domestic tasks to which Reinshagen pays such close attention become ciphers for an obsessive preoccupation with the small and manageable that do not so much ward off the destruction in the outside world as they replicate it. The rules and "principles" so important in Frau Wöllmer's life are the domestic ghostings of a machinery of murder that stands out most of all as a bureaucratic feat.

The scene in which Elsie and Lona prepare gooseberry preserves is juxtaposed with the eruption of armed violence. Inka and Konradi have been shot by the secret police, though the official version maintains that they committed suicide. Back in her kitchen, Elsie's mother tells the girls off for being sloppy:

This is not a matter of berries, I'm telling you: this is a matter of principle, to do one thing right and orderly, one *single* thing orderly, in the midst of this sloppiness everywhere. This neglect is going to kill me. It is like mold, once it starts somewhere it proliferates, I can't . . . stop it. (Reinshagen 1986, 330)

The violence of this "principle" becomes visible when Elsie pricks her finger with a needle in just the right manner "twice, here and here, all the way through," as her mother commands. The orderly way of life, Frau Wöllmer's defense against the "terrible dissolution" around her, is the counterpart to military violence.

It is the "sanity" of bourgeois women that represents a repressive mentality fostered by the war. The unquestioning make-do attitude of the *Trümmerfrau* [rubble woman],[15] from her happy appreciation of rare luxury items to the wedding dress made of the dead husband's suit, substitutes a shortsighted preoccupation with replacing what has been lost or destroyed for visions of a different future.

While Reinshagen historicizes this attitude as produced by a specific set of circumstances, she does not confine it to a clearly delimited historical period. On the contrary, German women's busy mending and restoring, enforced by the scarcity of goods during the war, is directly related to the economic miracle of the postwar period when the "desire to replace daily what was destroyed daily, suddenly produced a visible accumulation of objects, [. . .] when barracks became bungalows, houses, sky-scrapers" (Jäger 1977, 45). It is for this reason that the play's final scene is the most horrifying one—it marks the smooth transition from war to peace and from Nazi dictatorship to liberal democracy. Elsie's mother marries Rodewald, an opportunist school director. While Elsie's new stepfather proclaims "a new beginning," the women are preoccupied with the accoutrements of the wedding, the food, the decoration, and their dresses. Elsie is the only one who realizes the monstrosity of this mindless plodding that exposes the announcement of the "new beginning" as a delusion. When General Belius appears at the wedding in a suit that used to be a uniform, Elsie looks at him and "suddenly, she doesn't see an ex-general in a suit, but something horrible, frightful, like a monster" (Reinshagen 1986, 343). She attacks him; but her violent outburst is immediately brought under control.

The perspective of the child provides a critical vantage point toward the violent, insane world of the adults. Konradi articulates the belief in children's power to fantasize, to intuitively grasp the truth:

> Children never go insane. They already are. Every child, as long as it really is one, is a little fool . . . they have second sight, they live in a dream. . . . Like fools, they see the worst, most truthful meaning of things. . . . (Reinshagen 1986, 319)

The adult's "crazy notions" suffocate the children so that they die "before becoming like the others, the normal, living corpses" (Reinshagen 1986, 320). The microstructure of fascism operates at the levels of dreams, which, as Lenin said, "must be the beginning of everything, of change, of a new order, no matter for what kind of society" (Reinshagen 1986, 321). The possibility of a different Elsie, the one whose mutilation and silencing the play traces, and of a different Germany, which she embodies, remains the utopian gestalt of this text, and can only be represented as an absence.

The spectator's identification with Elsie poses a challenge to the audience's moral and political judgment because it presents her as both victimized and complicit. While in some instances Elsie's misjudgment in regard to Nazi atrocities is understandable in view of their scope, her confrontation with a Polish prisoner, in which she taunts him and speaks to him as to a dog, illustrates her acceptance of the dominant ideology that constructs the enemy as subhuman. While it is important to call forth the pain of the victim in order to embark on the "labor of mourning," which the Mitscherlichs demanded,[16] empathy with, and recognition of, the oppressor's mindset and motivation has been a delicate, but even more urgent, task. In order to confront the trauma of fascism, which would haunt the ostensibly democratic West German state as long as it was suppressed, Germans needed to come to terms with their previous embracing of Nazi ideology.

Reinshagen's representation of fascism shows the Third Reich as a set of social and psychological structures that continue to determine the contemporary ideological landscape of the Federal Republic of Germany. Rodewald, who toasts to the "new beginning" (Reinshagen 1986, 343), and General Belius, whose suit still betrays its original function as a military uniform, highlight "de-nazification" as a mere costume alteration, while the ideological body of the state, i.e., the hierarchical struc-

tures of the Nazi administrative, educational, legal, and military apparatuses, is left intact.

These characters are representative of postwar Germans. Historian
Wolfgang Benz characterizes the attitude of the general public toward
the Nazi era as an effort to "ward off the past" (Benz 1987). Any attempt
to deal with Nazism by taking on responsibility was denigrated as the
airing of dirty laundry, which should remain hidden from the neighbors'
eyes. Moreover, the totalitarian critique that dominated the cold war
discourse collapsed fascism with communism, effectively turning the
Third Reich into the history of the Other. In the conservative political-
cultural climate of the Adenauer era—that chancellor's slogan was "No
experiments!"—few critical voices disturbed a truce based on collective
suppression and historical amnesia.[17]

Eichmann's trial in Jerusalem and the Frankfurt hearings of
Auschwitz criminals in the early 1960s sparked a wave of public debate
about the Third Reich for which the theater provided a forum. The
construction of the Berlin Wall in 1961 brought home the entanglement
of the present with a past that, in Ernst Nolte's words, "does not want
to end" (Nolte 1987, 39). The renewed interest in German fascism and
its impact on the contemporaneous ideological landscape coincided with
the return of Erwin Piscator, the originator of documentary theater at
the Volksbühne during the Weimar Republic, to the Federal Republic
of Germany. Documentary theater as a presentational style revived
through the plays of Peter Weiss, Rolf Hochhuth, and Heinar Kipphardt.
Similar to the axioms of New Objectivism and its attendant Brechtian
aesthetics, the theater that sprang out of and fed the Left, claimed to
accurately represent an oppressive reality while openly advocating social
change. In the late 1960s, when Reinshagen wrote her first plays for the
stage, art and literature were taken to task by and for revolutionary
forces and causes.[18]

The historicization of the Third Reich occupied a crucial position
on the political agendas of both conservative parties and the conglomerate of leftist, progressive discourses and agencies that operated outside
the parliamentary institution. While the Right deployed a policy of containment and suppression, on which the image of West Germany as a
trustworthy partner in Western alliances rested, leftist theater workers,
historians, and activists during the 1960s began to question the official
representation of the Nazi period that portrayed the German people as

Hitler's victims, stressing aspects of continuity between the fascist regime and the liberal democracy. Documentary theater during that decade became an important medium to reopen the debate about West Germany's past.

The docudrama constructed a homogeneous subject characterized by a collective guilt shared by all Germans—guilt of the Nazi regime's atrocities and guilt of nearly twenty years of suppression and silence in regard to the past. That notion destabilized the assignment of roles within the oppressor-oppressed dyad. In 1968, Peter Weiss published his manifesto "The Material and the Models," in which he asserted that its purpose is to construct a "model of actual occurrences," i.e., reveal a truth that has previously been suppressed by the state. Its main tenet is its "authentic" nature: "Documentary theater refrains from all invention: it takes authentic material and puts it on the stage, unaltered in content, edited in form" (Weiss 1971, 41). The docudrama "takes sides" in order to affect social change, and thus becomes an instrument of agitation for political opposition. Its claim to an objective representation of history rested on a Brechtian poetics of distance.

Reinshagen's subjective, metaphorical style set her apart from a theatrical scene dominated by the docudrama's approach to representing history through so-called authentic facts. In an interview with Anke Roeder, she explained:

> For me, a play that wants to prove something is not a play. In order to stir up people, I cannot serve them with a theory and a solution to a problem, but I must hit them where they themselves could have been involved, and then let them draw their own conclusions. Rather, I would like to raise questions: How would I have reacted to a dictatorship, what is the effect of fear, what crimes result from what existential need, and what produces silence? Could I myself have been a criminal? (Roeder 1989, 34)

History, according to Reinshagen, is too complex and riddled with contradictions for a writer to be able to represent it in terms of simple problems or solutions. Instead, she experimented with dramaturgical models that could account for different orders of reality, and saw her writing as an attempt to search for ways to represent the social as complicated and multileveled.[19]

In some ways, Reinshagen's subjectivist style vis-à-vis an objectivist theatrical tradition resembles the political constellation in which Marieluise Fleißer found herself (and who, not coincidentally, was being rediscovered at this time); unlike Fleißer, however, Reinshagen's writing was not politically and aesthetically isolated. Her texts register and participate in the reconfiguration of Marxist theory and practice resulting from the dispersal of the homogeneous ideology and structure of the student movement into the heterogeneous discursive formation summarized by the umbrella term the New Left.[20] In political terms, this heterogenization marked a shift in focus from activism in the public spaces of institutions, universities, factories, and the street, to the subjective and interpersonal spaces of the revolutionary individual's consciousness and domestic relationships.

Aesthetic discourses reflected and instigated this shift by replacing the objectivist style of representation that the docudrama exemplified with the aesthetics of New Subjectivism. That discourse, however, itself comprised diverse aesthetic practices. Many male New Subjectivist writers recorded feelings of loss and disempowerment in their texts, which register the breakdown of authoritarian structures within the student movement and construct its demise as a failure (Adelson 1983). Reinshagen, however, viewed the lack of a common goal, or political program articulated by a Marxist vanguard, as an empowerment of the individual who would strive for social change in the micropolitical practices of everyday life.

In the polarized political climate of the 1960s and 1970s, the New Left had to wrench political agency from an all-powerful state that, under attack, displayed the military and legislative might of a police state. Oppositional forces found their radius of action radically diminished by state surveillance and repression. In 1975, the members of the first Rote Armee Fraktion, the so-called Baader-Meinhof-Group, were on trial in Stammheim near Stuttgart where Reinshagen's play *Sunday's Children* opened. Their trial, lasting several years until their deaths in 1977, posed the question of what constituted a "German": the reformer-turned-terrorist or the official representative of an all-powerful state. Both the defendants, physically and psychologically weakened through solitary detention and hunger strikes, and the prosecutors laid claim to a "German" identity by justifying their actions as being on behalf of the German people. In *Sunday's Children*, this constellation between the revolutionaries in chains and the state that condemns them parallels the quelling of the protagonist Elsie's imagination and dreams by the authoritarian structures that suffocate the fantasy of a different, better future. In response to this deadlock, the focus on everyday life and the mechanisms of ideological reproduction signaled the New Left's shifting ground of action: Since society could not be changed, the revolutionary subject must change itself.[21] Although some would contend that New Subjectivism in fact abandoned Marxist premises as the docudrama had defined them, this school of thought, itself a heterogeneous project, arguably filled a lacuna in a Marxist critique that had neglected the subjective dimension in the study of social change.[22]

While Reinshagen's texts share their concern with ideological microstructures and psychological mechanisms with New Subjectivism, her dramaturgy relies on Brechtian notions of the dialectic and its function to reveal contradictions; a dramaturgy that was emulated by the radical literature of the student movement. Her emphasis on social relations and the necessity of change is also informed by her continuing engagement with political issues and movements of the late 1970s. In contrast to orthodox Marxism, however, the absence of a proletarian (or feminist) agent prevents the closure of victorious revolution in her plays.

In this context, the theories of the Frankfurt School gained renewed significance, because they took into account the absence of a collective, historical agent that takes a position in social struggle. Theodor W. Adorno argued that no positive representations of social relations free from alienation and domination are possible because in a world contaminated by the homogenizing forces of reason, the Non-identical, the Other is corrupted once it is touched by the instrumentalizing force of the idea. If the Other appears in art, it does so as a crossed-out possibility, as a marked absence. Adorno vehemently rejected a literature of engagement (as the student movement propagated it), because it rests on the instrumentalization of the work of art for a social purpose. On the contrary, he claimed that art that serves a social function has no social truth value: "Art is societal in its immanent movement against society, not in its manifest stance" (Adorno 1973, 7:336). Reinshagen borrows Adorno's notion of the negative dialectic that theorized a position of resistance, thus becoming a useful strategy for claiming political agency within and against a hegemonic system. However, she does not share that theorist's condemnation of a literature of engagement, which registers his distance from any social movement. Her indictment of fascism does take a political stance and inscribes her proximity to an ongoing social struggle.

The lack of a forceful, assertive narrative of revolution in New

Subjectivist literature prompted derision on the part of some critics. In an essay entitled "Mutations in the New Drama" published in 1976, Reinshagen countered accusations of decadence and lethargy levelled at New Subjectivism, and posited the emergence of a dramaturgy that, despite its focus on petit-bourgeois apathy, is committed to social change. The new dramaturgy is characterized by "mutations of thought" and "cracks/leaps in consciousness."

The aim of this dramaturgy is not the presentation of "perfect counter-images, a boring utopia," but the "sudden change, which, unaccounted for and unpredictable in scientific discourse, can transform a character" (Reinshagen quoted in Weber 1979, 246). Such mutations, she asserted, could lead out of the impasse where theater endlessly rehearses the powerlessness of the resistant subject.

It is possible that the discovery of new qualities, beyond the first astonishment, beyond the first, tentative getting accustomed to them, could lead to new possibilities in the course of this process, it could perhaps result in new values, in persons setting their own standards, and it will provoke the more interest, since this experience will not be restricted to distant gods, or omnipotent rulers, but can happen to anyone. (Reinshagen in Weber 1979, 246)

The theater's "mutation" toward a New Subjectivist dramaturgy that strove to carve out pockets of resistance and agency through a shift of focus from the public and monumental to the personal realm of everyday experience participated in the reconfiguration of a heterogeneous, resistant subject that intervened in hegemonic, monolithic representations of German identity. One of the motors behind this political project was the feminist movement.

The collapse of the student movement and the heterogenization of the Left during the 1970s into a multitude of micropolitical organizations had opened a field of political action and theoretical discourses to women who until then had subordinated or rather sacrificed a gender critique to a class critique. Feminist scholars intervened in dominant constructions of identity in historiographical discourse and developed an increasingly complex subject equipped to deal with Germany's "ambivalent traditions" (Habermas 1988). They started to develop their own theories of fascism that refuted the simplistic position that most male historians had accorded women in the Third Reich. These studies carefully distinguished between different social, ethnic, political, and religious groups of women, tracing the "rewards" of the regime for those women who complied with it and uncovering various strategies of noncompliance and resistance.[23]

Sunday's Children's representation of the home and the relationships within it as political coincided with the emerging feminist discourse on fascism. Reinshagen's gendered perspective not only shifted the terms of inquiry into Germany's Nazi history to a differentiated spectrum of positions ranging from complicity to resistance but also advocated an empathetic confrontation with the past, which at the same time suggested a political agenda for the present. Reinshagen's focus on the domestic sphere and everyday experience replaced a representational style that stressed distance and abstraction with a mode of address that emphasized proximity and personal identification and that in feminist theory and practice has been described as "identity politics."

In U.S. feminism, identity politics provided the conceptual tools for eroding the monolithic notion of universal "Woman," enabling women to account for differences among themselves. The predominant discursive mode that developed concurrently was the testimonial, indicating a change in the relationship between the personal and the political. According to bell hooks, confession and memory become "documentary sources" for "constructing strategies of resistance and survival" (hooks 1989, 110) and they enable oppressed individuals and communities to deal with victimization.[24] The telling and naming of a traumatic experience empower the victims by placing experience in a political framework.[25] Since identity politics provides strategies for politicizing the experience of oppression, it also proves useful for the oppressors: It enables whites to come to terms with their own racism, men to learn about sexism, and Germans to understand their complicity with fascism.

Gerlind Reinshagen's play *Sunday's Children,* even if not strictly autobiographical, functioned as a testimonial. In 1977, she was awarded the prestigious Mühlheimer Dramatikerpreis (playwriting award) for *Sunday's Children.* It fulfilled the need to unearth and examine a past too ugly and frightening to be looked at. At a time when the state claimed that a critique of fascism equaled terrorism, Reinshagen's play allowed its audiences to pose questions that otherwise and formerly were not permitted to be asked. The characters in *Sunday's Children,* a realist narrative of Nazi fascism, occupy and represent a range of positions from engagement to denial; operating on the mimetic paradigm, the play constructs these same positions for the audience, thus serving to facilitate a discussion on whose urgency the Left insisted and which the Right suppressed. The play offers spectators the opportunity to confront the Nazi past and question the way it has overdetermined notions of national and gender identity; it necessitates accepting this as a problem in the present and dealing with it from a position of engagement and identification.

Striving to represent the exact mechanics of everyday life during the Third Reich, however, *Sunday's Children* repeats the exclusionary moves of that which it represents. Jews and other "asocial elements" remain invisible within this frame; the artifacts that point to their existence cannot be explained or integrated into this world. The mass killings of Polish Jews are as much beyond Elsie's imagination as are Konradi's reports about people exploding in the air. Reinshagen cannot do more than mark the exclusion. The extinction of a utopia brings the urgency to leap toward one.

Ironheart

In *Ironheart,* published in 1982, Reinshagen engaged with the debate conducted among the New Left during the 1970s in regard to the role of the imagination in relation to social change. While those who chose "the long march through the institutions" with the objective of reforming the system from within and deployed the imagination as a motor to sustain this project, others remained "autonomous" in order to avoid the trap of established, hierarchical power structures. To their mind, radical art and radical social practices function as a safety valve and therefore had to be abandoned in favor of confrontation and activism. The notion of utopia was reserved for the future; any oppositional fantasy or project in the present would merely defer the revolution. However, the women's movement intervened in this opposition because it practiced autonomy and focused on subjective change in everyday life, which emphasized the revolutionary potential of the individual.[26]

Likewise, Reinshagen's play can be viewed as an endorsement of antiestablishment politics, suggesting that social change cannot be effected from within the patriarchal-capitalist system at the same time that it locates responsibility for social change at the subjective level and in the present. The utopia of a nonalienated existence and female autonomy is no by-product of political change, as the male-dominated Left had posited, but must precede and complement an institutional critique.

Ironheart exemplifies the politics of socialist feminism, combining a class critique with a gender critique. Reinshagen casts gender as the determining factor of the subject's experience. Gender determines its degree of alienation from itself in its exclusion from, or access to, an objective and objectifying language; it determines its sexuality as either aggressive or submissive; and it determines its mobility, or lack of it, in the socioeconomic terrain of the capitalist marketplace. *Ironheart* articulates gender not only as sexual difference of women from men but also as differences among women, examining and highlighting the conditions of solidarity and support as well as competition and jealousy.

Ironheart is set in a clerical office, locating relationships among women in the workplace. The play largely lacks a conventional plot; a young man, Kolk, is offered a permanent position in the office, and a young woman, Bublitz, who loves him unrequitedly, leaves. *Ironheart* provides glimpses into its characters' inner lives, into their hopes and dreams, and into their interactions with each other. Dramatic structure, the building and resolution of conflict, is abandoned in favor of the characters' continuous rubbing against an oppressive and painful reality juxtaposed with their fantasies. The absence of dramatic development and the overall impression of stasis reflect the impossibility of change. The presence of another office, visible through the window of the one in which the main dramatic action takes place, underlines the ubiquity of these workers' experiences shaped by labor relations. The play maps out the conditions of stagnation by tracing the reabsorption of liberating fantasies into an oppressive material reality. Yet it does not indict the imagination as mere escapism from material reality but rather acknowledges its potential to create pockets of solidarity and compassion among the disenfranchised. At the same time, *Ironheart* maintains the utopian notion of an outside where autonomy and self-fulfillment are possible.

The mise-en-scène highlights the workers' subjective experience of labor. The ticking of the office clock and the noises of typewriters, adding machines, and the teletype punctuate the existence of the clerks. The extent to which machines dictate their time provides a measure of their alienation, which is most drastically illustrated in Billerbeck's accounts of her long, empty weekends. Labor determines the clerks' lives even when they do not work, showing how "leisure" is shaped by labor relations, instead of compensating for them somehow. They spend the Sundays regenerating themselves for the coming week, unable to maintain an identity apart from work. The rhythmical, repetitive pattern of the women's language mirrors the office sounds, and conveys the slow, almost imperceptible passage of time, highlighting the perpetual, tortuous return of the familiar.

The language of the play grounds the narrative in class and gender. The women's elliptical, fragmented utterances establish communality among them that rest on unspoken understanding and on a shared history and experience. The women communicate in an abbreviated code that seems unintelligible to the men, most notably Kolk. Among them, correct grammar is unnecessary for communication; moreover, the use of an intimate language reveals Kolk as alien to the group of women. He not only interrupts their dialogue but also remains outside a communicative process that relies on pauses and silences more than words.

Kolk's "accurate" language of science, counting, and measuring reflects his distance from the female workers. He is the one who attempts to translate the immeasurable boredom of wasted weekends into figures:

> BILLERBECK: I didn't go out all day. Can't do anything after a week like that. No energy.
>
> KOLK (*to* BILLERBECK): And how long, did you say, that's been going on? Your Sundays, like that? How many years? (BILLERBECK *shrugs. Silence.*)
>
> BUBLITZ (*softly*): For a long time. (*Silence*) Maybe . . . for as long . . . as this cabinet has been standing here.
>
> KOLK (*calculating*): That would be twenty-two times fifty-two, so more than a thousand, if I'm figuring right, one thousand one hundred Sundays, approximately?
>
> (Reinshagen, *Ironheart* 1992, 235)

The office itself provides the only frame of reference for the women, while Kolk has recourse to "objective" discourses circulating outside of it. Bublitz, who falls in love with Kolk and switches allegiances, fails to perceive his divisiveness; her loyalty to him jars her out of tune with the other workers and destroys the tenuous support system among them.

Ironheart designates language as the instrument of alienation, and locates the possibility of harmony, communality, and understanding in the nonverbal realm. Bublitz's dream of a magic language that could express her personal uniqueness holds out the possibility of healing the gap between the subject's desire for authenticity and a language that erases it. Her desire for a name that fits her, and for a signature that conjures up an autonomous, powerful being, eventually propels her out of a system that turns the impulse to escape into self-destruction and suffocates the desire to be different.

Billerbeck's remonstrations and continual calls for speed, efficiency, and obedience emphasize the class differences among the women. Billerbeck is both a countess and the office head, which bolsters her claim for authority; the flip side of her superiority is her isolation. Moreover, her dark, apocalyptic visions profess the decadence and depression associated with the aristocracy (Case 1988, 88). However, gender solidarity overrides class differences. During the recurring moments of crisis, the women assure each other of their support and affection. When Billerbeck breaks down, despairing of her loneliness and sole responsibility for the running of the office, Bublitz and Ada console her. Similarly, Billerbeck takes care of Bublitz in a moment of overwhelming angst, telling her to take a coffee break and offering to take over her work load.

The men, on the other hand, are incapable of compassion and solidarity. Kolk's attempts at forging exclusive bonds with Billerbeck and Ada disrupt the sensitive social fabric because he sows distrust, resentment, and jealousy. While Kolk's harrassment of Ada exploits her perceived sexual submissiveness, his advances to Billerbeck are more clearly recognizable as opportunistic careerism because he depends on the head clerk's approval during his time of probation. Rosinski's advances to Bublitz are overtly destructive when he offers her alcohol in order to secure her dependency on him.

Kolk and Rosinski, the office handyman who lurks mostly in the photocopy room adjoining the office, are both characterized by their cynical outlook on life. Kolk [crow], whose telltale name betrays his sadistic enjoyment in pessimistic remarks, continually rebukes the women's liberatory fantasies. In a key scene he ridicules Billerbeck's belief that "in every class—no matter how many there are—everywhere, everything is always possible. That's the miracle!"(248) by asserting that there are no miracles, and accusing her of self-delusion. Kolk's intellectual analysis of labor relations leads him to the conclusion that "if you stay you amputate yourself. . . . And to hold on to the illusion that you can still change something, that's ridiculous" (266). His ostensible radicalism masks economic and educational privilege. The women, whose belief in the possibility of change he ridicules, stay because they lack the option of a self-determined existence elsewhere. Their vacillation between despair and hope is shown as a strategy, a way to cope with the everyday experience of stagnation.

Reinshagen highlights the structural violence inherent in the patriarchal, capitalist system, and gender-specific responses to it. In dissecting the effects of oppression on the subjective level, *Ironheart* traces the assimilation of counterproductive impulses into the system. While the men turn their frustration and hostility against others—Rosinski harrasses and blackmails Bublitz; Kolk's free-floating aggression attaches itself to all of the characters in the course of the play—the women respond masochistically. In moments of crisis, Bublitz resorts to alcohol; Ada exhibits bruises and wounds as the visible signs of her masochism; Lissy, who sporadically visits the office as a messenger, is recovering from a suicide attempt; and Billerbeck heaps the others' workloads onto her own desk. Billerbeck's self-destructive reaction to alienated working conditions most clearly demonstrates the vicious cycle of violence fed by frustration and its effect on the worker. Her position of responsibility for the efficient running of the office produces a high amount of anxiety and isolation on her part; her response, however, only increases her despair and effectively perpetuates the system at the expense of her own sanity. Bublitz' nickname, Ironheart, which gives the play its title, suggests that women must steel themselves against violence and refuse to take it into their heart, the seat of subjectivity. Only then will they gain the strength to exit masochistic gender roles and seek out alternatives.

Lissy's suicide attempt exemplifies the women's lack of upward mobility. When Kastner, her lover, climbs the next step on the social ladder, he deserts the woman who has become inappropriate to his superior status. This sexist pattern also characterizes Kolk's career, which, like his male predecessor's and despite his lack of experience or ability, will eventually lead him into the higher echelons of the firm. The women remain stationary, forced to observe the careers of the men who pass through.

The women's sexuality is imprinted with prevailing power relations. The visible manifestations of Ada's masochism signal her desire to be "the centre of attention in the office—a painful bid for social power" (Case 1988, 88). In a monologue, Ada describes her sexual fantasy about a Turkish man, who in West German society inhabits the lowest social strata:

I see in the broken mirror how he's looking at me, as if I
wasn't . . . human. . . . Like he's trying to . . . figure me out, the way
he's looking, I'm sure of it, surprised, because he loves me. . . .
(Reinshagen 1992, 257)

This scenario exemplifies the eroticization of power relations, in
which the lowest position is constructed as female. Ada is a pawn in the
sexual fantasy that circulates among the office workers, which constructs
women as the willing "participants" in sexual abuse and men as the
aggressors. Her display of wounds, scars, and abrasions fuels her co-
workers' imagination as well as their belief that "she asked for it." The
entire office lasciviously participates in this fantasy, which Ada acts out.

The female subject's eroticization as the immobile object of male
violence casts women's social position in the workplace in sexual terms.
The sexual prowess of Kastner, another employee in the company, is
figured in socioeconomic as well as sexual terms; his potency is intricately bound up with his upward mobility. Masculinity is defined in the
sociosexual terms of domination, abuse, and objectification. For that
reason, Kolk cannot respond to Bublitz's bid for recognition as an individual; instead, he molests Ada, demonstrating his successful interpellation into the male position within this sexual economy.

Bublitz is the only character who manages to break free from masochistic role prescriptions. She rejects Rosinski's efforts to dominate her
and refuses to participate in her own sexual objectification. This narrative of liberation is central to *Ironheart;* in leaving the site of capitalist
exploitation and alienation, Bublitz also leaves the site of her feminization, rejecting Rosinski and Kolk's attempts to force upon her the role
of dependent victim. That ending, however, also suggests that in the
office business will continue as usual.

The task of the theater, Gerlind Reinshagen contended in 1976, is the
simultaneous representation of what is and of what can be.[27] This definition problematizes the capacity of realism to instigate social change. The
function of literature, the notion of utopia, and the proposed relation
between the two were hotly debated and underwent considerable change
during the decade following the emergence of the student movement and
the subsequent formation of the New Left. The representation of utopia
as a positive vision of the future gave way to a notion of literature's
potential to convey "anticipatory illuminations" located in the interstices
of the text.

The political theater of the 1960s, as self-proclaimed forum and medium for social change, found itself obligated not only to offer a critique of the status quo but also to provide guidelines toward reform or revolution. However, the function of the theater to formulate a political program changed radically during the 1960s and 1970s. Reinshagen's texts participate in the reconfiguration of social change on a local, subjective level, and implicitly critique the student movement for its dogmatism.

During the late 1960s, the theater's task to envision social change was complicated by the fact that at that historical juncture, the utopian function of art and literature had become ideologically suspect. The revolutionary students doubted the potential of the theatrical institution, the so-called *Theatertheater,* to directly effect social change; the impulse toward political activism was shifted outside the institution into the street.[28] The domination of the student movement by orthodox Marxism led to the instrumentalization of representational practices as tools in a political struggle with socialist goals.[29] The shift from a homogeneous political movement that recognized only one contradiction and one plan of action, to a heterogeneous field of political practices, also effected a rethinking of utopia and social change.

Reinshagen's aesthetic model registers what in the 1970s was frequently lamented as *Utopieverlust* [the loss of utopia]. However, the term *Utopieverlust* actually indicated a change in the meaning of *utopia,* which entailed, to varying degrees, the aestheticization of a notion that had been instrumentalized and, to the minds of some, overdetermined for the purposes of political activism. In a radical reversal of orthodox Marxist thought, Gert Ueding went as far as defining all literature as utopian (and therefore liberating) because it is not identical with reality.[30]

Thus, the meaning of the term *utopia* shifted from its traditional definition, i.e., the projection of an ideal state, to the notion of the "utopian function" of art.[31] Particularly the work of Adorno and Bloch provided impulses for a rethinking of utopia, which located it in the interaction of the reader with the text. Their models of "utopian production" replaced a positive representation of the future with the notion of a fragmented text whose gaps provide blank spaces for the reader's imagination. The shift of the site of production from author to reader extricated the utopian model from the authoritarian structures that dominated the student movement and, through this new mode of address, imbued the subject with responsibility for social change, comprising the public, institutional—as well as the private, subjective—dimensions. Reinshagen, like other New Subjectivist artists, attributed great power to the imagination as counterhegemonic agent.[32]

Bloch's theory provides the tool for reading Reinshagen's texts as examples of utopian production, despite their lack of positive *Leitbilder* [model images]. According to Bloch, art provides anticipatory illuminations of a better future. He articulated a processual notion of utopia as always in flux and interactive with material reality. Thus, hope becomes a "principle," or method, that can be disappointed but not cancelled. Because utopian thinking is grounded in the social conditions with which it critically engages, it is always strategic; utopia is contingent on the historical moment that gives rise to it but has no reified content, such as happiness, freedom, or a particular social order. Bloch asserted the potential of realization residing in that which not yet exists. The *Not-yet* became a central term in his epistemology, and the function of art is to render the Not-yet visible. Glimpses of the future as the possibility of the present appear in a momentary *Vor-Schein* [anticipatory illumination].

According to Reinshagen, the theater can represent the tension between the Not and the Not-yet through its own means that are specific to the medium. These are:

> (1) to find precise metaphors for a time, a person, a situation; (2) to force the spectator to concentrate on a certain aspect so that s/he automatically extrapolates, through the hyper-clear description of details—in the manner of the neo-realists. (Jäger 1977, 45)

The term *precise metaphor* is itself a contradiction, since the metaphor in its reliance on the image always ultimately resists its complete assimilation into language and intelligibility. The dissoluble conceptual "knot" that the metaphor presents inscribes at the same time its proximity to the historical moment in its complexity and contradictedness rather than permitting aesthetic distance (see Müller 1979, 55–57). Reinshagen's plays, which capture the Not-yet on the subjective level, operate in the realm of personal experience, from which the spectator is then invited to extrapolate a social critique.

Ironheart illustrates the notion of utopia as it had been reformulated by leftist theorists and feminists. The confrontation of the intellectual Kolk with the clerical workers plays out a common scenario of the student movement and its tactics of infiltrating the workplace. *Ironheart's* attention to the untapped energies of the subject's "sub-life" (Kässens 1983, 42) implicitly critiques the movements' attendant, linear notion of utopia that posited the resolution of contradictions in the future, thus legitimating the deferral of "peripheral contradictions" such as women's oppression. While retaining the hope for a different, better future in the dramatic development of Bublitz, who leaves the representational frame and the system it circumscribes, Reinshagen also maps the possibility of authentic, human relations in the subtext of the play.

Reinshagen maintained, "What should never be separated: the material appearance of a person and her utopia" (Reinshagen 1984, 189). This postulation contains a tenet that is central to her work: the inscription of a utopian gestalt into the text that shines through the cracks of a character's consciousness.[33] *Ironheart* dramatizes the dialectic between the visible and the invisible in the gradual destruction of the office's social fabric, and in the juxtaposition of a base of solidarity and understanding among the women with patriarchal mechanisms of control, domination, and abuse. However, Bublitz's decision to leave contains a strong utopian potential because she not only believes in the possibility of a nonalienated existence but decides to act on that hope.

Utopia is represented as gender specific. Rosinski and Kolk are locked into a rational discourse that denies change. "You don't want to understand that someone can change for the better," Bublitz tells Rosinski (243). Only the women have access to a support system that tacitly acknowledges and validates their visions of themselves. Their silent solidarity and respect empower Bublitz to take the step outside. Still, her leaving is ambiguous because it includes the possibility of failure. The suicide of the girl in office B, which Bublitz observes from her window, suggests that change cannot be wrought within the parameters of existing social conditions and relations. The girl's death can be read as a negative prefiguration of Bublitz's future, whose positive potential cannot realistically be represented.

Ironheart suggests an intangible realm of nonalienated human relations among women, which empowers them to strive toward autonomy and authenticity. In Reinshagen's plays, the female subject becomes the site of the impossible utopia yet denies the closure of an essentialized femininity. Bublitz is no conventional heroine promising to heal a violent, patriarchal world. She risks failure, even death, in leaving a system against which she rebels. Reinshagen writes around the fantasy of a different system in order to mark its absence from political and theoretical discourses. Her poetics of the "double vision" (Kiencke 1986, 38) mark the potentiality of her characters as unrepresentable, as that which has been destroyed, or as something that cannot yet be seen.

Elfriede Jelinek, courtesy of Gruner and Jahr. Photograph by Karin Rocholl

Chapter 5

Postmodern Inversions: Elfriede Jelinek

Elfriede Jelinek, an Austrian living in Vienna and Munich, is probably the best-known feminist writer in the German language today. Her work has been received in the context of the women's movement and the emergence of feminist theory in academia. She is also a popular figure and has, after the publication of her controversial novel *Lust* [Desire], become one of the few women who represent feminism to the broader public in German-speaking countries. Not only did her face appear on the cover of the feminist monthly *Emma;* her image was also the centerfold of the general news magazine *stern.*[1] The photograph of Jelinek in a femme fatale pose with spike heels, leather jacket, and cigarillo, reclining in an armchair, bore the legend "Men see me as the great dominatrix" and characterized the writer as "Austria's best-hated author."[2]

As Jelinek explained in interviews, *Desire* constituted the attempt to rewrite George Bataille's pornographic novel *The Story of the Eye* from a female point of view. The mass media gloatingly reported her "failure" to craft a "genuinely female, erotic language"; what *Desire* achieves is a meticulous description of power relations within which "woman is always the object, never the subject of desire" (Schwarzer 1989, 51), condensing the relationship between men and women into brutal images of sadomasochism. The title of her book is, of course, ironic, because it describes and analyzes the unrepresentability of female heterosexual desire.[3]

The *stern* centerfold enacts precisely the problematics of women in representation that Jelinek addresses in her work. The article marked her as a transgressor—as a woman writer and, what is more, author of a book notorious for its relentless critique of male heterosexual pleasure as pornographic. With the publication of *Desire*, Jelinek steps out of the role of being the object of the male gaze and looks back at the patriarchal apparatus that objectifies her. This aggressive and blunt stare has prompted critics to suspect Jelinek of possessing the "evil eye," and turned her into "Austria's best-hated author."[4] Clearly, what haunts this discourse is the specter of the witch, the traditional cipher of male castration anxiety. Yet the taunting image of the dominatrix manages to assuage this anxiety and recuperate her into a sexual economy threatened by her speech. Jelinek's eroticization as a centerfold calls attention to the precarious condition of women's authorship: as dominatrix, she has permission to speak—the legend quotes her—but only to men and in their terms: "Men see me . . ." Ironically, the *stern* article, which prominently displayed sexualized images of Jelinek and sensationalist, bold-faced captions interspersed with the text, rehearses the dangerous contradiction that Jelinek inhabits. Her claim that "it is impossible for women to speak about [desire] in a language that is not male" (Lahann 1988, 78) is proved by the layout of the article. The spectacle of a woman's body renders her voice inaudible.

The unorthodox introduction of this author through her image in the mass media allows me to approach Jelinek's work from the site that she has declared one of her main battlegrounds. She has also directed her derisive stare at the dominant discourses of classical high culture. Her inimitable style, which mixes the masterpieces of European culture with the TV slang of commercials and soap operas has (not surprisingly) angered those who wish to preserve the "purity" of the work of art and guard it against ideological contamination; however, Jelinek's reception in feminist criticism has been equally controversial, due to her absent female subject and her preoccupation with the "Fathers." Jelinek's texts gain their feminist momentum from the self-destructive dynamics of the master narratives but accord no agency to an oppositional or resistant subject.

I will first discuss generally Jelinek's stylistic and political development, her sense of dramaturgy, and its relation to feminist theory. This will serve as the groundwork from which to read two of her plays: *Clara S.* and *Illness or Modern Women*. The discussion of these plays will examine the usefulness of deconstruction as an ideological critique for a feminist politics. These two plays seem particularly appropriate because they best represent Jelinek's "negative" dramaturgy and politics; her first play, *Nora*, and its dissection of bourgeois feminist rhetoric seem slightly dated from a contemporary perspective, and *Burgtheater,* which deals with the Nazi past of that famous institution, is very specific to the cultural context of Austria and difficult to access for an American readership.

Elfriede Jelinek was born in Austria in 1946. She spent her adolescence in Vienna, where she studied theater arts and art history at the University of Vienna, as well as classical music at the Vienna Conservatory of Music. Her familiarity with the discourses and institutions of high art has informed her writing, most directly the play *Burgtheater,* and her novel *The Piano Teacher.* Her work as a novelist, poet, playwright, translator, and writer of radio plays and film scripts has earned her recognition in Europe in the form of numerous awards.[5]

Jelinek's early writing evidences the influence of the Wiener Gruppe [Viennese Group], which consisted of a number of avant-garde writers who worked together from 1952 to 1964 (Hoffmeister 1987, 107). The Viennese Group experimented with representational techniques. The collages of ready-made text fragments that the four artists Artmann, Achleitner, Rühm, and Bayer assembled and that they occasionally performed in "action-lectures" were organized around formalist principles rather than social criticism, though that was often implied.[6] In his history of the group, Gerhard Rühm stresses their efforts to "estrange" language and thereby create "new meanings," a project that emphasized playfulness and pleasure in the roaming of the imagination.[7]

Jelinek is presently a member of the Graz writers' association, an organization founded in 1973. Its constituency, among them the Grazer Gruppe [Graz Group], constitute the Austrian avant-garde. Jelinek's work evidences the influence of the Graz Group; it shares its topics and cultural critique while diverging from its politics.

The work of the Graz avant-garde writers, like that of their Viennese predecessors, revolves around pleasure.[8] The study of mass culture, influenced by the writings of Marshall McLuhann and Roland Barthes's theory of myths, precipitated these writers' focus on popular discourses, which they dissected and reassembled in dadaist fashion. The Graz artists view themselves as social outcasts, and tend to celebrate "non-conformism and anti-collectivism, which easily slipped into the cult of individualism and elitism" (Wiesmayr 1980, 32).

In the heated debates around the political function of literature, which were sparked by the West German student movement and its proclamation of the "death of literature" in 1968, many Graz authors, like the *manuskripte* editor Kolleritsch, took the position that

> revolution can only mean the victory of literature, of art in general. . . . [the *manuskripte*] angered, demystified, they instigated the shedding of masks and revealed the state of things better than a lengthy analysis of political conditions and their true structure.[9]

Kolleritsch argued, with Adorno, for the autonomy of the work of art, and met with severe criticism from writers who, like Jelinek, demanded a literature of engagement.[10]

Her novel *We're Decoys Baby* contained a user's guide that discouraged from reading the book those who already engage in "undermining the massive official organs of repression, and those who lack the will to deploy violence to this end" (Young 1987, 98). The reader's anticipated intervention in the text by rearranging its sequence or choosing a title was equated with her or his willingness to intervene in social institutions and power structures. The author viewed the electronic media as the late capitalist version of the Super Ego and in her novel rehearsed the insurgence of an "infantilized society." The faithful dog Lassie and the domesticated dolphin Flipper, ciphers of a contented consumer society and its capitalist values, suddenly become aggressive and evil; they invite the patricide that, to Jelinek's mind, is the precondition for social change.

In terms of formal considerations, her prose fiction has since evidenced a movement from the cartoon creatures of the media world toward social "reality," from the experimental collage to the narratives of *The Outcasts, The Piano Teacher,* and *Desire,* which take their material from historical events, autobiography, and everyday life.[11] In her dramas, however, the reverse movement is true: While her first play, *What Happened After Nora Left Her Husband,* a satirical deconstruction of Ibsen's *A Doll's House,* adheres to dramatic conventions by developing action through dialogue and unfolds a plot along the dialectic of personal and social contradictions, her later plays abandon these conventions. *Clara S.* explodes the notion of dramatic character modeled after the bourgeois individual's resting on an interior subjectivity. *Illness* presents sequences of speeches that do not add up to dialogues, illustrating the lack of communication between the sexes. Her latest pieces, *Desire & Driver's License* (1987), *Wolken. Heim* ([Clouds. Home] 1990), and

Totenauberg (1991) are prose texts that eliminate the notion of interpersonal conflict as the basis for dramatic action.[12]

Although the "material" for her collages comes from mass culture, Jelinek has been categorized as an avant-garde writer because she refuses to emulate traditional narrative and dramatic models. In some ways, Jelinek eludes the categories of "high" versus "low" culture, particularly since her novel *Desire* became a bestseller, a distinction that few avant-garde texts enjoy.

In terms of Jelinek's political alliances and positions, her work and her reception evidence a change of priorities from Marxism to feminism. Despite the fact that her novel *The Brassière Factory* became somewhat of a cult book of the women's movement during the 1970s, she refused to be categorized as a "woman writer" because at that historical moment the label denoted an essentialist politics and an aesthetic focusing on woman's body and emotions. In 1981, she still defined herself primarily as a Marxist, only secondarily as a feminist (Sauter 1981, 110). She insisted on the superior importance of a political fight against capitalism (Sauter 1981, 110).

While *Nora* still privileges a class critique over a gender critique, *Clara S.* was received as a "feminist play."[13] It is also significant that during the late 1970s, Jelinek started publishing in the feminist magazine *Die Schwarze Botin,* whereas earlier pieces appeared primarily in *manuskripte,* a literary journal that published the experimental writings of the Graz Group. That choice indicates Jelinek's changing political allegiance and signals her identification as a feminist. Several of her plays were directed by feminist directors: *Clara S.* and *Desire & Driver's License* were produced by Ulrike Ottinger, and Barbara Bilabel directed *Illness or Modern Women. Illness* was dedicated to German feminist theorist Eva Meyer, who responded with a critical essay, "Writing the Vampire" (Meyer 1989). Jelinek's plays, though addressing and deconstructing male master texts, were directed at and embedded in feminist discourse emerging in academia and in the countercultural spaces of feminist publications.

Jelinek occupies the poststructuralist position within the feminist critical spectrum. Woman appears as an image with no "substance" and is revealed as a male phantasma. She contends that women in the patriarchy cannot speak because they are always already spoken for and about. In her refusal to represent female identity, even as a utopian possibility,

Jelinek participates in the project of deconstruction, shifting the critical frame from material reality to the terrain of semiotics.

Clara S.

In her play *Clara S.*, written in 1981, Jelinek explores women's place in cultural production. She uses the Romantic discourse on woman and her place in the arts in order to illustrate mechanisms of control and exclusion. The figure of pianist Clara Schumann (1819–96), wife of composer Robert Schumann and later the "motherly muse" of Johannes Brahms,[14] epitomizes the Romantic heroine who sacrifices her art to her husband's genius in the name of love. Her biographers glossed over her frequent complaints about the heavy load of household management and the raising of seven children (one died young), the lack of time for piano practice, and Schumann's insistence that she not play when he composed (Litzmann 1918, 2:15). As recently as 1983, Joan Chissell wrote:

> [T]he woman in her longed for his comforting arms, and always intuitively realized that it was for his creative genius that her lesser career as a performer would eventually have to be sacrificed, or at any rate curtailed. (Chissell 1983, 59)

Before her marriage, Clara Wieck was not only a celebrated pianist but also a composer who performed her own pieces. Her "lesser" career secured her a place in musical history as the most acclaimed pianist of her times (Chissell 1983, 141), as a woman who single-handedly supported herself and her family before and after her marriage and contributed greatly to their welfare even while Robert Schumann was alive.

Clara S. offers a critique of the tragic, Romantic heroine by contrasting the image of prescribed femininity with the needs and ambitions of women artists. Although the play highlights the incongruity between material reality and representation, it does not suggest a place for women that is outside signification. Clara's suffering is cast in terms of heroic tragedy and sacrifice; like the classic heroine, Clara speaks the language of pathos and self-abnegation. Every tear is already coded; her failure to change the narrative, or history, is already programmed into the terms of deconstruction and its inability to dismantle the master's house with the master's tools.

The play anachronistically brings Robert, Clara, and Marie Schumann together with the Italian poet Gabriele d'Annunzio, in whose palace the play is set and who has gathered around him a group of poor women artists who are hoping for his financial support. The time is 1929, shortly before the fascist takeover. The historical Count d'Annunzio, an avid supporter of Benito Mussolini, was a celebrated war hero and fighter-plane pilot and became known as the inventor of the fascist greeting, the raised right arm. He was, however, also famous for his sexual conquests; he reportedly performed intercourse three times a day (Hensel 1982, 24).

Since Robert has become mentally disturbed and thus cannot deliver on the promise of a musical masterpiece in exchange for the money of the Commandante (as d'Annunzio likes to be called), Clara and Marie are expected to provide sexual services in lieu of the money. When it becomes clear that Robert, for whom Clara has sacrificed her career and artistic aspirations, is insane, Clara kills him. She dies at the piano.

Jelinek reconstructs a piece of women's history as Clara Schumann epitomized it and that not only is relevant to German women artists today but also speaks more widely to a still-virulent, bourgeois notion of femininity that is cultivated through music lessons and other artistic disciplines. Her materialist critique intervenes in the romanticized representation of woman as muse to great men, which mystifies the power structures governing the art market as well as the home; love and self-sacrifice mask competition, unequal access to the means of production, and exploitation. In representing the pianist's story as one of mutilation, dependence, and prostitution, Jelinek draws a bitter picture of the female artist. Clara is denied any claim to original genius and creativity because as a woman her domain is the body, not the mind; like the other women in d'Annunzio's palace—the dancer Carlotta Barra, and the pianist Luisa Baccara—she is restricted to the interpretive or performative arts, which forces her to become a passive receptacle for aesthetic artifacts created by men.[15] Clara and Robert Schumann's marriage, and the division of labor within it, serves as a model for gender relations in the culture at large.

The play posits women's exclusion from active, productive creativity as primordial and never changing by collapsing three historical moments into a misogynist continuum. The action takes place in 1929; the cast, however, consists of well-known historical figures from the nineteenth century. The epilogue is set in the present. The impression of a transhistorical continuum of women's oppression is reinforced by the set, which places elegant furniture in a stalactite cavern. The superimposition of the discourses of Romanticism and fascism, which mark the cusp of the patriarchal narrative, highlights the material stakes of the mutually exclusive construction of femininity and artistic production. The fascist regimes in Germany and Italy cemented the bipolar structure of naturalized gender difference into a rigidly segregated system that constructed women exclusively as mothers and developed sophisticated state apparatuses of eugenic control and forced reproduction. In Germany, the establishment of *Lebensborn*, government-run breeding institutions in which genetically viable women were used to supply "human material" for an aggressive, expansionist regime, marks the logical conclusion of a gender discourse based on women's exclusion from cultural production and their imprisonment in the reproductive sphere.

Jelinek represents Romantic aesthetics, with its simultaneous elevation of woman into an ideal image and exclusion of material women from cultural production, as a social/aesthetic paradigm still virulent in our time.[16] The "feminization" of culture often associated with Romanticism, and the increased activity of women artists, might lead one to believe that at that historical moment women were given permission to contribute to cultural production—a permission that can be directly read into the "positive" images of woman as sensitive soul, beauty incarnate, in short, as personification of those values held most highly in Romantic culture. An examination of late Enlightenment aesthetics which led into Romanticism, exemplified and codified in the writings of Kant, Herder, and Schiller, shows, however, that the so-called feminization of culture broadened the range of artistic expression for men by allowing them access to the realms of emotion and sensibility formerly reserved for women while engraving women's exclusion from creative production into the very terms of aesthetic theory (Bovenschen 1979). This becomes particularly clear in Kant's explorations of "genius," a central term in Romantic art that is coded male. Kant's notion of genius inscribed women's exclusion because their lack of critical reason foreclosed the possibility of their inhabiting the position of autonomous aesthetic subject. Since the genius represents the harmonious merging of reason and sensibility, women lack the anthropological prerequisites for geniality.[17]

In spite of the common preconception that the eighteenth century was a "time of equality" for women (Mayer 1975, 40), the proliferation of female images stands in curious contrast to the scarcity of women artists, writers, and philosophers even though much of their work has recently been excavated. Women were granted cultural competence in receptive sensibility, not sensible productivity (Bovenschen 1979, 201). Their role was thus effectively restricted to that of either muse to or interpreter of men's artistic production. For Robert and d'Annunzio, their female companions' only function consists of their ability to inspire them and provide the material for their creative production.

   Clara S. describes in terms of capitalist labor relations the Romantic privileging of the mind as the seat of the critical faculties on which genius is predicated. The specialization of the (male) artist as a "mind-worker" effects a discursive fragmentation of the subject and alienates him from his body and its products. Anything corporeal, repressed in the male subject in pursuit of abstraction, is projected onto woman as Other and incites fear and hatred. Clara, mother of eight children, views men's exhortations to women to bear children as a ploy that prevents women from effectively competing with men because their continual pregnancies consume a great deal of energy. At the same time, the gendered mind-body split inscribed in this aesthetic model takes its toll on the male subject as Robert's insanity illustrates. Men's constant repression of physical needs and their projection onto women ensure male superiority as well as pose the danger of mental collapse.

   Since woman is defined by her reproductive functions her social place is the home and the family. These role prescriptions are coupled with strong polemics against her participation in cultural production; the woman artist or scholar is viewed as monstrous and unnatural.[18] The association of biological gender and intellectual-creative abilities legitimated the inscription of fundamental difference and foreclosed the possibility of social change in terms of gender relations.

   CLARA *desperately:* When woman's abilities develop beyond the
   norms of the time, the result is a monstrosity. She violates the
   property rights of him, in whose service the she-animal must put
   herself. Woman's mind is devoted to *in extreme agitation* the invention of new dishes and the disposal of waste.

                                                      (Jelinek 1984, 94)

   In *Clara S.,* the division of gender roles, which is mystified as "natural," is revealed as a function of material relations characterized by the unequal distribution of property. Jelinek focuses on material everyday reality in which the scenario of women's exclusion plays itself out. "Every time I approached the piano in order to compose, I found the apparatus occupied, by you!" Clara accuses Robert (93). The double referent of the term *apparatus*—the Schumann's piano as well as the apparatus of musical production in the capitalist art market—highlights their marriage as paradigmatic for patriarchal-capitalist practices.

In Romantic discourse, woman's representation as beauty incarnate fixed her sphere of influence and power in the realm of sexuality. The male imagination attached itself to the feminine as the projection screen for conflicting needs and fears. Sexuality in this system is revealed as a compound of male monomania and misogyny and registers the constant flickering between horror, fear, and fascination. Moreover, since the only currency conceded to women in the patriarchal-capitalist system is their bodies, their sexuality, overdetermined within the heterosexist economy as a means to attract and control men, acquires demonic power. D'Annunzio speculates:

> In all probability, Woman is rather Nothing. Nothingness! One cannot really touch her. Rather stare into the pure flame than work one's way into Woman. The fact is, Woman possesses an inexhaustible greediness which man can never satisfy. The result: fear! Therefore, one must turn Woman into something disgusting, possibly even something putrifying, so that she repels. (84)

The desire to transform woman into a "pure flame" to be worshiped is entwined with the desire to figuratively, and literally, kill her. These contradictory impulses produce the complex and conflicted figure of woman as Virgin and Vamp behind which the material reality of women disappears.

In *Clara S.*, the violence of the discourse on gender is dramatized as Logier's Contraption, a training machine for piano players that Clara's father, himself a famous pianist and teacher, used as a pedagogical tool. The piano and the training apparatus attached to it appear as instruments of discipline, which apply physical force in order to inscribe gender on the subject's body. The pain this machine inflicts on the player, Clara's daughter Marie, in order to ensure the correct posture, stresses the process of becoming feminine not only as continued labor but also as a crippling ordeal that purposely deforms the student's body and mind.[19] Significantly, the daily rehearsal, aimed at the girl Marie's perfect performance of feminine sensibility, results in her intellectual retardation; at age five she can scarcely speak. Contrary to the Enlightenment discourse on man's self-fulfillment through education, the learning of womanliness involves the violent and deliberate inhibition of all but one of the girl's talents, skills, and needs. Ultimately, she is turned into a pair of skilled hands, signaling her alienation from her own body, which has been turned into a specialized tool: a woman. The violence of Logier's Contraption, which disciplines the body into femininity, is symbolic as well as material; interpellation into gender occurs through physical force.

The play's sexual economy revolves around the male subject. The Commandante's sexual fantasies about Clara project a scenario in which she comes to substitute for the masters whose work she plays:

> COMMANDANTE: *touches her.* I painfully regret never having had this pianist after a great triumph on stage, still warm from the breath of the audience, sweaty, gasping and pale. For instance after the Hammer Piano sonata. Or after the exhausting Tchaikovsky-concert.
>
> (69)

The pianist thus becomes a pawn in the exchange among great men, exposing a socioeconomic structure that can be characterized as homosocial and that is predicated on the circulation of women as objects of property. In the Commandante's fantasy, Clara also comes to stand in for the masses who breathe life into her, as it were. This image of the gullible feminized masses adoring an all-powerful master resonates with the fascist-imperialist rhetoric that becomes more explicit in part 2:

> COMMANDANTE: Man strives for conquest, he conquers either a foreign region, as far away as possible, a woman, or a corridor in the air-space. The gullible masses applaud him. The masses are body-oriented, like woman. One can occupy them if one chooses to.
>
> (88)

In this fantasy, woman appears as a blank screen reflecting the male subject's desire back to him. Thus, she *is* nothing in herself but is solely determined by his idealized perception of her as Nature, the Masses, or Beauty.

Gender relations are articulated exclusively in heterosexual terms and characterized as exploitative. This is not surprising, since women in this system have no desire of their own, but must conform to male representations of it. As patriarchal capitalism recognizes only one subject, which is configured as masculine, and one desire, namely that of the male, the discursive universe that Jelinek represents on stage revolves around the phallus. However, she carefully distinguishes between the phallus as signifier of male privilege and patriarchal power and the penis as the male subject's pawn in the phallocentric economy by juxtaposing d'Annunzio's financial might with his dysfunctional penis. In *Clara S.*, d'Annunzio's wealth, rather than his sexual prowess, signifies his masculinity.

Jelinek places the Commandante center stage and focuses on his sexual activity, which extends to all female characters with the exception of his wife. The Commandante's lack of command over his penis—he is impotent—undercuts the biologistic discourse on "natural" gender as an active-aggressive, passive-submissive dichotomy. His sexual transactions occur in the context of unequal power relations and financial dependency, which demystifies heterosexual love as prostitution. This is exposed when d'Annuncio patronizes a local sex-worker.

> COMMANDANTE: I represent a gigantic financial and even greater ideal power. Also, the new regime recognizes my high prestige, it couldn't be higher. [. . .] *He has trouble breathing. To the uncomprehending village-girl:* Speak! Answer me! Tell me that you could not bear to see the dawn without me, just as I could not without you! Answer me! *Aélis motions the girl to say yes, which she does.*
>
> (81)

Due to his phallic power, the Commandante is able to dictate the terms of sexual desire to the "uncomprehending" object of his attention. Although unable to master his penis, he is empowered to command the discourse of love that he assigns to the obliging sex-worker who otherwise remains mute. In the context of material relations in which the male possesses all the power, heterosexuality is represented as obscene. Women's bodies are objectified and used as sex toys.

D'Annunzio's ability to perform sexual intercourse at all is contingent on drugs that his housekeeper Aélis administers to him, which further highlights gender as artificial rather than "natural." The efforts the women take to conceal d'Annunzio's impotence from him underscore their complicity with dominant ideology; their tribute to the penis is their only avenue of access to the phallus. All of the female characters are portrayed as masquerading subjects who deliberately don the mask of femininity both to hide their possession of the phallus and "to avert anxiety and the retributions feared from men" (Riviere 1929, 303). Therefore, they are invested in maintaining the illusion of the Commandante's potency, which keeps the phallocentric universe stable and intact. They participate in the system because they have no alternative. Luisa Baccara calculates, "Only 120 more surrenders! At the most!" (70) until she can go off on her concert tour that d'Annunzio has promised her.

The woman artist is continually confronted with the necessity to abnegate her talents and skills in order to avoid male criticism and hatred. In feminist theory, this specifically female position has been described in terms of masquerade and credited with liberatory potential. *Clara S.* opens the feminine image of compliance and complacency to inspection and glee by showing the women as entrepreneurs dealing femininity as their currency. Some of the most comic moments of the play occur when the women plot their masquerades—dividing up roles such as the solemn priestess, the regal Phoenix, and the little deer.

As Case points out, the masquerading position that Rivière first described and that has been further developed in contemporary feminist film theory, is marked by passivity and phallocentrism, reinscribing traditional gender roles into this supposedly liberatory model. As a compensatory gesture performed for the male, the heterosexual female's masquerade leaves the phallic regime intact in return for some stolen moments of power. *Clara S.* denies the possibility of constructing female or feminist agency on the basis of masquerading practices. The women's clever wielding of femininity as a tool designed to trick the Commandante may momentarily provoke laughter, a liberatory feminist laughter that can only emerge from a place outside of dominant ideology, yet the humor remains grim because the women's failure is already programmed into the scenario. What is at stake in Clara and Marie's performance of gender is economic survival, not just material privileges. Ultimately, the performance of femininity can only defer, not compensate for, their being taken to task and invariable loss. Because, as Clara realizes, given the oversupply of women, the sexual value of her body barely outlasts its consumption.

Woman's personification of beauty extricates her from historical processes[20] and deprives her of the status of subject-agent: "She is beautiful and captivates and that is enough" (Kant 1960, 93). She has access neither to knowledge nor to morality, and therefore lacks the prerequisites to impact material reality, history, or social change. The mother-daughter relationship in *Clara S.* illustrates the absence of a developmental notion of history predicated on the autonomous, male subject's pursuing its quest of self-fulfillment and mastery. Rather, the exact repetition of behavior patterns from one generation to the next depicts women as nonsubjects outside of history and powerless to change it.

Jelinek's postmodern style renounces a mimetically accurate representation of reality. Instead, her plays address the world as text, and examine the way that gender is constructed by specific discourses. Jelinek's writing applies some insights of French feminism—the dominant critique used in German academic feminism—such as the critique of phallogocentrism. However, she does not share the search for an ideological outside with these critics who attempt to mobilize the powers of the feminine, the unconscious, and the Id, in order to destabilize naturalized bipolar differences. Rather, Jelinek's texts retain a negative stance and refuse to posit a feminine "truth" lodged in the body or in the drives. The purpose of her critique is the destruction of the theatrical institution and humanist philosophy as they continue to dominate the contemporary construction of gender—not the utopian representation of an alternative system in positivist terms.

Illness or Modern Women

While *Clara S.* traced women's exclusion from representation in a diachronic movement from prehistoric times to the present, *Illness* provides a synchronic view of discourses whose pattern and hierarchies map the cultural terrain of Austria in the 1980s. The play deconstructs the dominant sex-gender system as it is constituted in the languages of psychoanalysis, capitalism, humanist philosophy, religion, and mass culture. It describes various positions of investment in the cultural apparatuses that (re)produce the ideology of gender and distinguishes not only between the genders but also between two women. The play suggests two strategies that subvert, or rather invert, the place of the feminine in the dominant sex-gender system. While the traditional figure of the ill woman, once reversed into its negative, evacuates the feminine, the vampire destabilizes the ontological base of discourses organized around dichotomies and celebrates the order of "equivalence" and "indifference." *Illness* reveals the theater's ideological implication in the (re)production of the humanist subject with its imperialist, fascist underpinnings, thus signaling its end.

Illness is set in the present. The lesbian vampire and poet Emily (Brontë), engaged to her employer Dr. Heidkliff, a dentist/gynecologist, seduces his client Carmilla who has come into his practice in order to deliver her sixth child. Heidkliff and Carmilla's husband, the tax consultant Benno Hundekoffer, unite in their pursuit of the undead couple in order to force them back into the previous heterosexual alliances. They chase the women from the bedroom to their final refuge, a public restroom. In the course of the hunt, the vampires kill all of Carmilla's children and decide finally to leave the scene. They reappear as a monstrous "double creature," which the men manage to shoot. The final image shows the men sucking at the throat of the creature and commanding the audience to leave.

The stage is split into two separate areas that signify the division of nature and culture: While one half depicts the wuthering heights of Emily Brontë's invention, the other half changes from Heidkliff's office to the women's house to the public restroom. During the course of the play, however, both sides of the stage gradually decay and fill with weaponry, garbage, and corpses covered with bloody shrouds.

Fascism, here in its Austrian manifestation, figures prominently within this ideological landscape, erupting occasionally but regularly like the occasional but regular scandals that briefly expose a public figure's Nazi past to international scrutiny—a well-known example is the Austrian president Dr. Kurt Waldheim, to whom the play alludes as the "man from Linz"—to quickly fade into blissful political amnesia. Silenced, the discourse of fascism nevertheless pervades this text. The Nazis' "Off with his head!" situates the men's hunt for the vampires in the context of the Holocaust; Carmilla's query to her husband, of whether he has "given his child a human appearance. . . . So that it could later be recognized as human. So that one won't obliterate it or gas it" (17), exposes the racist underpinnings of the genesis legend; and the juxtaposition of Goethe's "More light!" with the Nazi's expansionist slogan "More Space!" illuminates the imperialist base of Enlightenment thinking.

A further characteristic for the Austrian ideoscape is the prominence of the Catholic church and its alliance with capitalist ideology and practices in the configuration and perpetuation of the dominant sex-gender system. The biblical myth of woman as man's handmaid and receptacle of his semen cements capitalist relations of ownership. Carmilla expresses her gratefulness for her husband's investment in her reproductive capacity: "Thank you very much for putting this loaf into my stove. Thank you very much for baking this roll."[21]

The third discursive complex that signifies contemporary Austria is the juxtaposition of the rhetoric on nature with the late capitalist military-industrial technoscape. As a country whose economy is largely dependent on tourism, Austria's affluence relies to a great extent on the rhetorical purity of nature whose referent is constructed by the leisure industry and has thus been technologically transformed into its own simulacrum.

The technological (re)production of nature and its products is, of course, the more significant because of that term's proximity to woman and the body in Enlightenment discourse and the shared status of obstacle and object within it. Like nature, which has been colonized and transformed into the setting of so many ski jumps, woman is reconfigured as "MotherMachine" (to quote the title of a book on reproductive technology published in 1986, the year the play was written). The much-decried contamination of the wine, one of Austria's prime export products, with chemicals parallels the contamination of mother's milk. Both instances of pollution are mentioned in *Illness* on several occasions. The body is represented as the postmodern technobody, or, in Donna Haraway's words, the cyborg who crosses the borders of organic and anorganic (Haraway 1990). The loss of the natural reveals gender as a simulacrum without any referent in the "real." Instead, characters acquire gender markers for tactical purposes and attempt to approximate mass media images of masculinity or femininity.

Jelinek's theater deconstructs the humanist subject. Humanist philosophy defines the "I" through a series of exclusionary operations that oppose it to an Other—woman, nature, the body—which it simultaneously desires and dominates.[22] While the history of this subject has been narrativized as a teleological progress toward an ever-higher degree of civilization,[23] the flip side of this progress has been repressed: women's lack of agency and exclusion from subjecthood, the pollution and destruction of nature in the process of cultivation and industrialization, and the fragmentation of the body into a machine park for capitalist production and reproduction.

Particularly, the scholars of the Frankfurt School have theorized the conquest of nature, one of the central tenets of Enlightenment thought, as a totalitarian notion that directly contributed to the advent of German fascism. Adorno viewed the hegemony of reason, which distinguished the Cartesian subject as ultimately fascist because it assimilates the truth, i.e., social relations free from alienation and domination, to the instrumentalizing force of the idea (Horkheimer and Adorno 1972). Likewise, Jelinek exposes the destructive teleology of these Enlightenment narratives of "progress." Their logical conclusion is the icy landscape of the epilogue in *Clara S.*, the scene of the heroine's death. *Illness* situates the conclusion of Enlightenment discourse in the military-industrial wasteland of the nuclear age at ground zero.

In recycling the linguistic, gestural, and visual sign systems of dominant discourses and the attendant theatrical traditions, Jelinek's dramaturgy is highly intertextual and self-reflexive. The classical stage appears as a factory of images and sentences, a site at which labor is exerted but pretends to be play. Jelinek's theater reveals its machinery; it stages the expenditure of energy. The discourses, practices, and apparatuses that constitute the theater as the locus of ideological (re)production manifest what Teresa de Lauretis termed a "technology of gender."

De Lauretis coined this term as a revision and radicalization of Foucault's theorization of a "technology of sex" (Foucault 1980):

like sexuality . . . gender is not a property of bodies or something originally existent in human beings, but "the set of effects produced in bodies, behaviors, and social relations," in Foucault's words, by the deployment of "a complex political technology." (Lauretis 1987, 3)

The theater as it is realized in Jelink's writing and theatrical practice exposes its own history as a sophisticated machinery designed to interpellate subjects into what feminists have called the "sex-gender system" as "both a sociocultural construct and a semiotic apparatus.[24]

The material weight of this apparatus calls attention to semiosis as a (re)production of power relations, of material oppression, and also to the varying degrees of investment in it. In this scenario the men guard the dominant sexual order from which they profit. Exasperated, they command: "Don't be the way you are! Be hygienic! Follow your nature! Scrub! Scrub! Scrub! Scrub!" (Jelinek 1987, 52).

The women's transgression of prescribed gender roles ruptures the seamless semiotic system. Its frantic attempt to mend itself accelerates semiosis and causes the system's overproduction. What appears in the process is its repressive machinery in excess and its fallout in the form of "garbage... weapons... a military trash heap... mountains of corpses covered with shrouds" (65, 71). The "texting" of the world in *Illness* operates against the postmodern lack of referentiality. In deconstructing the humanist-imperialist narrative of progress, it unearths the unsightly excrements of Western civilization. In doing so, the play insists on the material stakes of representation for those who have been rendered invisible.

Jelinek's postmodern style registers her Marxist training and insists on the notion of material oppression, which all too often disappears from the poststructuralist critique but which nevertheless remains a central term within the feminist movement. A materialist critique of ideology, in contrast to much poststructuralist theory, maintains a focus on oppression and its effects on the body. Within this critical apparatus, Teresa de Lauretis argues, the material object retains more "weight" than in post-Saussurian semiotics whose focus on the arbitrariness of the sign has led to the disappearance of social "reality" from many poststructuralist models (Lauretis 1987, 39). While de Lauretis's theory does not posit a primordial "reality" outside signification, it insists on "an overdetermination wrought into the work of the sign by the real, or what we take as reality, even if it is itself already an interpretant; and hence the sense that experience... is indissociable from meaning" (Lauretis 1987, 41, 42). The close imbrication of semiotic systems and social reality can account for gender as more than "différance," as de Lauretis ironically remarks, namely as oppression. This critique renders the material effects of discourses and their function to engender the subject recognizable as violence, the "violence of rhetoric."

Jelinek stages the semiotic construction of Austria as the violent enforcement of bipolar systems but reintroduces that which has been repressed in the process. The suppressed material reappears as waste and debris; the signs of oppression therefore continue to refer to the processes of signification that structure the cultural field into the visible and the invisible. The garbage heap that covers the stage exposes oppression as a violent, semiotic process that conceives of the "real" as fabricated rather than positing it as a pristine place outside, and untouched by, signification.

The cyborg-vampires, who haunt this technoscape by flaunting their blasphemous artificiality and "unnatural" desire for each other, effect the destabilization of its ontological structure and the dissolution of the dichotomies between life and death, nature and culture, and man and woman that are inscribed at its base. Case, in her essay "Tracking the Vampire," celebrates the queer vampire as a trope empowered to "pierce the ontological sac" of Platonic organicism, which bolsters the dominant equation of nature with fertility and with heterosexuality (Case 1991). The right to life that this formulation evokes is tied to the preservation of "pure" blood enclosed in wholesome bodies free from racial or sexual contamination. Like capital in a Swiss bank account it must be hidden in order to generate profit. In *Illness,* blood flows freely across the stage expending the myths it nourishes. Jelinek restages them, "in order to bring into play, one last time, their traumatic seductiveness, and play out their last authentic expression" (Meyer 1989, 99).

The figures of the ill woman and the vampire illustrate Jelinek's deconstructive method as one of inversion, though both figures demonstrate different, almost opposing, strategies in regard to their effect on the ideological system in which they intervene. Carmilla, who celebrates illness, the mark of woman's lack, in order to prove her existence ultimately reinscribes her own marginalization and exclusion from the patriarchal system: "Illness is beautiful. . . . I am ill and therefore legitimate. Without illness I would be nothing" (44). Carmilla's logic highlights the precarious conditions for women's visibility within the discourses of humanism and psychoanalysis, which converge in her claim "I am ill therefore I am" (44). It calls attention to the omission in humanism's claim for Man's emancipation while remaining silent about women's oppression. Within the boundaries of this discursive ground, woman's illness as the prerequisite for her appearance, her visibility, and, by extension, her survival is contingent on the display of her castration, an equation the play makes frequently. Yet it must be noted that Carmilla's illness (like her curls) has nothing "natural" to it. It does not reify or correspond to woman's "wound," as Heidkliff and psychoanalysis would have it—the mark of her castration that constitutes her as mutilated, inferior, and hence ill. Carmilla's illness is a simulation. She makes a "mockery of illness," as she points out (44). Claiming the place assigned to her within the patriarchal economy, Carmilla is awarded the tenuous pleasure of the masquerading subject: "I am ill, and I enjoy it. I am suffering, and I rejoice" (45).

Her exit from that system, on the occasion of her sixth childbirth and with Emily's help, opens up the pleasure of inversion. This exit is situated within technology: A male-owned reproductive technology that renders woman obsolete as breeder and that signifies both climax and logical conclusion of the ill woman's narrative. Her figuration as Lack, which can only be attenuated by her child, is cancelled out by the shift of reproduction onto the site of the unnatural. Because conception and birth can be performed technologically, woman is released from the yoke of reproduction.

This reversal of previous functions and assignments is effected by Emily's artificial fangs. Here, woman's desire for the penis fails to inter-pellate her into the oedipal triangle, the site of patriarchal reproduction. It turns instead toward another woman, a woman equipped to display desire. The gender signifiers in the modern technoscape, from Emily's phallic tooth to the lesbian couple's freezers (those "cold wombs" that house the remnants of Carmilla's children), are grotesque mockeries of dominant gender codes that revel in perversion.

From then on, Carmilla refuses to do her duty. Dr. Heidkliff is outraged at this twist in the *grand récit* of psychoanalysis: "You have lips, and what do you use them for? For what? For speaking! *(Barks terribly)*" (57). The flow of Carmilla's blood, which so far she has spilled in a "pretty rhythm," is interrupted and reversed. She remarks:

> I notice how this life differs from my previous one. Before, hungry mouths had to be fed. Now the maxim is: to feed on them in the most efficient way. I do not choose among beverages any longer, there are only blood and minerals now. Thank you, that'll be all for me. Before, I have treated myself to face creams. Now I mistreat others. (45)

Carmilla, the vampiric incarnation/inversion of the girl Mircalla from Sheridan Le Fanu's novella, reverses the image of the Happy Housewife without claiming an "other" truth. If Carmilla is marked by illness, lack, and thus, negation, the inversion of that image yields no positive posi-tion but, on the contrary, evacuates it. Marlies Janz points out,

> [The text] rather performs a negation of a false image, which it seems impossible to articulate in positive terms. Jelinek's perver-sions persistently point back to the always-already false, i.e., to the feminine as a male projection, which can only constitute the femi-

nine as the Other *of the masculine*—and thereby as dependent and secondary to it. (Janz 1990, 82)

In her eagerness to deflect from the lesbian narrative embedded in *Illness*'s text, Janz misses precisely the point that those false images, faithfully reflecting the male subject's projections back to himself, (temporarily and partially) exit the male-centered specular economy. With her gaze firmly fixed on the male subject, it is then difficult for Janz to recognize the differences between the two female figures and the possibility that what is true for Carmilla may not be so for Emily.

The lesbian Emily refuses and challenges the traditional role assigned to women, and announces: "My feelings are autonomously lesbian and sadistic" (70). In contrast to Carmilla, whose illness engages and unravels the misogynist languages of psychoanalysis and humanism, the figure of the vampire predominantly operates against the sex-gender system as it is constituted at the intersection of capitalism and Catholicism. The lesbian vampire is the counterimage to the Christian capitalist who is "prohibited from drinking anyone's blood but his boss's" (47). Benno, the tax consultant and member of the Christian Party, is one of those who "take it from the living" (24). Consequently, Benno feels betrayed by Carmilla's vampirism, which twists around the positions of activity and passivity on which relations of ownership and profit rest. Now she claims her revenue, leaving her husband to lament: "I should not have entrusted her with my seed. I should not have stuck anything in her soil" (50).

The capitalist property relations are bolstered by Catholic ideology that legitimizes man's mastership and woman's servitude, constituting her as appendage, maid, inanimate receptacle. The asymmetry in the Christian sex-gender system hinges on the representation of blood. According to the doctrine of transsubstantiation, the body and blood of Christ are purified, consumed, and celebrated during Communion; women's bodies and women's blood, however, are denounced as soiled and are denied representation. The lesbian vampire's bite upsets the taxonomy of blood drinking as it constitutes and regenerates the community of believers in the spirit of an authoritarian, patriarchal ideology. It renders transparent the interpellating function of this ritual in which the subject recognizes itself in, and swears allegiance to, the divine Subject.

Emily, who describes her personality as "in every respect: inexora-
ble opposition" (22), announces her interest in Carmilla with an untrans-
latable twist—"*Ich gebäre nicht. Ich begehre dich*"[25]—and displays lesbian
desire as contingent on inverting—perverting the place of the feminine
in the symbolic order like the consonants in that phrase. Emily's consumption of Carmilla's blood mocks the myth of transsubstantiation and
calls attention to its gender markings. Heidkliff fears, "whoever lives off
someone else's blood removes that Other one from the world and turns
her into her opposite" (50). However, the vampire is unable to reassign
her object a positive space within ideology. Mimicking Catholic rhetoric, she promises, "Immortal be whose flesh I eat" (22), and, "You will
not be a handmaid, once I will have fed on you" (22). Carmilla no longer
is a "maid," as Emily has announced, yet she is no master either. Rather,
they are coupled in negativity, quadrupling lack, absence, and invisibility. And exceeding it.

The arithmetic of the feminine is too complex—"One would have
to work very hard to make [it] simple again" (22)—for woman to completely disappear. She reappears, "busy with disappearing" (5). Though
it has become clear by now that her reappearance, momentary and tentative, hinges on her doubling, her lesbian coupling. That arrangement
not only releases the women from their bondage to the male, which
replicates gender as sexual (in)difference; it also abolishes the inscription
of passivity in woman as other/mirror to man. Woman, who in mimetic
systems has been configured as mirror to the male, refuses to reflect
"back to him—*thereby demonstrating the truth of his centrality*—his own
image, his Self-Same" (Diamond 1989, 59). As vampires, the women
step out of the mirror trope that governs mimesis. They gaze at each
other and, in a key scene, do each others' hair and makeup. In other
words, they control each others' images (54).

The lesbian vampire manages to disrupt the ontological base of the
discursive formations in question, precisely because she has no positive
space in it. This strategy does not reinscribe woman's difference but
destabilizes the difference(s) on which her exclusion rests. The vampire,
like the ill woman, "mocks" sexual difference but, unlike the ill woman,
openly claims the phallus, albeit an artificial one, floating free from all
biological reference:

I want these two fangs to be ejectable! They should be able to
protrude and disappear. Like myself. I need an apparatus similar to

the one you men possess! I want to impress. I want to display desire! I have juices, but they aren't worth much in everyday life. I, too, want to function according to a principle! (33)

The principle according to which this cyborg vampire functions is that of replication rather than reproduction with its heterosexist inscription. Christian theology describes reproduction in terms of mimesis, in which man, analogous to God who created him, generates offspring in his image. Benno, for instance, has succeeded in "reduplicating" himself in his latest product, just like his other children (17). The hierarchy of images is abolished in serial production, which obliterates the "original reference."

The problem of [the signs'] uniqueness, or their origin, is no longer a matter of concern; their origin is technique, and the only sense they possess is in the dimension of the industrial simulacrum. Which is to say the series, and even the possibility of two or of *n* identical objects. The relation between them is no longer that of an original to its counterfeit—neither analogy nor reflection—but equivalence, indifference. (Baudrillard 1983, 96, 97)

Illness locates the production of gender as sexual difference within late capitalism, or, in Haraway's words, the era of the cyborg, "hybrid[] of machine and organism" (Haraway 1990, 191). While the men strive to enforce mimetic reproduction, the female vampires practice cyborg replication in the realm of the undead, which not only reverses existing gender roles but threatens attendant social formations and semiotic apparatuses organized hierarchically in relation to the transcendental Subject, God, Man, the Model.

The expenditure of myths that Jelinek stages agitates discursive structures of "violent protection," as Heidkliff puts it (49); it dissolves the partitions between the seen and the unseen that secure the system of representation and the assumption of "authenticity" on which it operates. The sociosemiotic order of "equivalence" and "indifference" that the vampire instigates provokes the wrath of those who are invested in hierarchy, asymmetry, and domination because they profit from the unequal distribution of power between the sexes: the men. It is no wonder, then, that their pursuit of the undead becomes a matter of life and death.

The men's violence against women and against the body is conveyed in a manically cheerful language that operates in the name of science, truth, and decidability. Their tennis game is overlayed with the following dialogue:

> HEIDKLIFF *impassioned:* Yes! Yes! Yes! Yes! The grating sound of the stake as it penetrates the bone, the body writhing in agony, the bloody foam at the mouth, the vomit. We may remind ourselves: It has to be. It serves mankind. So do I, as a doctor.
>
> (48)

Illness highlights language as constitutive of the subject, and thus also the site at which sexual difference is inscribed and performed. Benno asks his ally: "Where, do you think, was gender before people talked about it, Heidkliff?" (53). The dramatic action that defines the characters is language and their relation to it in terms of ownership and exclusion. Dramatic development occurs in the characters' changing linguistic gest—the women's move toward a more emphatic, imperative speech, and the men's loss of coherent, grammatically correct language.

The men's increasing aggression and threats against the women is accompanied by the fragmentation and depravation of their dialogue. On the level of meaning, the signifier *woman* accumulates any meanings that are culturally devalued, including *communists, croupe, pollution, skin disease, allergies, smog, foreigners,* etc. On the syntactic level, their speech is first interrupted by barking, then rapidly fractures into short phrases and single words punctuated by exclamation marks. Their tirades culminate in the demand, "Be deadead once and for all! Wewe need space! More space! Give! More light! More! Momore light! More listen! Bark! Bark! Bark!" (64). In this short speech, Goethe's last words ("More light!") and the Nazi slogan "More space!" are herein collapsed into a homogeneously imperialist demand that signals the climax and end of Enlightenment discourse and its theater.

At this, the women must exit. Their flight has led them from the bedroom, site of a transgressive sexuality, to the place where gender contestation calls forth the greatest anxieties: a public toilet. The reassertion of gender renders perversion invisible. Cornered in this heterosexist locale, Emily and Carmilla vanish into separate stalls. A female subject that, as Carmilla phrases it, won't "be sucked at any longer," that, Emily

proposes, "takes care of herself," and no longer "makes any appoint-
ments," cannot appear on this stage (71). So, at Emily's invitation,
Carmilla takes leave and says her good-byes.

At the site of gender as the bathroom inscribes it, the counterdiscourse the couple articulates is eclipsed by the heterosexist category of
woman that they had abandoned.[26] Now, back in the dominant terrain,
they repossess that term with a vengeance. What appears after the
women's exit is a double creature. It cannot speak, but displays a volup-
tuous femininity, consuming its picnic on the mounds of military and
industrial waste. Its immense size makes it easy game for the men, who
shoot it and proceed to suck its blood out. As "the sex that is not one,"
but multiple (as Irigaray suggests), woman is here transformed into pure
sign, pure image, mute. Its excessiveness and monstrosity "crosses out"
the vampires from the field of representation. Their transgression is
transformed grotesquely by the dominant gaze.[27]

The creature's death, though preprogrammed in a discursive structure organized around sexual (in)difference and bent on the suppression
and exclusion of one of its terms, signals the end of patriarchal discourse.
The extinction of the sign "woman" marks the end of the classical,
humanist, realist theater as a technology of gender. The lesbian vampire
challenges a system bent on the obliteration of the Other, causing it
finally to implode. With the image of the male hunter sucking the blood
out of a wholly artificial, excessively feminine creature, the humanist
drama takes its leave.

The dramatic style through which the (male) humanist subject has
traditionally reproduced itself as hero has been the theater of psychological realism. Historically, it established itself in Germany in the form
of the bourgeois tragedy that rehearsed the role of woman as noble
victim who sacrifices herself for love. Jelinek rejects realism as the dominant discursive mode and insists:

> Ultimately, the goal is not to create the illusion that what you see
> on stage are entities, autonomous subjects inhabiting and owning
> their own space, their own time, their own action. They are not
> masters over their own fate, no unified wholes. They constitute
> themselves purely through/in speech, and they speak what they
> would not say otherwise. It speaks through them. . . . speech seeks
> a site of enunciation. (Jelinek in Roeder 1989, 151)

In Jelinek's writing, "characters" are highly artificial constructs, no longer mimetic signs of human individuals but discourse machines, relays for the ideology of gender. What speaks there can no longer lay claim to an "I," or unified whole that could guarantee the truth of an utterance, but serves as switchboard for a multiplicity of discourses. Characters cannot rely on a stable identity, or historic authenticity; all dialogue is quotation, undercutting the notion of a private subjectivity bolstering the dialogue in the form of a psychological subtext. By commenting on and interpreting their actions, they ironically anticipate and preempt any attempt on the part of the spectator to construct a subtext when they announce, for instance, that they will demonstrate female radicalism by climbing up a phallic symbol. This device dispels the illusion of a spectatorial "subjectivity" that can construct meaning by decoding messages. Instead, the spectator is situated as mere consumer whose every critical response is preprogrammed.

Likewise, Jelinek rejects the notion of authorship as the expression of original genius and stresses instead the "repetition of the always-familiar" (Roeder 1989, 152), the trivial, and the banal. The author, like the characters, becomes a switchboard for dominant ideology.

Jelinek's dramaturgy rejects realism as a dramatic style, because that form invests in a stable representation of "reality"—no matter how critical of it—that resists change (Diamond 1989, 61). However, one might ask if a feminist politics operating in the postmodern hyperreal risks forfeiting any purchase on material relations. The endless repetition of Kristeva's "this isn't it" and "this is still not it" (Kristeva quoted in Roeder 1989, 180) has effectively reinscribed the dominant notion of gender as sexual (in)difference, an aesthetics whose pleasure resides in the expenditure of what has never been real (Meyer 1986, 66). The "incessant production" of signifiers implodes an economy of meaning that rests on the secure separation of interior and exterior through which "identity" constitutes itself. Emptying words of meaning, however, makes them useless for the politics of argumentation in a parliamentary democracy in which relations of power are negotiated. The dissolution of identity also marks the end of identity politics, a strategy that can account for, and operate against, sexism and its institutions.

Moreover, the deconstruction of gender as sexual (in)difference ultimately keeps intact the master's house; as a critical practice with a material, historically accumulated weight, it has produced its own blind spots by effacing differences among women, many of whom are not willing to forgo the stable foothold of identity politics in order to intervene in social relations. It is significant in this regard that women of color, particularly Turkish and Afro-German women, are largely invisible in German feminism. However, at this historical moment one can scarcely speak of feminism, much less feminist deconstruction, as a dominant discourse in German or Austrian culture.

The categorical refusal to frame gender in positivist terms and the resulting freeze of a feminist critique in a stance of negation, however, have produced a rising number of "endgames" celebrating the end of humanism, the sovereign subject, and its technologies. In that respect, Jelinek's aesthetic closely resembles that of Heiner Müller and Thomas Bernhard, though her financial success as a playwright falls far short of theirs. Like Beckett's impossible heaps, their plays announce and demand their own disappearance but continue to occupy the stage, refusing to evacuate their privileged position within the frame of representation.

The play carves out a spectatorial position that can be defined as feminist. The spectator is addressed within dominant ideology, situated vis-à-vis a technology of gender that only allows for two positions— male or female. Jelinek's plays retain the focus on gender as sexual difference (of women from men) and remain within a male-centered scopic economy. At the same time, her theater resists dominant ideology because it disturbs the function of the apparatus to interpellate the subject through recognition or, in the language of dramatic criticism, identification and empathy. She offers neither characters with whom to identify nor a storyline in which to invest. Instead of inviting the proximity of empathy, Jelinek's texts allow for a spectatorial position of distance that is—temporarily and partially—outside dominant ideology. From this angle the spectator can catch glimpses into the "wings" of the representational frame. From that feminist point of view she can perceive the absences and invisibilities within the system. By marking those, Jelinek intervenes in an ideological apparatus bent on concealing its seams and suppressing its contradictions. It is a crucial undertaking for understanding oppression as the control of the cultural imaginary.

The subject of feminism, which de Lauretis envisioned in constant motion between the "critical negativity of its theory and the affirmative positivity of its politics" (de Lauretis 1987, 26), should not be reified as a formalist prescription for the construction of feminist texts. Rather it should describe a discursive terrain of which deconstruction is an integral part.

Chapter 6

The Palatheater of the Mouth:
Ginka Steinwachs

Ginka Steinwachs is the final author in this study because of her accomplishments as a postmodern feminist writer, theorist, and performer. Her work engages with the contemporary debates in feminist theory on the tension between essentialism and poststructuralism.[1] That debate turns on the question of whether *woman* as a patriarchal construct still yields enough political efficacy to warrant its continued use for a feminist activist rhetoric or whether it has turned into a liability and should be evacuated. Steinwachs, a postmodern maverick, navigates between identity politics and its deconstruction and transcendence toward the hermaphroditic "third sex," demanding "everything plus a tomato" in the name of women, while simultaneously refuting the notion of female identity (Nowoselsky-Müller 1989, 32). Crossing gender as well as genres, the writer commits tactical acts of critical piracy by raiding diverse theoretical systems and theatrical traditions for their subversive potential, rather than committing to a stable political or aesthetic strategy. Freud's query "What does woman want?" is answered by the demand for equal rights at the same time that the terms of inquiry are contested; since woman as autonomous desiring subject does not exist except as man's Other, she cannot want but him/the child/the penis. Therefore, the question must be simultaneously answered and refuted. Steinwachs's skill and agility in addressing the complex issue of women in representation can be attributed in part to her intellectual involvement, as a university-educated woman, with the theoretical issues mapped out in these debates.

Steinwachs completed an extensive education and thorough academic training that spans the theoretical spectrum from Marxism to poststructuralism, including, as well, German and French cultural contexts. Steinwachs studied philosophy, religion, and comparative literature in Munich, Berlin, and Paris. From 1967 to 1974, she lived in Paris and studied with Roland Barthes, one of the most influential poststructuralist theorists. Her dissertation on André Breton, a surrealist artist and writer, earned her a doctoral degree. Supporting herself from writing and lecturing, Steinwachs now lives in Hamburg and Mallorca, an island in the Mediterranean that is also one of the settings in her play *George Sand* (1980). She writes theory, criticism, and fiction, and has published three novels and four plays. In addition, she is a performance artist and has appeared at theater festivals in Germany.

Steinwachs's thinking is strongly influenced by the French poststructuralists, among them the feminist theorists who developed the notion of *écriture féminine*. Due to the diversity of positions among the theorists generally categorized under the heading "French Feminism," it is difficult to speak of them as one school of thought. Hélène Cixous, author of "The Laugh of the Medusa" and *The Newly Born Woman*, is the theorist most often associated with *écriture féminine*; Julia Kristeva is the writer whose texts clearly had the greatest impact on German feminist theory. In my application of "French feminist theory" to Steinwachs's texts, I refer mostly to Luce Irigaray's early books *Speculum* and *This Sex Which Is Not One* because her metaphoricity shows affinities with Steinwachs's writing. In the parameters of this chapter, however, space considerations make it impracticable to differentiate among those theorists in every instance.

Borrowing from the French feminist critique of phallogocentrism, Steinwachs calls attention to patriarchal language and culture as repressive and proposes to unleash what had been forced into invisibility and incoherence. *Ecriture féminine* assumed the existence of primordial, unstructured forces outside of the Symbolic order; an assumption that carves a position of agency outside patriarchal ideology. Its liberatory moment as a political practice lay in its emphasis on pleasure, sensuality, and a playful eroticism. However, this academic theory failed to account for oppression experienced by women as social beings. Nor could it account for other material categories, like race, class, or ethnicity—thus recording its distance to the feminist movement and its activist prerogatives.

While Steinwachs's feminist aesthetics show the influence of the theorists of *écriture féminine*, it must also be read in the context of the

German feminist movement and the market of women's literature that movement fostered. Her writing shares the celebration of the female body with the aesthetics that the German women's movement developed in the late 1970s. Women's literature at that time created the sense of a woman-centered eroticism, along with the awareness of social and economic structures that govern the circulation of representations. In addition, Steinwachs's politics evidences her intellectual roots in Marxist thought. She insists on a materialist analysis of an oppressive system that excludes women from cultural production. Steinwachs raids both critiques, French poststructuralism and German materialism, balancing their political efficacy and their blind spots. *George Sand* illustrates this critical-cultural compound. In that text, Steinwachs develops a strategic model of feminist intervention in representational practices.

German feminism, while sharing some of its vocabulary with the French theorists, rested on a different set of assumptions and priorities. It evidenced a greater concern with women's oppression in economic, social, and cultural terms, addressing issues such as the gendered division of labor, reproductive rights, rape, pornography, etc. Women debated measures such as paid housework, demanded abortion rights, and imagined a woman-centered eroticism to be developed in separatist environments. With the growth of an autonomous women's movement and counterculture, one that endeavored to carve out alternative niches within the patriarchal economy, women's writing, rather than *producing* a feminist reality, was viewed as an objective reflection of changes in women's self-perception at that historical moment. Likewise, Steinwachs posits that the subversion of the Symbolic through representational strategies must be accompanied by social change wrought by feminist activism. However, she does not wholeheartedly share the radical feminist tenets of the German women's movement. Two terms in particular will serve to elucidate Steinwachs's position vis-à-vis French and German feminist discourses at that time. Both *écriture féminine* and German feminism privileged the body as a repository of truth, and both philosophies revolved around femininity as a key concept. However, these terms mark French-German differences rather than similarities because they carried widely divergent meanings within their respective contexts.

Around the mid-1970s, the women's movement in Germany developed an aesthetics that was often summarized and simplified by the slogan "writing the body." It rested on the assumption that women's

bodies held the key to the previously suppressed truth of "female subjectivity." To write the body, bypassing the censorship of the intellect, was
viewed as a strategy to express oneself authentically as a woman. Language became suspect because it alienated women from their own feelings and desires and from their sexuality. In 1975, Verena Stefan published the groundbreaking novel *Häutungen* [Shedding]. In its preface,
she states:

> while writing this book which has been long overdue in this coun-
> try, i ran up against the existing language, word by word, term by
> term. . . . Language fails as soon as i want to describe new experi-
> ences. seemingly new experiences which can be represented in the
> language, cannot really be new. articles and books on the subject
> of sexuality, which do not address the problem of language, are not
> worth anything. they maintain the status quo. (Stefan 1978, 3)[2]

Shedding provides a feminist hero who sheds layer by layer her
patriarchal indoctrination and in the process develops a feminist consciousness, a new relationship to her body, and a lesbian identity. The
novel's authority rests on the narrator's personal experiences. By recog-
nizing her experience of oppression not as singular and individual but as
the product of patriarchal oppression, Stefan's heroine develops a political critique. She articulates this newfound consciousness in terms that
she has to invent because traditional language fails, and she develops a
lyrical, often flowery "woman's" language. Stefan posited "femininity"
as the core of female essence lodged in the body and waiting to be
expressed—a core at one with nature, woman-loving and untainted by
patriarchal ideology.

   In contrast, French poststructuralism defined "femininity" as "a
complex of drives which remain outside of cultural structuration. . . . a
real which threatens to submerge not only the female subject but the
entire order of signification" (Silverman 1983, 186–87). The French
theorists conceptualized the gendered subject as an effect of signification;
hence, representation became the privileged site of feminist practice. To
write the feminine, then, was a radical political strategy that could be
deployed by male writers and theorists just as well as by female ones.
For the German writers, the body and femininity were inextricably
bound up with "real" women and their life experiences, but the French
theorists, even the feminists among them, did not necessarily privilege

women's issues or texts (although some seem close to it); femininity is a disembodied force, a theoretical construct operating against the equally uncorporeal phallocentrism. The French feminists' object of study was the text; representation was divorced from the material world of male and female subjects.

While French feminism failed to acknowledge oppression on a material level, German feminism neglected to account for the way that symbolic systems construct and reinforce sexual difference, since (according to the Kristeva, Iragaray, and Cixous) the speech act itself is already predicated on a masculinized position within the patriarchal realm of the Symbolic. The speaking subject trades intelligibility and meaning for the price of radical difference, a revolutionary femininity threatening to submerge the paternal order. In contrast, Stefan posited that gender oppression could be countered by valorizing previously devalued concepts and terms, reforming patriarchal language as it were.

German feminist authors at the time experienced the appropriation and transformation of language as liberating. Writing lent to them a sense of authority and power. For the first time, women collectively perceived themselves as the authors of their own representations. Moreover, the emerging network of feminist presses and publications granted women control over the ownership and distribution of their texts.[3]

Stefan's book became a model for feminist writing and publishing for several years to come. Her publisher, a small women's collective, managed to establish itself as the leading feminist press in West Germany. The book revealed the existence of a feminist counterculture, which it in turn helped to create and expand. This alternative cultural space constituted a market for women's writing that had as yet been untapped. Several feminist presses, journals, and magazines were founded. Major publishing houses followed suit by establishing a women's series. Women writers' conferences and special feminist issues of progressive journals became forums for postulating and codifying a feminist aesthetics. Between 1974 and 1977, women's writing established itself as a "discursive event" (Weigel 1989, 49). In 1977, Ginka Steinwachs began contributing regularly to the feminist magazine *The Black Messenger,* placing her within the development of this discourse. Her play *George Sand* was published by the Berlin feminist press, Medusa, whose name recalls Hélène Cixous's feminist manifesto.

Steinwachs refuses to subscribe to the essentialist notion of an "authentic," "natural" female language. Her training in poststructural-

ism put a critique of language at her disposal, which perceives the production of meaning as a process of installing differences and hierarchies
that repress the "body" of language, its material sensual quality. At the
same time, Steinwachs ties the return of *das Leibliche* [the sign-body], to
the pleasureful sensuality of *das Weibliche* [the feminine Id], and to actual
women and lesbians. Phallogocentrism is associated with the male subject's speech and aesthetic practices, with his material privilege and
vested interest in maintaining the dominant system of representation.
Thus, the term *body* in Steinwachs's writing resonates both with French
poststructuralist discourse and with the body that German feminists
were trying to write. Similarly, *femininity* comes into play both as a
structural force and as the celebration of a historical woman, her courage, and accomplishments, in short, as the celebration of women's difference and superiority.

The popular theatrical traditions and styles with which Steinwachs
aligns herself, such as the baroque *Hanswurstiade* and the puppet theater
with its cast of animal characters, share her dramaturgy of corporeality
and excess as well as the refusal of the bourgeois drama's didacticism.
The transformation of the stage as a "moral institution" (Schiller) into
an "oral institution" (Steinwachs), however, renders the representation
of hierarchical, oppressive relations across a social spectrum difficult.
The allegorization of class and gender differences as "aristomcats" and
"prolopussies" and the visualization of the flow of capital as hot and cold
water are somewhat simplistic within the frame of her cartoonish fable
world. The division of her cast into animal choruses as audience and foil
to a few monumental figures as well as her focus on nineteenth-century
aristocrats as liberating models have prompted criticism on the part of
German feminists (Alms in Nowoselsky-Müller 1989).

The crossover between French and German feminist critical theory
makes Steinwachs's writing an interesting example of "operational
essentialism,"[4] enabling her to represent oppression as well as constructing an empowering position of agency for a subject outside dominant
patriarchal, heterosexist ideologies. While at times, she posits women's
radical otherness, she also argues for gender equality from a socialist-
humanist perspective and refuses to agree to essentialist distinctions. She
critiques the Freudian hierarchy of libidinal stages and champions androgyny as well as stressing the politics of object choice when she proclaims a "lesbian credo." The notion of "operational essentialism" will

be worked through in the following discussion of both her theory of dramaturgy and of her play *George Sand*.

Dramaturgy

Steinwachs has postulated her own dramaturgical theory, a poetics that she characterizes through (at times neologistic) attributes such as excessive, terrorist, pleasurable, and bombistic. Its politics center on the explosive potential of sexuality, agitating the rigid opposition of gender both at the level of social and dramatic roles and at the semiotic level of the production of meaning. In particular, the key notions "explora-terrarism" and "theatorality" provide insights into Steinwachs's aesthetics and politics. These concepts illustrate the author's expert maneuvering between contrary arguments within French and German feminist theories in regard to sexual difference and equality. They also emphasize the operation of gender in theatrical communication where it is not explicitly present and work toward a feminist intervention in the phallogocentric production of meaning in classical German theater. Her attention to the production, proliferation, and liberation of signs, while informed by French surrealist theories of writing, attests to the revision of surrealist concepts within a feminist critique of semiosis.

The figure of the explora-terra-rist voraciously consumes continents (Nowoselsky-Müller 1989, 32), a gesture that represents the world as a material text to be incorporated through the mouth and transformed as it passes through the explora-terra-rist's digestive system. She is both an explorer and a terrorist who invades the terrain of male-dominated knowledge and representation and deconstructs it in the traverse, thus embodying the active-aggressive potential of Steinwachs's literary production. It perverts the traditional image of woman as the dark continent to be conquered by the male hero. The explora-terra-rist signals the will to inhabit these previously forbidden continents and wield male privilege and power. The trope of explora-terra-rism operates within the egalitarian paradigm that rests on a symmetrical division of power between the sexes, an argument that has been criticized for its lack of a fundamental critique of social structures and institutions.[5] The egalitarian discourse, which demands women's integration into the extant social and political system, risks participating in that system's oppressive aspects, as the imperialist connotations of the term *explora-terra-rism* illustrate.

Steinwachs balances the egalitarian argument with the insistence on women's difference, a position that enables a radical critique of patriarchal, capitalist institutions and the semiotic codes and technologies that (re)produce them. Her concept of theatorality calls into question patriarchal notions of gender and theater and dissolves them through the revolutionary force of the feminine. Her short essay "The Theater as Oral Institution" illuminates the notion of theatorality as a feminist strategy. Since it is central to her theatrical theory and practice but unavailable in English, I will quote it in full:

It is a stage truth that every author reinvents the theater for himself. Büchner is such an inventor, Brecht is another one, to name but two German dramatists starting with a B. Paradoxically enough, Brecht properly belongs to the 19th, and Büchner to the 20th century. I mean that in the sense that Brecht operates at the level of the branches of the tree of language, and Büchner erodes the roots. This erosion (*Ab-Arbeit*) already belongs to the order of the theatoral theater, or of the theater as an oral institution. That's what the bell has tolled. It takes its toll on a theater for which the stage means the world. Because the stage has stopped meaning. Curtain. The stage has dissolved, no matter if as box, revolving or open air theater, period. Because: it has shifted from the actors (players) to the spectators, whose participation has turned them into spect-a(c)tors, with emphasis on the second, so-called active "c." Stage in the auditorium? Nes. Auditorium as stage? Yo. We (singularwe, plurall) want to come on to that question with the cutlery of the tongue. The augmentation of the culinary theater is the—restaurant. The spect-a(c)tors' (plural) mouth is watering, because persons and things grow slippery in the flow of saliva. It dishes up, bite-sized in all courses: language. As the dialect of emotion, steering against the high language of reason. As the regional specialty of the soul. For instance the entrée: a champagne-sorbet, the Plat-de-Résistance: crabs from the Atlantic and herbed chicken, the dessert: creme tarts and liqueurs. (That is the menu of the first four scenes of *George Sand*.) Taste, a suppressed sense, is given permission to speak, seconded by the smell of tobacco- and hashishpipedreams. Equally seconded by the tactile sense, or tact, which used to be somebody in the beginning but now threatens to drop out of fangshion, because singularwe and plurall have become incapable of corporeally perceiving it. Curtain. It blows through the curtain like a forest. The theater as oral institution is oral. Orality in the Freud-Lacanian theory of the libidinal stages denotes a regression to the first and lowest of three (among which there are two higher) stages. All progress is regressive, says Wiesengrund. That indirectly attests progressivity to the theatoral theater. An oasis in the desert, I*d* capital I italic d, liquifidates a l(M)anguage as dessiccated as frozen assets. Articulatory relishing of words. In every instance, wallowing precedes swallowing. Babblebanquets, speechfeasts. Open your eyes. Open your mouths. Curtain up. The play begins behind the fences of the teeth under the hard palate. The stage is soft as wool. The tongue-rug is wet and cool. An open-air-festival in dewey grass. Mash the moist wordmush. Titillate the papillaries, tease the taste-buds, appease the players', participlayers' and spect-a(c)tors' appetite after a detour over the gullet, stomach and intestines. Behind the fleshy curtain of the lips, the actors and spect-a(c)tors live and let live, chitter and chatter. I*d* capital I italic d speaks, I*d* articulates itself, I*d* gesticulates. In the case of George Sand, I*d* is historical. It answers the question, "How do I take a stance and signal resistance," after a failed relationship, after fleeing the province, before the decisive literary success andsoonandsoforth. Prehistory of modernity. Curtain. Wrong. Instead: the modernity of prehistory. Curtain. Correct. My history as a writer who will soon swim down the river of time to "Sappho in Palma," your history as women who shake the worndations, our history of participlayers who will continue to call George Sand back into the witness stand. The palatheater of the mouth bears a Klaus Heinrich-emblem: the Bocca della Verità. (Berlin 1979) (Steinwachs 1984)

The classical German theater, functioning according to the bourgeois imperatives of morality and enlightenment, is revealed as a technology that represses pleasure. That process of repression characterizes the production of meaning (which privileges sense over sensuality), the mapping of gender on the human body (which supplants anal and oral stages with genital sexuality), and the construction of the humanist subject (which installs morality over pleasure). Steinwachs calls attention to the intersection of three discourses—phallogocentrism, psychoanalysis, and humanism—that conspire in that repression.

Steinwachs, who declares the death of the classical humanist theater and announces the age of theatorality, subverts the function of the institution as a tool of dominant ideology by inverting the process of subject construction. Since progression (to the genital, heterosexual stage) provides the rationale for the repression of alternative sexualities, she proposes regression as a revolutionary strategy. The chain of oppositions that Steinwachs constructs in her manifesto juxtaposes the Ego, "the high language of reason," with the Id, "the dialect of emotion"; communication with sexual and culinary pleasure; the intellect with the senses (taste, tactile, smell); stasis, frozen assets with flow (saliva, digestive juices); death, the desert with life (moisture, the oasis). Steinwachs inverts the traditional hierarchy that subordinates the second term to the first. The mouth, formerly restricted to articulation, regains its sexual and culinary functions. Her corporeal language translates the phallogocentric critique of *écriture féminine* into a performance aesthetic that stresses excess and *jouissance*. Steinwachs's theater invites the spectator's imagination to play, to become a spect-a(c)tor, rather than assigning to her the traditional position as the passive recipient of ideas.

Steinwachs's poetics is largely dependent on the construction of the subject in psychoanalytic discourse, particularly in the writing of Freud and Lacan. Psychoanalysis describes the process of the subject's interpellation into the dominant sex-gender system; Freud lists the oral, anal, and genital stages as stations on the subject's itinerary toward a complete and "healthy" gender identity locked into heterosexuality. Steinwachs proposes the "regression" to the oral stage as the one of least differentiation between self and other, in which in fact the subject perceives itself as boundless, "oceanic" (Freud). Consequently, what speaks in her theater is not the Ego, the site of consciousness, control, and reason, but the Id, that complex of drives situated in the unconscious.[6] The Id is anarchic and chaotic and obeys solely the pleasure principle.

Steinwachs's playful texts proceed from the pre-Symbolic from whence semiotic material erupts into sounds and images that are not yet disciplined by or in the Name of the Father. Her theoretical writing, her plays, and her performances liberate the sensual, erotic quality of the sign from the jacket of singular, nonambiguous meanings that celebrate "complexity, heterogeneity, negativity, multiplicity, liquefaction of oppositions" (Meyer 1983, 30). Her language subverts the hierarchy of denotative meaning over sound. Replete with puns, neologisms, assonances, and rhymes, Steinwachs composes the meaning of her text through the word as *Klangkörper* [sound-body] rather than as an abstract unit of communication. Her dialogue is constructed through association and connotation, emphasizing the relations among words rather than the denotative tie between stable sign and referent. Through this textual play, Steinwachs's dramatic language remains fluid and does not congeal into fixed meanings.

Like Irigaray, whose "twolips" have become notorious, Steinwachs deploys the metaphoricity of the female body in her emphasis on the lips/labia. For *George Sand,* she explained in an interview, she envisioned a "mouthscape, in which all twelve scenes are staged in a differently arranged mouth, a mouth that sometimes looks like a vagina" (Nowoselsky-Müller 1989, 38). Mouth, lips, and tongue become the stage that Steinwachs stimulates to make words spill like vaginal juices. The mouth as the site of speech and sex, the slippage of lips and labia, exemplify both as transgressive for the female, queer subject heretofore invisible in the paternal domain.

Steinwachs' theater voraciously consumes and transfigures language, sucking it into its vortex from whence "bilabial streams of language" can begin to flow (Nowoselsky-Müller 1989, 37). The slippage of the signifiers that sets the text in motion, as Sigrid Weigel has pointed out, "follows a dynamic of the *senses,* rather than the creation of *sense*" (Weigel 1989, 341). The Id that speaks in Steinwachs's palatheater does not produce different messages, but rather engenders "a different logic, a movement she calls 'flow'" (Weigel 1989, 342).

The notion of "flowing" as the process of liquification of oppositions, resonates with the juices that flow from and within the female body and with the traditional iconography that associates woman with water, liquids, and the ocean.[7] It celebrates femininity as excess, a principle central to Steinwachs' aesthetics. She calls it "the theater of plenitude,"[8] "maximalism," and "bombism" (Nowoselsky-Müller 1989, 111). It privileges the ornament over the essential, artifice over the "authentic," fantasy over truth. This gender critique of maximalism has certain affinities with the discourse of camp in its privileging of appearance and excess, and its ironic, witty tone.[9] Steinwachs aligns the subordination of pleasure to meaning with the instrumentalization of sexuality for the purposes of heterosexual reproduction in the oedipal family. She reclaims the theater's function of awarding pleasure for the sake of pleasure, mockingly conceiving of it as a "restaurant."

Steinwachs's notion of theatorality echoes Barthes's exploration of textual pleasure. Barthes theorized a text of bliss, which articulates desire from a preoedipal position and speaks an "unweaned language. . . of an undifferentiated orality, intersecting the orality which produces the pleasures of gastrosophy and of language" (Barthes 1975, 5). Bliss, as opposed to pleasure—though these two terms are in contiguity as often as they are in opposition—"imposes a state of loss," and thus brings about a rapturous abandonment of the self and of culture, bringing to a crisis the reader's "relation with language" (Barthes 1975, 14). Barthes suggests two conditions for the eruption of bliss:

> In short, the word can be erotic on two opposing conditions, both excessive: if it is extravagantly repeated, or on the contrary, if it is unexpected, succulent in its newness (in certain texts, words *glisten,* they are distracting, incongruous apparitions. . . .) In both cases, the same physics of bliss, the groove, the inscription, the syncope: what is hollowed out, tamped down, or what explodes, detonates. (Barthes 1975, 42)

"The Pleasure of the Text" captures the stylistic principles of repetition/ similarity versus the unexpected/difference on which Steinwachs's writing operates. Steinwachs reformulates them as association/dissociation or attraction/repulsion. While the microstructure of her text functions as associative chains, in which words are varied and compounded along assonance and similarity, the macrostructure of her play is antithetical and organized around difference. The title of *George Sand,* "a woman in motion, the woman of stature," not only outlines the poles between which the title figure is suspended but announces the pattern of opposites that structure the play into complementary scenes, as for instance in "Homolulu" and "Heterogonia." This technique reveals the structural analogy of text and machine by describing writing as a magnetic field (Steinwachs 1975, 205).

Steinwachs theorized literary production as the work of the "poetrymachine." This notion of writing aligns her with the theory and practice of (French) surrealism, which she studied closely (Steinwachs 1971). The poetrymachine refutes the notion of authorship as an expression of original genius by processing texts, words, and language fragments that are already in circulation. The texts this machine produces undertake a traverse of culture, crossing a great number of discourses from philosophy and art to popular wisdoms and trivia. The poetrymachine "finds"; it does not "invent" (Nowoselsky-Müller 1989, 39).

This terminology aligns her with the surrealist/dadaist bricolage based on the collection and arrangement of raw material and found objects.

In contrast to the surrealist practice of automatic writing that sought to circumvent the writer's consciousness, however, Steinwachs does not disavow or abdicate authorial agency through the concept of the poetry-machine. She mixes historical material, namely elements of George Sand's biography and its settings, with lyrical passages, and quotations from George Sand, Gertrude Stein, André Breton, Lévi-Strauss, Deleuze/Guattari, etc., as well as set phrases and clichés (Steinwachs 1975, 206).

Steinwachs is conspicuously present in her writing. She imprints her texts with her signature by weaving her name into words and phrases. Her writing becomes an anagram. Her name becomes the instrument with which she appropriates the world. Rather than emptying language and marking it as that which excludes women, Steinwachs inscribes herself into the world-as-text, transforming it in the process. She invades the domain of the father, mimicking the voices of the great men of art and science and transforming the *Originalzitat* [original quotation] into a campy *Originkalzitat*.

George Sand

George Sand's twelve scenes, divided into two parts entitled "A Woman in Motion" and "The Woman of Standing,"[10] unravel and agitate received images of Amantine Lucile Aurore Dupin, née Dudevant, alias George Sand: the prolific author trying to live off her writing; the woman who wore pants in public; the first woman in European history to win back her premarital property in a divorce trial; the notorious bisexual lover of many famous men and women; hostess of her own artistic salon; activist in the 1848 revolution; and explorer who crossed the Alps alone and on foot. An early rediscovery of the women's movement, George Sand is shown not in the manner of the traditional dramatic hero embattled by (and overcoming) adverse social forces. Rather, the play, like the drunken sculptor at the opening of the play, zooms in on various facets of this monumental figure, guided not by chronological or psychological principles but by the dialectic of desire and social structures, sex and text.

It is the process of writing itself—on the part of Steinwachs as well as Sand—that unlocks moments of creativity, ambiguity, and excess frozen in the monumental marble statue of the woman author, effecting altered states: the metaphorical transformation of *Stein* [stone] into sand. That play on and with names, signs, and matter illustrates Steinwachs's project as the productive reception of literature and history, one that transforms notions of gender as it works through their patriarchal manifestations. The main subject of *George Sand* is the woman writer; the main dramatic action is that of writing, underlining the centrality of cultural production as sociopolitical intervention in French feminism. However, the text stages the impact of diverse feminist strategies on patriarchal structures that resist the forces of change, strategies that do not rely on the power of hysterical writing alone.

The title announces a dialectic between motion and stasis that serves as the organizing principle of the text. The play begins and ends with the motif of the statue which Alexandre Manceau has created and installed on a pedestal.[11] Each scene is divided into at least two parts: A prose section in capital letters introduces the reader to the setting and offers historical data as well as an interpretation of the action that follows. The capitalized passages broadly outline the clash and move of sociohistorical forces dramatized in the ensuing scene, often using metaphors rather than offering literal stage directions. In that way Steinwachs's creative rather than mimetic approach to Sand sets off a process of theatrical production that proceeds through association and imagination, necessitating director, designer, and actors to invent theatrical images of their own rather than executing or illustrating authorial commands.

Many scenes are segmented by film clips and use a music soundtrack while some contain directions as to the use of smells, turning the play into a multimedia event designed to please the senses, pique the imagination, and stimulate speculation, rather than teach moral lessons. The text playfully fractures into a multiplicity of sense impressions that may be imagined simultaneously instead of following a chronological, much less causal, arrangement. This style illustrates Steinwachs' dramaturgy of "bombism," and undergirds the specta(c)tor's emancipation from her traditional position of passive reception.

Each scene places George Sand in relation to specific patriarchal discourses, ranging from libertinage to the literary market, marriage to the antiporn "moral majority," fashion, narrative, and the legal system. The heroine is aided at times by diverse progressive forces, including the artistic avant-garde, her lovers, and the communist revolutionaries in midcentury Paris. The following discussion will proceed through three thematic problematics: literary production, sexual politics, and revolutionary agency.

Many scenes address the material conditions surrounding the process of writing. The literary marketplace is characterized as a swamp roamed by predatory crocodiles, allegories of "press-czars" and "journalist-mandarins" like Sand's editor Buloz-Snout, who determines the monetary value of her books. In "My Horse for a Pair of Pants," the socio-Darwinian notion of the survival of the fittest that the swamp image calls up demands the combat skills that are being rehearsed by Split Britches and Spiderwoman, women artists who practice karate. The reference to two well-known feminist theater companies resituates the question of George Sand's cross dressing within the contemporary United States, calling attention to the continuity of male domination of cultural production across centuries and genres in the new as well as the old world.

The scene unties the signs of gender and attendant social privileges from biological sex. It also sets up a certain pace, emulating the technique of the jump cut with its rapid switching between literary, theatrical, and filmic discourses. "My Horse," in which Sand conquers the capital, shows how codes of fashion and the rules of the literary jungle conspire to prevent women from active participation. In both discourses women serve as the objects of men's designs, beautifully adorned in the fiction as well as the costumes invented by men. George Sand gallops through Paris and into the men's clothing store The Handsome Horseman, where she purchases a pair of pants. Her manipulation of gender codes through the practice of drag capitalizes on the stability of signs in a naturalized taxonomy of truth and appearance that enables her to gain access to male power, as the indignant manager realizes. Underlaid with the ring of The Handsome Horseman's cash register, Sand reasons that in order to live off her writing and fulfill her many financial obligations she must invent "the fashion of women's trousers on economic grounds. split britches. i am merely poor and in no way impudent." (Steinwachs 1992, 300)

The emphasis on the combat skills on which a writer's survival in the literary "mudclub" is predicated challenges the Romantic notion of the genius-artist and its built-in gender bias. Sand's appropriation of male privilege is motivated by economic necessity. However, the woman author in drag is not only materially equipped to enter the patriarchal battlefield; her subversion of dominant gender codes gains part of its momentum through its alignment with certain subcultural practices, which resituate this performance in the camp space of queer subjectivity and desire. In a dominant heterosexist context of reading, drag could be interpreted as a strategy of limited use, empowering individual impostors while leaving male privileges intact. The historical practice of cross-dressing in homosexual subcultures, however, unlocks representation from dominant gender ideology and shifts the focus from center to margin. The gender-specific meanings of drag are emphasized by the two male dandies who patronize The Handsome Horseman on the one hand, and by the reference to Split Britches in the film clip on the other, a troupe that frequently deploys cross-dressing in the context of butch-femme role-playing in the streets and on stage.

The scene "Sauna of the Crocodile-Revue" further elaborates the metaphor of the literary jungle. In the office/sauna of the crocodile Buloz-Snout, the flow of capital is dramatized as the circulation of hot and cold water. Buloz, sitting in his command post, the bathtub, controls the faucets. Steinwachs's "materialist" analysis of the literary machinery emphasizes the material effects (heat and cold, moisture and dryness) of its operation on the senses and bodies of actors and spectators.

In the machinery commanded by Buloz, writers are treated as commodities and classified according to the profit they yield. George Sand is Buloz's prime asset: Her prolific production has earned her manager a considerable amount of money and real estate. But Buloz's press-imperium is only a small part of the larger capitalist machine, the stock market. Because the value of all commodities is determined by interrelationships, any transaction reverberates throughout the system and affects its other parts. The notion of the literary market as a subset of the capitalist stock exchange dispels the myth of the author as autonomous individual and master of his or her fate. Not "talent" or "genius" determine the value of the literary commodity (author or book), but diligence and compliance with the rules. Buloz is devastated at finding out that George Sand has left the country and gone to Mallorca in the midst of a stock-market crisis. What is at stake in Sand's disobedience is the smooth functioning of the machine that controls Buloz as well.

"Opera-Express of Art" illuminates George Sand's position within the literary market from another angle. It examines her assimilation into, and simultaneous effacement within, the French canon of high art. The train, conducted by Victor Hugo, becomes a metaphor for nineteenth-century French literature. It is operated by Balzac and Flaubert, who incessantly feed the engine with coals. It moves from scene to scene, surrealistically connecting the Paris Opera house, Homolulu, and LE CROISSET. The image of the literary machine as a train is a visual pun on the word *Kohle* as "coals" and "money." As in "Sauna," value is represented in terms of physical labor and its material effects. The stokers puff and sweat, exerting themselves in the process of production that keeps the wheels turning.

The scene examines the reception of women's writing in popular discourse of gossip and in the context of high art and canon formation. The displacement of moral judgments and prejudices, voiced by a mob of aristomcats and prolopussies, onto supposedly neutral critical categories espoused by Balzac and Flaubert on the train, and the concomitant shift in focus from the author to the text, renders invisible the mechanisms of control that govern processes of ideological regulation in literary reception.

Sand's leap from the volatile position of a queer woman in the literary marketplace onto the supposedly safe, all-male space of nineteenth-century French literature historically effaced her from the canon. Although famous and popular in her time, George Sand's writing was eclipsed by the train's male passengers; her texts were deemed worthless by critics who defended the values of patriarchal culture. The reception of the equally prolific Balzac's work as high art as well as the acceptance of the sexually ambiguous Flaubert exemplify the double standards operating in critical discourse and the resulting effacement of women's writing from the literary canon.

A gondola ride through Venice shows another kind of swamp where Sand and one of her male lovers battle over narrative structures and the prerogative of speech. In the scene "Heterogonia: The Great SRI," George and Alfred de Musset drift slowly through Venice in a gondola driven by a musical gondolier. The young man entertains his lover by telling her a story involving sexual pursuit and conquest, couched in the orientalized language of the Arabian Nights. In the story, the powerful Caliph of Stanbul orders the great SRI to find and capture the most beautiful woman of Venice. Musset, who assigns himself the role of the great SRI while casting George as the nameless object of the caliph's desire, eroticizes the active-passive gender positions that the story rehearses not only in its relation of (male) subject and (female) object but also in the division between active narrator and passive listener, author and actor.

The scene highlights the connection between gendered narrative elements and the material preconditions of narrating, calling attention to the conditions of speech by inviting such questions as Who gets to tell the story and who has to listen? Who is invested in telling the same stories over and over? What are the possibilities of feminist intervention?

Under Musset's direction George is reduced to kissing on cue. She continually resists this assignment by either interrupting his story, by telling a story of her own, or by not complying with his directions. At the moment when the narrative moves toward the conquest of the beautiful woman, George interrupts three times by giving the servants orders before the exasperated Musset can at last resume his tale and achieve closure. Her assertive stance as the one in command at this crucial moment highlights their power struggle as one of authority and authorship; in order to rebuke Musset's striving for dominance, George must intervene in the plot. That moment also underscores the violence of traditional narrative that engenders the positions of hero and object-obstacle as male and female. The representation of difference between self and other as conflict, and its resolution as conquest, shows that women have nothing to gain from these narrative structures.

Steinwachs trains her materialist critique on the discourses that prohibit and hamper women's entrance and competition in the literary training ring/swamp/train and mobilizes countercultural images, such as the amazon warrior and feminist cross-dressers, against them. Steinwachs's writer-warrior declines to forfeit the sites and prizes of patriarchal culture that excludes her. Her demand for participation and equal opportunity, however, is grounded in a feminist politics that refuses to be co-opted into a superficial integrationism.

In *George Sand,* the production of literature cannot be thought of apart from sexual politics. The following section addresses writing specifically in its relation to sanctioned and proscribed sexual practices. While some of the play's most potent and liberating moments are associated with lesbian sex and texts, Steinwachs eschews the equation of heterosexuality with patriarchal oppression (as "Heterogonia" suggests) and of homosexuality with liberation from it (implying, too, the renunciation of privileges dispensed). What Steinwachs would seem to advocate is the utopian figure of the "hermaphrodite child of sun and moon" that keeps reappearing as a bigendered, bisexual position.

Steinwachs develops two counterstrategies to women's exclusion from cultural production. One is exemplified by a materialist analysis of the cultural apparatuses; the other is the text of bliss, which ruptures the structural fabric of phallocentric discourse and its repression of sensuality.

"Homolulu," the sexual centerpiece of *George Sand*, executes both moves in a complex dialectic of feminist strategies. In German, *Treibhaus* [hothouse] puns on the noun *Trieb* [drive] and the verb *treiben* [grow], clearly marking it as the pre-Symbolic realm of the Id governed by the pleasure principle. In heat and humidity opposites begin to slide, signifiers to flow, and sexual desire to well up. The smoke of hashish wafts off the stage and signals altered states of consciousness inducing *jouissance*. However, Steinwachs achieves a double-exposure effect in the twofold setting of the scene as simultaneously a hothouse and a coffeehouse frequented by ladies and gentlemen of high society. While the untamed, tropical growth of the hothouse designates it as the domain of femininity, the presence of "high society" under whose gaze the lesbian love story play itself out dramatizes a topographical model of the subject that denies the primordiality of the drives but represents them as implicated in, and coexistant with, the social structures that inhibit them. It endows the lesbian subject with a twofold agency: its slippery bliss constructs it as antiphallic, destroying the fabric of the Symbolic order from the outside; but it is also granted a position of agency *within* the patriarchal economy, which enables her to claim and appropriate male privilege and power and challenge male ownership of representations.

Under the disapproving eyes of the ladies and gentlemen of high society, George and Marie Dorval, an actress at the Comédie Française, enter as a butch-femme couple: George in a high hat and tails, Marie in curls and frills. Entering Baudelaire's *paradis artificiels,* they move into an altered state in which words start flowing, unfolding in the dialogue between the lovers and charged with an eroticism founded on the liberation from sense. Words become pure sounds, hilarious nonsense in which rhyme follows rhyme in a dance of seduction:

> george: MARIE: criminal clitoral cannabis.
> marie: GEORGE: critical clitoral credo.
> george: the cradle of critical chaos.
> marie: chaosmosis. cosmos.
> marie: a clitoral oratorium.

> (312, 313)

The flow of femininity submerges the social order and the couple drifts away under the patronizing eyes of the Anita Bryant chapter of the moral majority and their last offer of "assistance." The first film segment, a lesbian reinterpretation of the legend of Snow White, stages *jouissance* in the coming together of folktale and film as popular discourses of the nineteenth and twentieth centuries. Here, lesbian sexuality peaks in two technologies that have traditionally repressed it when George becomes the prince who saves the paralyzed princess through cunnilingus. The flow of saliva and vaginal fluids between lips and labia, butch and femme, prompts their flight from, rather than return to, the king's palace. The unleashing of the repressed also blurs ontological divisions between natural and unnatural, living and dead: The coffin, animated, "enters the water and drives forward on silver waterwings" (313).

However, *jouissance* in this scene is not only represented as the undermining of language as communication and the celebration of the erotic charge of the sign; the third segment of "Homolulu" articulates sexual transgression in terms of property relations. The lesbian actor Marie rejects the icons of womanhood created by great men and asks George to author her roles. The second film segment visualizes the double politics of bliss and materialism, both of which intervene in the Symbolic, in the women's flight from the hothouse to the top of the Paris opera where they celebrate their love.

Unlike the lesbian subject of psychoanalysis, Steinwachs's lesbian is not condemned to unintelligibility, but is empowered to invade the phallocentric regime and demand a space within it. Whereas French feminism, for the most part, leaves the terms of ownership of phallocentric culture intact and monolithic, Steinwachs reconfigures culture as heterogeneous. "Homolulu," with its fourfold division into segments that overlap, amplify, and complement each other, is one of the most complex scenes in *George Sand,* and constitutes the play's pièce de resistance.

Yet the bulk of the drama investigates Sand's somewhat dysphoric relationships with men as "Heterogonia" illustrates—a state of affairs that has less to do with the protagonist's affections or preferences than the weight of sociohistorical forces bearing on individual instances or proclamations of heterosexual love.

"G(e)orge of Fontainebleau" explores two models of institutionalized heterosexuality as the context of women's cultural production and suggests autonomy as the prerequisite of women's authorship and self-determination. George Sand, straddling the Gorge of Fontainebleau, is suspended between the alternatives of marriage with Baron Dudevant and libertinage with Jules Sandeau. For a woman, however, either role entails exploitation and subordination—with Dudevant that means the "contractually guaranteed use of the other sex" (305); with Sandeau, it means her financing his bohemian lifestyle. In other words, either relationship is organized around male needs and privileges. When husband and lover, equipped as mountain climbers, approach her from opposite sides and catch her in their ropes, she looses her bearings and plunges down the abyss. Her exit from false alternatives prompts her recognition that what is called "passionate love" is in fact a question of property. Her new position at the bottom of the gorge carves a space outside heterosexual institutions from which to speak. This new foothold empowers her to author her own narrative instead of letting men control it.

In Steinwachs' text, two positions are particularly empowered to terrorize the paternal regime. Her recurring phrase of the "hermaphroditic child of sun and moon" calls attention to the bisexual and the child who can challenge the dominant, heterosexist order. The games of Maurice and Solange, George Sand's children, serve as models for preoedipal pleasure and a refiguration of gender within representation. In "G(e)orge," they run across the stage, crisscrossing George's left-right schema. They cavort naked in a rivulet, remarking on each others' genitals. Steinwachs stages the moment at which the girl supposedly perceives her lack of a penis as a sign of castration and inferiority. This is a crucial moment for feminist theory and politics as well. The Freudian notion of penis envy ties gender to heterosexuality, causing the girl who accepts her gender as lack to desire the male (lover or son) as compensation. Conversely, the absence of penis envy signals an infantile sexuality, i.e., one not based on object choice. This model makes gender unthinkable without heterosexuality. It also renders femininity inconceivable apart from inferiority and dependence: A femininity conceived as strong and autonomous appears either as regressive or as lesbian, in effect conflating both. Solange does not conceive of her sex as inferior; this does not, however, preclude her from articulating heterosexual desire.

For the most part, Steinwachs deploys *jouissance* in a dialectical relation with the Symbolic order that represses it. "DIVORCE MARCH

TWO THREE," however, achieves an almost complete dissolution of patriarchal, phallocentric structures in the discourse of law by shifting the terms of inquiry into woman's "nature" and "desire" onto the slippery ground of femininity without performing the contrary gesture of claiming a place for women within extant structures.

The trial scene aligns the patriarchy with reactionary social forces bolstered by marriage as institutionalized oppression in opposition to women's equality as a program of progressive, oppositional forces. George demands back her property from her husband, who automatically gained ownership of her money and estate through the marriage, in order to support herself and her children.

Whereas "G(e)orge of Fontainebleau" represents marriage and "free" love as false alternatives, the trial scene highlights the strategic usefulness of libertinage because it enables women to align themselves with the rhetoric and the political clout of oppositional forces as Sand's advocate represents them. Again, Steinwachs refutes a feminist politics in absolutist terms, but emphasizes the need to argue strategically.

Within the trial, the speeches by Maître Thiot de Varennes, the advocate of the patriarchy in general and Baron Dudevant in particular, and Maître Michel Everard de Bourges, advocate of the Leftist opposition and George Sand, illustrate the poles of the masculine and the feminine in language. Thiot de Varennes constructs a forceful argument around the perpetuation of extant gender relations and against their transgression; what is at stake, he argues, is male power and privilege in general. Thus, the lawyer is able to solicit the sympathy of the all-male jury. His speech culminates in a tirade against women's autonomy:

WOMEN IN DRAG WHO PURSUE THE MUSE, WOMEN ARTISTS WITH AMBITIOUS VIEWS, are and will always be an abomination to us, the BLACK PANTHERS of the FRACTION of THE BLACK PANTHERS in the GOVERNMENT. long live the PHALLUS. long live the PHALLUS. down with the mannish women. fear our malice. genital supremacy. MAL DE SIECLE. (325, 326)

George responds with a claim to human rights: "THE MEASURE OF WOMAN'S FREEDOM IS THE MEASURE OF A SOCIETY'S FREEDOM" (326). The egalitarian rhetoric of the Enlightenment provides a philosophical, legal foothold for her argument. However, her exclamation meets with the court's disapproval. Any utterance is interpreted as a disruption; the mere act of a woman's speaking is viewed as an aggression and sets off a machinery of discipline and control.

Whereas Thiot de Varennes's plaidoyer is applauded by the court, Michel Everard de Bourges is admonished even before he starts speaking. De Bourges, who attempts to build his argument symmetrically to his counterpart, cannot make a positive claim to women's position. While the male subject is firmly supported by the Law of the Father and its institutions, woman in that system is coded as Other, Lack, Nothing. She cannot be called "subject" because if she speaks, she can only do so with a male voice; she is doubly split in language. Consequently, de Bourges's argument falters. His speech remains coherent only as long as he bases his defense on the liberal humanist rhetoric of civil rights. As soon as he begins to isolate women's cause from the general plight of the disenfranchised, he fails:

> but this woman here is a . . .
> indiscernible: no common . . . but a . . . and what a . . . and i tell you:
> ominous . . . voluminous . . .
> serious . . . monstrous . . .
>
> (327)

Since only the Law of the Father guarantees intelligibility, any attempt to contest it results in incoherent babble.[12] George, excluded from the order of meaning and communication in which power relations are negotiated, loses consciousness. The drama symbolically shifts to the slippery realm of the unconscious. The supreme judge falls into a trance; the jury follows. Echoing the lovers' dialogue in "Homolulu," the authorities enter the dangerous, seductive territory of femininity:

> supreme ass, absent-minded:
>   rejoice, rejoice:
>   sweet air grows moist.
> second presiding ass, likewise:
>   orchids bloom, wafts of perfume.
> third: explore the borders of the jungle of feeling its
>   bottom its ceiling.
>
> (328)

Although the play sets received images in motion in order to render visible the phallocentric mechanisms of exclusion, the utopia of a liberated language is but momentary. The dynamic of motion and stasis is arrested in the image of the statue that awakens and rigidifies under Manceau's hands. While the poetrymachine starts to foam like the champagne in the bottle of Veuve Cliquot, the palatheater of the mouth desiccates in the final scene; its lips close.

In a radical move out of the French feminists' psychoanalytic model, Steinwachs refuses to accept their—for the most part uncontested— equation of culture with the Symbolic order under the rule of the Phallus and the concomitant equation of signification and castration. The representation of culture as synonymous with the paternal law precludes a heterogeneous model of culture that would allow for the articulation of desire in nonphallic terms, and reconfigure sexual difference not as the difference of female from male but as a difference from gender and heterosexuality. The invisibility of the lesbian within the psychoanalytic model has prompted Irigaray to formulate that position in materialist terms: "But what if these 'commodities' refused to go to 'market?'" (Irigaray 1985, 196). Likewise, Steinwachs situates the lesbian simultaneously within the pre-Symbolic and the Symbolic, granting her *jouissance* as well as the privileges *jouissance* supposedly compensates for. The explora-terra-rist is the electric rider and the woman in pants, the resistant object of the great SRI's desire and the butch author. This strategy stresses motility, the swift raid, the evasion of stability and arrest. She has no essence, no ontological home from which to strike; all she leaves behind is a trace, a wink, a trail of cast-off masks.

The theoretical foothold for the feminine in the "Semiotic," (Kristeva) or the pre-Symbolic, all denoting an "originary space *before* the sign" (Spivak 1988, 146), risks to reinscribe women's exclusion from language and culture. Historically, what these theorists had been at pains to construct as a textual operation, rather than an ontological category, was assimilated into the conventional bifurcation schema that feminine writing had attempted to circumvent. Sigrid Weigel points out that in the popular discourse on a "feminine aesthetic," the textual operations of *écriture féminine,* cataloged as nonphallogocentric, "semiotic" (as opposed to symbolic), and metonymic (as opposed to metaphoric), have again been subsumed under a dualist notion of gender so that a text possessing certain formal characteristics can be categorized as "feminine."[13]

The convergence of feminism and psychoanalysis that *écriture fémi-nine* performed constituted the object of its analysis as "a psychic topog-raphy of oppression as opposed to external structures of coercion," privi-leging representation over material relations (Kipnis 1988, 152). What this aesthetics concealed is its own implication in historical structures of domination, thus effecting the "aestheticization of the political," as Laura Kipnis suggests. Ultimately, the displacement of political activism onto aesthetic strategies of resistance leads to the confinement of postmodern criticism to the text, which "comes to operate as a transcendental signified, as an ultimate meaning" (Kipnis 1988, 160). Meaghan Morris calls it "the Library," which, in its denial of referentiality, eclipses the critique of social, material relations of power (Morris 1988, 211).

Steinwachs integrates the categories of experience and oppression into the French critique, balancing a materialist analysis located in the Symbolic with the strategy of disruption/*jouissance* in the pre-Symbolic. Rather than viewing writing as a subversive, political practice per se, Steinwachs expounds on the material conditions of authorship, the "abyss of one's own." The explora-terra-rist resides in the lacunae of linear narrative models outside the literary market that declares war on her.

The alliance of French feminism and modernism has produced avant-garde writing practices that, like the leftist vanguard politics to which they have been opposed, have often incurred the accusation of elitism (see Kipnis 1993). While Steinwachs insists that both avant-garde art and leftist rhetoric remain necessary and effective, she marks these strategies as partial and unstable within our postmodern present. As an eminently open text, *George Sand* invites "mistranslations" into feminist stage practices, as they have already been undertaken, and demands fur-ther de-(euro)centerings from the perspective and with the tools of popular culture.[14]

Steinwachs calls attention to the alliance of the theatrical institution with the ruling class, suggesting that the uprising must resort to the amateur stage and, like *George Sand,* build its aesthetics from the perfor-mance traditions of the popular, nonbourgeois theater. A revolutionary theater can show images of social conditions that are not yet possible outside it. It must fly ahead and provide glimpses of the Not-yet:

MESDAMES, MESSIEURS, THE END OF THE PERFOR-MANCE WEIGHS HEAVILY, BECAUSE WHAT IS ALREADY

POSSIBLE ON STAGE CANNOT YET BE REAL IN REAL-
ITY. THE THEATER FLIES AHEAD: FOLLOW IT FOLLOW
IT FOLLOW IT. (331)

Notes

Introduction

1. In Günther Rühle's three-volume anthology of the drama of the Weimar Republic, *Zeit und Theater,* Marieluise Fleißer was the only woman represented. F. N. Mennemeier in his two-volume collection of essays *Modernes Deutsches Drama* mentions only three women playwrights. The omission of women, exemplified by these two standard works, is shared by all collections on twentieth-century German theater, which would be too numerous to mention. For feminist literary historians, see both Bovenschen 1979, and Weigel 1989.

2. Michaela Giesing's article *"Theater als verweigerter Raum"* [Theater as a Space Denied to Women] situates women's playwriting within the women's movement. Although she does not explicitly deny any previous significant dramatic production on the part of women writers, this historicization implies that only the women's movement enabled women's incursions into the theater. Giesing 1989.

3. Roeder 1989, 7. Roeder actually locates the emergence of women playwrights after World War I and mentions Else Lasker-Schüler, Marieluise Fleißer, Anna Gmeyner, and Ilse Langner as the first dramatists in the German language.

4. See for instance Gisela von Wysocki's book *Die Fröste der Freiheit: Aufbruchsphantasien,* which includes a chapter on Fleißer and whose title quotes from Fleißer's autobiographical essay "Avantgarde."

5. Gayatri Spivak quoted by Butler 1990, 325.

6. A small number of plays by women was published in the East German journal *Theater der Zeit,* and two articles existed that addressed East German women's drama: Heukenkamp 1991; and Hildebrandt 1986.

7. See *New German Critique* 46 (Winter 1989) on minority discourse.

Part 1

1. These writers are only the most well known of a large number of women playwrights. Sue-Ellen Case's introduction to *Divided Home/Land* provides a brief account of the life and work of Christa Winsloe, a playwright who ad-

dressed lesbian concerns in plays such as the classic *Girls in Uniform* (first published as *Ritter Nerestan* in 1930 and later turned into a film starring Therese Giehse, among others) and *Aiono* (1943). Anne Stürzer (1993) documented more than two hundred plays written by women during the Weimar Republic.

2. The German state under Bismarck had a parliament, which was, however, relatively powerless. Moreover, it consisted predominantly of conservative parties. The only leftist party (the social democrats) was banned from 1878–90.

3. From an article on women's liberation that originally appeared on January 1, 1933. Reprinted in Rühle 1973, 176.

Chapter 1

1. Unlike the work of her contemporary Ödön von Horvàth, however, Fleißer's work has not been translated until recently and is therefore almost unknown, whereas Horvàth's plays have been produced in the United States.

2. The term can also be translated as "non-synchronism" (Jack Zipes), "non-contemporaneity," or "non-concurrence." Bloch 1991, 97–148; and Bloch 1975, 1–9.

3. This notion was particularly relevant to the post–World War I years and again in the late 1920s when the capitalization of the agrarian economy and the impoverishment of large parts of the petite bourgeoisie in the cities resulted in a severe economic crisis. Bloch claims that the inability of communist rhetoric and activism to take the ideological and economic disparities between provincial and urban communities into account was one of the reasons why the Nazis found such wide support among the agrarian and petit-bourgeois population.

4. See Eva Pfister's discussion of this motif especially in consideration of Fleißer's last essay, a piece about Jean Genet entitled "Orphan and Rebel." Pfister 1981, 42–49.

5. See for example Walter Hasenclever's play *Humanity,* which earnestly portrays the protagonist Alexander as a savior. For a discussion of the Christ-motif and the Passion-play structure in expressionist drama, see Sokel 1963, xx–xxi.

6. See also Angelika Führich's discussion of expressionist elements in Fleißer's writing. Führich 1992, 94.

7. In 1936, Max Horkheimer first published his essay "Authority and the Family," which develops that concept. The impact of Horkheimer's work only began to be felt decades later, in the reception of the Frankfurt School's critical theory by the Left in the 1960s.

8. The critique of fascism as a dimension of the patriarchy emerged in the 1970s. See also my discussion of feminist theories of fascism in the chapter on Gerlind Reinshagen. A well-known work analyzing the fascist constructions of masculinity is Klaus Theweleit's two-volume study *Male Fantasies,* 1987. Theweleit notes the misogynist effect of fascism's homosocial structures combined with a heterosexist ideology, which designates women as objects of exchange between men.

9. The term was coined in 1925 by G. F. Hartlaub, a gallery director in Mannheim who put together an exhibition entitled "Die Neue Sachlichkeit." Willett 1978, 111.

10. See the "expressionism debate" in which many of the exiled Marxist artists engaged that is documented in Schmitt 1973.

Chapter 2

1. Synchronization refers to the official prohibition of any cultural, religious, political, or social organization that did not subscribe to Nazi ideology. Dissenting groups either had to disband (and go underground) or join Nazi organizations.

2. See Marianne Krüll's perceptive biography of the Mann dynasty, *Im Netz der Zauberer: Eine andere Geschichte der Familie Mann* (Zurich: Arche, 1991), especially the chapter "Der große Bruderzwist," pp. 229–38.

3. Erika Mann 1984, 253. See also her letter to the Immigration and Naturalization Service from December 1950 in which she withdraws her application for citizenship, pp. 275–80.

4. *Die Sammlung* appeared monthly from September 1933 to August 1935. *Decision: A Review of Free Culture* existed from 1940 to 1941.

5. Keiser-Hayne refers to Susanne Gisel-Pfannkuch's study of the Peppermill's Swiss reception, *Die Pfeffermühle in der Schweiz 1933–1936* (unpublished MS, Munich City Library).

6. See also my discussion of the *Volk* as a highly contested notion in the chapter on Marieluise Fleißer.

7. See for instance reviewer Wilhelm Hausenstein of the *Münchener Neueste Nachrichten* (January 1933), quoted in Keiser-Hayne 1990, 32. In spite of the male drag in which Mann appeared, Hausenstein praised her "feminine charm" and "graceful distinction," demonstrating the overdetermination of the medium in terms of sexual objectification.

8. Hans Hyan and Peter Hille, a "street vagabond and impressionist poet" who was friend and mentor of Else Lasker-Schüler, performed in Der Hungrige Pegasus. Appignanesi emphasizes the courage of these early cabaret artists in the context of the Wilhelmine police state: "Hans Hyan's chansons on the unemployed, on adverse social conditions and the fate of the poor, then seem truly remarkable. This first German socialist rebel in song, who opened his own cabaret, would take on the voice of the dispossessed and yell out: 'Damn you all. / We want to know / Why you're full / And we have to go hungry.'" Appignanesi 1976, 35.

9. Wysocki 1977, 295. Likewise, Marieluise Fleißer described the Girl as a product of fashion, a type to which women had to conform in order to succeed in the marketplace: "Time hung a banner over them on which the name of this creature was written: Girl. Men loved the Girl, precisely because she did not think." Fleißer 1972, 3:79.

10. Otto and Rösler 1981, 78. Budzinski estimates the number of establishments in early 1920s Berlin at fifty. Budzinski 1982, 110.

11. The latter was a theater critic who, after 1925, regularly published a "Kabarett-Kolumne" at the *Berliner Tageblatt,* a major daily. Many of his reviews, including those of the Wild Stage, are collected in Völker 1988.

12. Appignanesi 1976, 140. Hermann-Neiße spells her last name Haase.

13. Brecht's concept of a "smoker's theater" took shape during the mid-1920s.

14. See Brecht 1964, 87, 153. Erwin Piscator used those stylistic elements in his shows *Revue Roter Rummel* ([The Red Revue] 1924) and *Trotz Alledem!* ([In Spite of Everything!] 1925), which were sponsored by the communist party. See Willett 1978.

15. In the Wild Stage, the stout, comic Hase appeared in the role of the fallen woman.

16. See Valeska Hirsch's remarks on rehearsal methods and collective operation in Keiser-Hayne 1990, 58. Likewise, Lotte Goslar stressed the artistic autonomy she enjoyed when working with the Peppermill. Keiser-Hayne 1990, 84.

17. Berber's "dances of vice" focused on transgressive sexual roles and figures. Against the backdrop of the female body's increasing sexualization in mass entertainment, Berber's dances claimed sexual autonomy and pleasure for women and expanded the range of physical expression from a position of defiance. Her kinesthetic expression of an "authentic," perverse subjectivity eschewed the dualism between the natural and the unnatural that formed the base of the protofascist versions of *Ausdruckstanz.* Lothar Fischer 1988.

18. See Manning's examination of *Ausdruckstanz* in relation to fascist ideology and the arts. Manning 1993.

19. Peter Panter, *Die Weltbühne* 17:17 (1924), quoted in Hermann-Neiße 1988, 75.

20. Keiser-Hayne characterizes Goslar's work as congenial to Mann's, because, "like Mann in her texts, she used dance to tell stories; satirical, accusatory, poetic, anecdotal, also slapstick-funny, burlesque and grotesque. . . . She danced small dramas, fairy-tales, stories." Keiser-Hayne 1990, 83.

21. In an effort to describe Pina Bausch's style to an American audience, Manning locates her in relation to Brecht and Artaud. However, Manning's own scholarship suggests that one might place Bausch (and Hoffman and Linke) in a female, even feminist, genealogy including Valeska Gert, Mary Wigman, and other expressive dancers like Anita Berber. To identify "epic" with Brecht effaces the influence that dancers like Gert had on Brecht. Manning 1986, 61.

22. The documentary movie *Desire* estimates that in the 1920s, there were more than fifty lesbian bars in Berlin (1990).

23. Ebinger's approach, her appeal to the middle-class spectator's conscience through the realistic and sometimes morbid depictions of poor girls, brings to mind Hans Fallada's novels of the same period, for instance *Little Man—What Now?* and *A Man Gets Ahead,* both set among the detritus of a capitalist society forging ahead.

24. In the fall of 1934, when Mann wrote this sketch, the Peppermill was under constant attack from the *Frontisten* (Swiss fascists), who sabotaged and disrupted the performances. In addition, the German embassy attempted to have

the Peppermill banned. The program of which *Vienna Atmosphere* was a part was the Peppermill's most radical to date and the last to be presented in Switzerland. Shortly afterward, the troupe left the country.

25. The American speaks English. Spelling and punctuation errors are in the original Peppermill script.

26. The main character of the novel is only thinly disguised as the actor-director Gustaf Gründgens, whose successful career during the Third Reich is represented as political opportunism. The first edition of the book was published by the East German Aufbau Verlag (1955). In 1965, Mephisto appeared in the West, only to be banned a year later, at the behest of Gründgens' heir. This ban was in effect until the 1980s.

27. Mutter Wolffen in Hauptmann's *Biberpelz* became one of her most-performed roles. She appeared in almost all of his plays. Dürrenmatt had her in mind when he created Fräulein Doktor Mathilde von Zahnd in *The Physicians*.

28. On materialist feminist playwrights in Britain, see Case 1988, chapter five, and Reinelt 1986. On the history of materialist feminist acting in Britain, see for example Hanna 1978 and Wandor 1981; on the theory of a materialist feminist stage practice, see Diamond 1988.

Chapter 3

1. This was the diagnosis of a newspaper in 1910, which prompted Lasker-Schüler to sue them, only to have the paper's evaluation confirmed by a court of law. See Klüsener 1980, 73–74.

2. Ulrich Linse argues that the so-called sexual question resulted from the fear of venereal diseases spread by prostitutes; next to abortion, venereal diseases were regarded as the primary reason for the demise of the race and the nation, causing a decrease in the population and therefore a threat to German supremacy. Linse 1985, 250–51.

3. Lasker-Schüler mythologized that character in *Die Nächte der Tino von Bagdad* (1907).

4. Fritz Martini and Helmut Kreuzer define the Bohème as an intellectual subculture characterized by the rejection of dominant, i.e., bourgeois, norms of lifestyle, particularly in sexual and artistic practices. The bohemians based their lives and their art on the Romantic idea of an "existence in pure art," and often transformed their own lives into works of art. The movement sided with popular art forms the bourgeoisie devalues, i.e., the circus, the fair, cabaret, and varieté, and rejects artistic conventions such as the well-made play. See Kleemann 1985.

5. Both Hessing and Bauschinger point to the distance between the lyrical I and her people, which is expressed in the image of the brittle rock from which springs a lonely brook and in the dissonance between the isolated, praying voice and the community's collective scream to God. Nevertheless, the I is bound to the collective from which it flees. See Hessing 1985, pp. 91–119, and Bauschinger 1980, 170–71.

6. Kuckart constructs the position of the androgyn for Lasker-Schüler, which seems problematic insofar as it implies asexuality: "The androgyn is self-sufficient, because he no longer requires a social or emotional complement." Kuckart 1985, 101. Note the masculine pronoun.

7. Some feminists have interpreted Lasker-Schüler's cross-dressing for several of her parts either as a sign of her "male identification," a common conflation of heterosexist categories with homosexual practices, or as a result of the "lack of female role models." Hasecke 1982, 35.

8. See for instance Hessing's censorious remarks about her sexuality. Hessing 1985.

9. Hasecke mentions Antinous and Hadrian and David and Jonathan as other homosexual couples, some of them from biblical mythology. Hasecke 1982, 36. See her reading of "*Urfrühling*" and "*Nebel*" in Hasecke 1982, 17, 74.

10. The image of the heartstage is reinforced by a heart-shaped curtain. I chose not to hyphenate the English translation to convey the lack of distance between these two poles.

11. Lynda Hart underscores the liberatory potential of spectacle for women performers because it defies "the warning generally given to women to avoid having attention drawn to themselves, a prohibition against being publicly seen and heard." Hart 1989, 1.

12. The first two have telltale names: "glassy Amadeus" points to that character's heart of glass; "Frederic-with-the-pendulum" indicates his bared genitals; "Long Anna" wears a woman's name.

13. Martha's nude photograph is never clearly visible, Heinrich's attraction for the underage Lieschen only emerges during his alcoholic intoxication, and her incestuous relationship with her brother August is but alluded to.

14. The last act is divided into two scenes, thus creating six acts, as it were. In her letter to Jessner, Lasker-Schüler asked him not to lower the curtain during the play, not even at the end. Lasker-Schüler 1962, 2:659.

15. See especially her essays in *Gesichte,* which contains detailed, enthusiastic descriptions of circus, cabaret, and variety shows. Lasker-Schüler 1962, 2:139–216.

16. Hasecke calls attention to the dualism of "femininity" and "genius," which either automatically excluded women from the realm of "world literature" or, by according women like Lasker-Schüler exceptional status, again reinforced the universal truth of the dualism. Hasecke 1982, 91–92.

17. See for instance Klüsener 1980, 120, and Middell 1981, 637.

18. In 1938, Herschel Grynspan assassinated the German ambassador in Paris.

19. At the opening of act 6, a spectator asks her: "Did you . . . write . . . this play . . . all by yourself?" Lasker-Schüler 1992, 173.

20. See Bryant-Bertail's excellent analysis of Piscator and Brecht's production of *The Good Soldier Schwejk,* which used stage machinery to comic effect. Bryant-Bertail 1991, 19–40.

21. Bauschinger comments on this scene: "The figure of Marte Schwerdtlein ended up more stupid than intended. The beginning of the fifth

act, with the silly dialogue Marte Schwerdtlein-Goebbels exceeds the limit of good taste." Bauschinger 1980, 282–83.

22. This self-description appears in a letter to Martin Buber. Lasker-Schüler 1969, 1:117.

23. For instance, her work was published in the expressionist journals *Der Sturm, Die Aktion*, and *Die Neue Jugend*. The radical leftist press, Malik-Verlag, was named after one of her novels.

Part 2

1. In a panel discussion preceding the opening of *Illness or Modern Women*, Heiner Müller observed: "Texts that run ahead of the theater have a hard time making it to the stage, and rarely do so. I am interested in the resistance Elfriede Jelinek's texts pose to the theater as it is." Back cover of Jelinek 1987.

2. Laura Kipnis argues that feminism provides the political conscience of postmodernism. Kipnis 1993.

3. See Löffler 1986.

4. Steinwachs's dramaturgical theories are examined in chapter 6; Reinshagen addressed metatheatrical concerns in many published interviews and in the dramatic essay "*Die emanzipierte Mariann*," included in her volume of collected plays. See Elfriede Müller's ironic dramolett *Damenbrise* (1989).

5. In 1969, Ulrike Marie Meinhof wrote a documentary play entitled *Bambule* for television that had to wait twenty-five years until it was finally broadcast in 1994. See Case's discussion in the introduction to *Divided Home/Land*, 16.

6. Nelly Sachs' play *Eli* is included in Eleanor Fuchs' anthology *Theater of the Holocaust*.

7. On the one hand, Bohrer responds to the entanglement of some intellectuals with the policing agencies of the erstwhile GDR, on the other hand, however, I argue that the suppression of politically engaged art, associated with GDR culture, constitutes part of the current revision of German history. For Bohrer's argument, see Anz 1991. For a discussion of the changing role of culture in the new Germany, see Huyssen 1991.

8. This scenario is familiar from Rainer Werner Fassbinder's *Katzelmacher* (1970), in which a Greek "guest worker" is confronted by a gang of Bavarian youth. See Fassbinder 1985.

Chapter 4

1. Reinshagen, Jelinek, and Steinwachs all published novels and radio plays as well as stage plays.

2. See also Kiencke-Wagner's bibliography on Reinshagen 1989, 431–37. Apart from *Ironheart*, none of her texts has yet been translated.

3. *Heaven and Earth* was produced at thirty-four theaters and achieved a total of 490 performances. *Sunday's Children* was shown at sixteen different houses for 255 performances. Kiencke-Wagner 1989, 430.

4. She received the Schiller-Award (1974), the Mühlheimer Dramatikerpreis for *Sunday's Children* (1977), the Andreas-Gryphius Award (1982), and the Hrotsvith of Gandersheim Award (1988).

5. Weigel points out that it was not until the midseventies that aesthetics became a major feminist issue. She entitles the first chapter of her book "Non-Synchronisms" (Bloch), referring both to the gap between political activism and a politically committed literature in the early 1970s and to the inability of the women's movement to take into account aesthetic practices that did not fit its needs and norms. Weigel 1989.

6. *Lebensraum* was also the term used by Hitler to justify German expansionism and the annexation of states, especially in Eastern Europe. He claimed that the German race needed more space in order to survive.

7. Frau Belius, a socialite, calls herself a (literally) "social cannon," and continues: "I am the cannon and he is the bolt." Reinshagen 1986, 286.

8. Koonz brings this paradox to a point: "The organization that inspired them with self-worth by telling them they belonged to the elite also told them, when they reached maturity, that they must settle into the dull life of a mother. How could the thought of selecting "racially fit" husbands, cooking wholesome food, keeping house, and bearing many children excite them after the years of sports, hiking, camping, and adventure that had attracted them to the movement?" Koonz 1987, 196.

9. The Bund Deutscher Mädel [League of German Girls] was the equivalent to the Hitler Youth for boys. "It is planned to set up work communities for gymnastics, handicrafts, folklore, foreign affairs, games and music, health service, and the like. The groups meet weekly, and once a month the meetings take the form of evenings-at-home which are devoted to discussions of cultural life and the structuring and guidance of one's personal life." Quoted in Mosse 1966, 45.

10. Koonz 1987, 311. By "mainstream opposition," Koonz refers to church leaders, organized resistance in groups such as the "Edelweiss Piraten" and the "White Rose," and the *Putsch* attempt instigated by Count von Stauffenberg.

11. Koonz demonstrates the ubiquity of this apparatus when she points out that "[t]he most common crime for which women were arrested during the early years of the Third Reich was making offensive comments." Koonz 1987, 313. The new "Law Against Malicious Gossip" furnished the basis for these arrests, whose effectiveness relied to a great extent on the atmosphere of fear and terror it created.

12. See different redefinitions of "resistance," Koonz 1987, 316.

13. All theories and explanations of women's acceptance of, or even affinity with, fascism take for granted what many feminist studies in the 1980s disproved: neither did women vote for Hitler in the same proportions as men, nor did they support the regime to a greater extent than their male counterparts. For a discussion of this issue, see Bridenthal, Grossman, and Koonz 1984, 37.

14. The film *Die Wannsee Konferenz*, based on original transcripts, is an excellent example for the rules-and-regulations-happy administration of the Jewish genocide, particularly Heydrich's role in it.

15. *Trümmerfrauen* [rubble women] were those women who did the bulk of the cleaning-up work that was done after the bombings.

16. Mitscherlich 1975.

17. The theater was instrumentalized for the purposes of the West Germans' ideological "re-education." In his study of the German theater during the four years of Allied occupation, Wigand Lange examines the cultural policy of the United States and their "department of theater" as an instrument of indoctrination, and the recasting of the German spectator-subject from enemy (who had to be instilled with democratic values) to ally in the fight against Communism. Lange 1980, 10, 11.

18. Her first play, *Double Head* (1967), explores the issue of class alliances and conflicts. It was produced at the Theater am Turm in Frankfurt, famous for its controversial performances. *Double Head* is Reinshagen's only play with a male protagonist.

19. In an interview, she explained: "The conflict between idea and reality, the stubborn pursuit of an inner image and the failure of this attempt—I want to find a form for this. I have tried to do so in various ways—either through the interjection of dreams, or through the appearance of a fictional interlocutor, or through a collage of different levels of language." Roeder 1989, 30.

20. This conglomerate of organizations and discourses spans the antinuclear movement, the citizens' initiatives, antiauthoritarian pedagogy, the sociosexual experiments of the Berlin communes, terrorist groups such as the RAF (Red Army Faction), and the emerging women's movement. Mewes explicitly excludes the German communist parties from the New Left. The New Left, according to Mewes, is characterized by its nonorthodox stance toward Marxist ideology, refusing to "identify historical materialism with the theory or practice of (any) party or socialist state." Second, the New Left operates within the "spaces of freedom created by bourgeois parliamentary democracy [which] make for an important prerequisite for creative socialist work." And finally, the New Left is "characterized by its awareness of the most subtle forms of psychological controls and oppression found in advanced capitalist society, and the concomitant efforts for emancipation necessary to break such new patterns of domination." Mewes 1973, 23, 24.

21. *Alltagsforschung*, the study of everyday life, emerged as a discourse that attempted to locate subjective agency in the interpersonal domain. In September 1975, *Kursbuch* published a special issue on this topic.

22. See also the writings of Peter Schneider and Uwe Timm on this point. They were influential writers/theorists/activists during the later 1960s and early 1970s, who proclaimed that the function of literature is propaganda and agitation. Its purpose is to channel revolutionary energies into acitivism rather than catering to escapist fantasies. Schneider 1969.

23. Three examples are Tröger 1977, Bock 1979, and Frauengruppe Faschismusforschung 1981. For a more recent study by an American historian, see Koonz 1987.

24. "Confession and memory can be used constructively to illuminate past experiences, particularly when such experience is theorized. Using confession

and memory as ways of naming reality enables women and men to talk about personal experience as part of a process of politicization which places such talk in a dialectical context. This allows us to discuss personal experience in a different way, in a way that politicizes not just the telling, but the tale." hooks 1989, 109.

25. After World War II, testimonial has been an important tool for Jewish survivors of the Holocaust. See Katz and Ringelheim 1983.

26. The sociosexual experiments of the Kommune I and II in Berlin garnered much attention in this context, because they explicitly made such "private" issues as sexual relations, child rearing, division of housework, etc., the base of their politics. See Hübner 1977.

27. In an interview, Reinshagen asserted: "I believe that every play since Aischylos that is worth any consideration, shows this existential situation, this utmost isolation, the most extreme despair. But any play deserving consideration also indicates a counter-possibility, what could be, an inkling, the trace of happiness, of insight." Reinshagen and Laube 1975–76, 101.

28. Hüfner lists at least four street-theater troupes that sprang up in conjunction with the protest actions in West Germany during the summer of 1968. The communist writer Peter Schütt claimed that "the street is still the only news organ for the opposition that is not subject to censorship, and offers space for proclamations and demonstrations of all kinds, for posters, murals and graffiti, for improvised scenes, documentaries and agit-prop. If the ruling class wants to prevent the people from listening, public streets and spaces remain the last school for the nation." Schütt quoted in Hüfner 1970, 8.

29. In their manifesto "*Thesen zu einem politischen Theater*," Wolfgang Anraths and Victor Augustin postulated: "The projected activation of the audience must be articulated within the play through the presentation of possible activist strategies." Anrath and Augustin in Hüfner 1970, 257.

30. Ueding 1978. In a similar vein, Peter Handke argued for the power of poetic language to disrupt the symbolic order and therefore appropriate the future, conceptualizing all literature as inherently utopian, because it liberates the imagination. After receiving the prestigious Georg-Büchner Preis, Handke in his speech asserted the "anti-conceptual and therefore utopian power of poetic thinking." Handke 1983, 45.

31. Kiencke-Wagner outlines the history of that term from its early manifestations to contemporary practices. Kiencke-Wagner 1989, 99–111.

32. Adelson notes that "everyday life was also considered a potential source of emancipatory strength because it contains at least some elements that are neither ruled nor structured by market forces. It opens certain "free spaces" [*Freiräume*] of experience and fantasy." For further reading, she refers to Negt and Kluge 1972. Adelson 1983, 11.

33. The German expression "*Sprung im Bewußtsein*" puns on the double meaning of *Sprung* as "crack" and as "leap." A crack in consciousness means at the same time a leap in consciousness.

Chapter 5

1. The July 1989 issue contains an article in which Alice Schwarzer inter-views Jelinek. Schwarzer, like Gloria Steinem in this country, is a figurehead of the women's movement. As chief editor of *Emma* and author of several books, Schwarzer has shaped and articulated feminist thinking in Germany for more than two decades. Her books have become seminal texts in the women's move-ment.

2. Lahann 1988. The article mentioned the existence of other photographs of Jelinek in chains and ropes "like an ironized Justine, the Marquis de Sade's chastised virtue," photographs that Jelinek, however, had asked not to be pub-lished.

3. Nevertheless, the *stern* located her in the tradition of great pornographic literature; references to de Sade, Henry Miller, and even Erica Jong abounded. Although Jelinek's bitter and painful representations of women's sexuality have little in common with Jong's celebration of the "zipless fuck," these differences were swept aside by the mass media's insistence on regarding her as a "great dominatrix," as the voice of a feminist eroticism. See Schober 1989.

4. See for instance Burger 1983. This motif has become a standard trope in the reception of Jelinek.

5. Gürtler's critical anthology on Jelinek includes a list of all her awards. Jelinek received her first award, the Lyrik-und Prosapreis der österreichischen Jugendkulturwoche [Award for poetry and prose sponsored by the Austrian youth culture] in 1969; the most important ones were the Roswitha-Gedenkme-daille der Stadt Bad Gandersheim [Hrotsvith-memorial award of the city of Bad Gandersheim] in 1978, and the Heinrich-Böll-Preis, awarded in 1986. See Gürtler 1990, 162.

6. Walter Klier describes the political efficacy of the Austrian avant-garde, reduced to the slogan "the critique of language = the critique of society," as "questionable." Klier 1987, 423.

7. Rühm's criteria for the collages which the groups often produced collec-tively, remain vague and formalistic: "selection and order, and the sensitivity that grows from the tension between contiguous sentences, make up the special quality of this sort of poetry. . . . we played with each other, bouncing sentences off of each other like balls." Rühm 1967, 22.

8. In their 1965 manifesto "HAPPY ART & ATTITUDE," they proclaimed that this philosophy will revolutionize society by liberating the pleasure principle from the hegemony of the reality principle. Its goal is "the gentle world revolu-tion." Wiesmayr 1980, 26–27.

9. Kolleritsch, the editor of the journal, instigated a heated debate about the function of art vis-à-vis social change, which corresponded with contemporary debates in West German journals such as *Kursbuch*.

10. The Marxist writer Michael Scharang became Kolleritsch's most promi-nent opponent in the debate. See Wiesmayr's account of the discussion. Wies-mayr 1980, 40–41.

11. For a complete bibliography of her work, see Gürtler 1990, 163–73.

12. Jelinek 1987. For a critical analysis of Jelinek's dramaturgy and its development, see Hoff 1990 and Caduff 1991.

13. A review of *Clara S.*, published in the news magazine *Der Spiegel,* was subtitled "SPIEGEL-Redakteur Hellmuth Karasek über das feministische Stück 'Clara S.' von Elfriede Jelinek." Karasek 1982.

14. Her biographer Berthold Litzmann has been most influential in shaping the image of Clara Wieck-Schumann as the embodiment of Romantic virtues. Litzmann 1918. Later biographies do not significantly digress from Litzmann's portrait. Chissell puts a greater emphasis on Clara's accomplishments as a pianist but nevertheless remains close to her received image as a "dedicated spirit" to the men around her, introducing her as "a grateful daughter, a devoted wife, a caring mother, a loyal friend." Chissell 1983, xi.

15. Despite Clara's claim to her art as "original" rather than merely imitative, her critical reception as a pianist persistently focused on the *skill* aspect, denying it the status of *talent:* "People only saw my special gift of pressing down keys, and in the right order. Anyone can do it with some practice. The more you practice, the better you become." Jelinek 1984, 76.

16. Kant's admonitions to women illustrates the dilemma of constructing femininity and aesthetic competence as mutually exclusive: "Laborious learning or painful pondering, even if a woman should greatly succeed in it, destroy the merits that are proper to her sex, and because of their rarity they can make of her an object of cold admiration; but at the same time they will weaken the charms with which she exercises her great power over the other sex." Kant 1960, 78.

17. See Kant 1957, 10:405. Bovenschen applies a gender critique to the Kantian notion of genius. Bovenschen 1979, 238.

18. Schiller's poem "Die berühmte Frau" [The Famous Woman] derided that cultural type as "a hybrid between man and woman . . . in-between the sage and the ape" which threatened to disrupt the natural order. Schiller 1965, 1:137.

19. In comparison, the trope "becoming feminine" in postmodern discourse signifies a subversive position vis-à-vis dominant discourse, which can be claimed by the male theorist. See de Lauretis 1987, 24.

20. In Kant's discourse, the postulates of beauty and nobility are subsumed under the gender dichotomy; while woman receives beauty as Nature's gift, nobility for man constitutes an imperative, something for which he has to strive. See Kant 1960, 81–83.

21. Jelinek *Illness,* 1987, 17. Luce Irigaray elucidates the casting of reproduction in capitalist terms, "Matrix—womb, earth, factory, bank—to which the seed capital is entrusted so that it may germinate, produce, grow fruitful, without woman being able to lay claim to either capital or interest since she has only submitted 'passively' to reproduction. Herself held in receivership as a certified means of (re)production." Irigaray 1985, 18.

22. This operation characterizes the writing of Descartes, Locke, Kant, and Hegel, to name but a few. For an analysis of the construction of the subject in Enlightenment discourse, see Belsey 1985.

23. See for instance Rousseau 1953. In *The Dialectic of Enlightenment,* Horkheimer and Adorno view this "progress" as the establishment of an all-enveloping, totalitarian system of domination.

24. de Lauretis 1987, 5. Gayle Rubin coined the term "sex-gender system." Rubin 1975.

25. "I don't reproduce. I seduce." Jelinek *Illness,* 1987, 21.

26. I am indebted to Amy Robinson's work on bathrooms, gender, and sexuality.

27. Case has elaborated this figuration in Case 1991, 9.

Chapter 6

1. For detailed discussions of this debate, see Alcoff 1988 and Kipnis 1988. For an examination of the debate in relation to theater and performance, see the introduction to Case 1990.

2. Stefan's preface, a manifesto of feminist writing, is missing from the English translation of the novel.

3. Sigrid Weigel's book *Die Stimme der Medusa* is an excellent study of the history of women's literature, focusing on the German debate around a feminist aesthetic, and documenting the growth of a women's network of presses and publications. Weigel 1989.

4. Judith Butler quotes this term from a lecture given by Gayatri Chakravorti Spivak. Butler 1990, 325.

5. German feminist Cornelia Klinger traces the two competing paradigms, egalitarian and dualistic, through the first and the second women's movements in Germany. Klinger 1986, 57–72. Silvia Bovenschen uses the terms "equality theorem" and "complement theorem."

6. In her analysis of Freudian theory, Kaja Silverman provides an overview of two models of the subject; they differ in their alignment of Id, Ego, and Superego with the categories of the unconscious, preconscious, and conscious. Silverman 1983, 132–49.

7. Where *Illness* inverted and parodied this imagery in Emily's renunciation of her invisible juices in favor of a phallic apparatus, it is integral to *George Sand.* The French feminists claimed that imagery and celebrated its blurring of limits, borders, and oppositions. See for instance Irigaray 1977.

8. See for example the title of Anke Roeder's interview with Ginka Steinwachs. Roeder 1989, 109–22.

9. For theories on camp, see Case 1988–89, Bronski 1984, and Newton 1972.

10. The translation of Steinwachs's *George Sand* includes seven out of twelve scenes from the massive, book-length text. The second part, "The Woman of Standing," is represented by two scenes only in Steinwachs 1992.

11. That motif is taken from Ovid's *Metamorphoses,* in which Pygmalion breathes life into an ivory statue.

12. Judith Butler explains this phenomenon, and articulates her critique of it: in Lacanian theory, sexual difference is instituted "as the reified foundation

of all intelligible culture, with the result that the paternal law becomes the invariant condition of intelligibility, and the variety of contestations not only can never undo that law but, in fact, require the abiding efficacy of that law in order to maintain any meaning at all." Butler 1990, 329.

13. This has led to the discussion of male authors as major proponents of "feminine writing"; see for instance Cixous 1980 and 1991. Sigrid Weigel calls attention to this phenomenon. Weigel 1989, 203–4.

14. See Case's discussion of a staged reading of *Monsieur-Madame,* a condensed version of *George Sand,* sponsored by the Goethe House New York in 1991. That reading, performed by Split Britches, the Five Lesbian Brothers, and two members of the Bloo Lips company at the Cafe La Mama, brought a uniquely queer and American pop cultural interpretation to this eurocentric text, a perspective that was praised by Steinwachs and many of the (German and U.S.) feminist critics present at the occasion. Case 1992, 284.

Bibliography

Adelson, Leslie. "Subjectivity Reconsidered: Botho Strauss and Contemporary West German Prose." *New German Critique* 30 (Fall 1983): 3–60.

Adorno, Theodor W. *Gesammelte Schriften*. 20 vols. Frankfurt: Suhrkamp, 1973.

———. *Ohne Leitbild: Parva Aesthetica*. Frankfurt: Suhrkamp, 1967.

Ahrens, Ursula. "FiT (Frauen im Theater): Women in Theater." Trans. K. Sieg. In *The Divided Home/Land: Contemporary German Women's Plays*, ed. Sue-Ellen Case. Ann Arbor: University of Michigan Press, 1992.

Alcoff, Linda. "Cultural Feminism Versus Poststructuralism: The Identity Crisis in Feminist Theory." *Signs* 13, no. 3 (Spring 1988): 405–36.

Althusser, Louis. "Ideology and Ideological State Apparatuses." In *Lenin and Philosophy*, trans. Ben Brewster. London: Monthly Review, 1971.

Anz, Thomas, ed. *"Es geht nicht um Christa Wolf": Der Literaturstreit im Vereinten Deutschland*. Munich: Edition Spangenberg, 1991.

Appignanesi, Lisa. *The Cabaret*. New York: Universe, 1976.

Aust, Hugo, Peter Haida, and Jürgen Hein, eds. *Volksstück: Vom Hanswurstspiel zum sozialen Drama der Gegenwart*. Munich: Beck, 1989.

Bänsch, Dieter. *Else Lasker-Schüler: Zur Kritik eines etablierten Bildes*. Stuttgart: Metzler, 1971.

———. "'Ich bin Jude. Gott sei Dank.' Else Lasker-Schüler." In *Im Zeichen Hiobs: Jüdische Schriftsteller und deutsche Literatur im 20. Jahrhundert*, ed. Gunter E. Grimm and Hans-Peter Bayerdörfer. Frankfurt: Athenäum, 1985.

Barthes, Roland. *The Pleasure of the Text*. Trans. Richard Miller. New York: Hill and Wang, 1975.

Bartsch, Kurt, and Günther A. Höfler, eds. *Elfriede Jelinek: Dossier*. Graz, Vienna: Droschl, 1991.

Baudrillard, Jean. *Simulations*. Trans. Paul Foss, Paul Patton, and Philip Beitchman. Foreign Agents Series. New York: Semiotext(e), 1983.

Bauschinger, Sigrid. *Else Lasker-Schüler: Ihr Werk und ihre Zeit.* Heidelberg: Lothar Stiehm, 1980.

Becker, Peter von. "Letzte Nachrichten aus dem deutschen Niemandsland—und eine neue Dramatikerin: Kerstin Specht." *Theater heute* 1 (January 1990): 28–29.

Bellmann, D., W. Hein, W. Trapp, and G. Zang. "'Provinz' als politisches Problem." *Kursbuch* 39 (April 1975): 81–127.

Belsey, Catherine. *The Subject of Tragedy: Identity and Difference in Renaissance Drama.* London: Methuen, 1985.

Benjamin, Walter. *Gesammelte Schriften.* Vol. 2.1. Ed. R. Tiedemann and H. Schweppenhäuser. Frankfurt: Suhrkamp, 1980.

Benz, Wolfgang. "Die Abwehr der Vergangenheit: Ein Problem nur für Historiker und Moralisten?" In *Ist der Nationalsozialismus Geschichte? Zu Historisierung und Historikerstreit,* ed. Dan Diner, 17–33. Frankfurt: Fischer, 1987.

Berger, Renate, and Inge Stephan, eds. *Weiblichkeit und Tod in der Literatur.* Cologne: Böhlau, 1985.

Berlin Museum, ed. *Eldorado: Homosexuelle Frauen und Männer in Berlin 1850–1950. Geschichte, Alltag und Kultur.* Berlin: Fröhlich and Kaufmann, 1984.

Bloch, Ernst. "Gespräch über Ungleichzeitigkeit." *Kursbuch* 39 (April 1975): 1–9.

———. *Heritage of our Times.* Trans. Neville Plaice and Stephen Plaice. Cambridge, England: Polity, in association with B. Blackwell, 1991.

———. *The Principle of Hope.* Trans. Neville Plaice, Stephen Plaice, and Paul Knight. Cambridge: MIT Press, 1986.

———. *The Utopian Function of Art and Literature: Selected Essays.* Trans. Jack Zipes and Frank Mecklenburg. Cambridge: MIT Press, 1988.

Bock, Gisela. "Frauen und ihre Arbeit im Nationalsozialismus." In *Frauen in der Geschichte,* vol. 1, ed. Annette Kuhn and Gerhard Schneider. Düsseldorf: Pädagogischer Verlag Schwann-Bagel GmbH, 1979.

Bossinade, Johanna. "Haus und Front. Bilder des Faschismus in der Literatur von Exil- und Gegenwartsautorinnen. Am Beispiel Anna Seghers, Irmgard Keun, Christa Wolf und Gerlind Reinshagen." *Neophilologus* 70 (1986): 92–118.

Bovenschen, Silvia. *Die imaginierte Weiblichkeit: Exemplarische Untersuchungen zu kulturgeschichtlichen und literarischen Präsentationsformen des Weiblichen.* Frankfurt: Suhrkamp, 1979.

Brecht, Bertolt. *Brecht on Theater.* Ed. and trans. John Willett. New York: Hill and Wang, 1964.

Bridenthal, Renate, Atina Grossmann, and Marion Kaplan, eds. *When Biology Became Destiny: Women in Weimar and Nazi Germany.* New York: Monthly Review, 1984.

Brockett, Oscar. *History of the Theater.* 4th ed. Boston: Allyn and Bacon, 1982.

Brockgreitens, Annette. "YoYo-TA: FrauenKörperTänzerinnen." Master's thesis, University of Gießen, 1990.

Bronski, Michael. *Culture Clash: The Making of Gay Sensibility*. Boston: South End, 1984.

Bryant-Bertail, Sarah. "*The Good Soldier Schwejk* as Dialectical Theater." In *The Performance of Power: Theatrical Discourse and Politics*, ed. Sue-Ellen Case and Janelle Reinelt. Iowa City: University of Iowa Press, 1991.

Buck, Theo, and D. Steinbach, eds. *Tendenzen der deutschen Literatur zwischen 1918 und 1945 Weimarer Republik, Drittes Reich, Exil*. Literaturwissenschaft/Gesellschaftswissenschaft, vol. 69. Stuttgart: Ernst Klett, 1985.

Budzinski, Klaus. *Pfeffer ins Getriebe: So ist und wurde das Kabarett*. Munich: Universitas, 1982.

Burger, Rudolf. "Dein böser Blick, Elfriede." *Forum* 352 (1983): 48–51.

Butler, Judith. "Gender Trouble, Feminist Theory, and Psychoanalytic Discourse." In *Feminism/Postmodernism*, ed. Linda J. Nicholson. New York: Routledge, 1990.

Caduff, Corinna. "*Ich gedeihe inmitten von Seuchen": Elfriede Jelinek—Theatertexte*. Frankfurt: Peter Lang, 1991.

Canning, Charlotte. *Working from Experience: A History of Feminist Theater in the United States, 1969 to the Present*. Ph.D. diss., University of Washington, 1991.

Case, Sue-Ellen. "Brecht and Women: Homosexuality and the Mother." In *Brecht: Women and Politics*, eds. John Fuegi, Gisela Bahr, and John Willett. Detroit: Wayne State University Press, 1985.

———. *Feminism and Theatre*. New York: Methuen, 1988.

———. "Introducing Karl Valentin." *Yale Theater*, Fall/Winter 1981, 6–11.

———. "Towards a Butch-Femme Aesthetic." *Discourse* 11, no.1 (Fall/Winter 1988/89): 55–73.

———. "Tracking the Vampire." *Differences* 3, no.2 (Summer 1991): 1–20.

———, ed. *The Divided Home/Land: Contemporary German Women Playwrights*. Ann Arbor: University of Michigan Press, 1992.

———. ed. *Performing Feminisms: Feminist Critical Theory and Theatre*. Baltimore: Johns Hopkins University Press, 1990.

Chissell, Joan. *Clara Schumann: A Dedicated Spirit*. London: Hamish Hamilton, 1983.

Cixous, Hélène. "*Coming to Writing" and Other Essays*. With an introductory essay by Susan R. Suleiman; ed. Deborah Jenson; trans. Sarah Cornell. Cambridge: Harvard University Press, 1991.

Cixous, Hélène, and Catherine Clément. *The Newly Born Woman*. Trans. Betsy Wing. Minneapolis: University of Minnesota Press, 1986.

Cocalis, Susan. "'Mitleid' and 'Engagement': Compassion and/or Political Commitment in the Dramatic Works of Franz Xaver Kroetz." *Colloquia Germanica* 14, no. 3 (1981): 203–19.

———. "The Politics of Brutality: Toward a Definition of the Critical Volksstück." In *The Divided Home/Land: Contemporary German Women's Plays,* ed. Sue-Ellen Case. Ann Arbor: University of Michigan Press, 1992.

———. "'Weib ist Weib': Mimetische Darstellung contra emanzipatorische Tendenz in den Dramen Marieluise Fleißers." In *Die Frau als Heldin und Autorin: Neue kritische Ansätze zur deutschen Literatur,* ed. Wolfgang Paulsen. Bern: Francke, 1979.

———. "Weib ohne Wirklichkeit, Welt ohne Weiblichkeit: Zum S elbst-, Frauen- und Gesellschaftsbild im Frühwerk Marieluise Fleißers." In *Entwürfe von Frauen in der Literatur des 20. Jahrhunderts,* Literatur im historischen Prozeß, Neue Folge, vol. 5, ed. Irmela von der Lühe. Argument-Sonderband AS 92. Berlin: Argument, 1982.

Cocalis, Susan, and Ferrel Rose, eds. *Euterpe's Daughters: German Women Dramatists from the Eighteenth Century to the Present.* Tübingen: Günther Narr, forthcoming.

Daly, Ann. "The Thrill of a Lynch Mob or the Rage of a Woman?" *The Drama Review* 30, no. 2 (Summer 1986): 46–56.

Davies, Cecil W. "Working-Class Theater in the Weimar Republic, 1919–1933: Part 1." *Theatre Quarterly* 10, no. 38 (1980): 68–96. "Part 2," 10, no. 39 (1981): 81–96.

Dawson, Ruth P. "Frauen und Theater: Vom Stegreifspiel zum bürgerlichen Rührstück." In *Deutsche Literatur von Frauen,* vol. 1, ed. Gisela Brinker-Gabler. Munich: Beck, 1988.

Denkler, Horst. "Sache und Stil: Die Theorie der 'Neuen Sachlichkeit' und ihre Auswirkungen auf Kunst und Dichtung." *Wirkendes Wort* 18 (1968): 167–85.

Diamond, Elin. "Brechtian Theory/Feminist Theory: Toward a Gestic Feminist Criticism." *Drama Review* 32, no. 1 (Spring 1988): 82–94.

———. "Mimesis, Mimicry, and the 'True-Real.'" *Modern Drama* 32, no. 1 (March 1989): 58–72.

Dolan, Jill. *The Feminist Spectator as Critic.* Ann Arbor: University of Michigan Press, 1991.

Domin, Hilde. "Nur die Ewigkeit ist kein Exil." In *Preis der Vernunft: Literatur und Kunst zwischen Aufklärung, Widerstand und Anpassung,* ed. Klaus Siebenhaar and Hermann Haarmann. Berlin: Medusa, 1982.

Drewitz, Ingeborg. "Gerlind Reinshagen." In *Neue Literatur der Frauen: Deutschsprachige Autorinnen der Gegenwart,* ed. H. Puknus. Munich: Beck, 1981.

Drucker, Peter. "The Monster and the Lamb." *Atlantic Monthly,* December 1978, 82–87.

Ecker, Gisela, ed. *Feminist Aesthetics*. Boston: Beacon, 1985.

Ende, Amalie von. "Neunhundert Jahre Frauendrama." *Bühne und Welt* 1, no. 2 (1899).

Enzensberger, Hans Magnus. "Geimeinplätze, die Neueste Literatur betreffend." *Kursbuch* 15 (November 1968): 187–97.

Faderman, Lillian, and Brigitte Eriksson. *Lesbians in Germany: 1890s–1920s*. Tallahassee: Naiad, 1980.

Fassbinder, Rainer Werner. *Plays*. Ed., Trans., and with an introduction by Denis Calandra. New York: PAJ Publications, 1985.

Fischer, Lothar. *Tanz zwischen Rausch und Tod: Anita Berber, 1918–28 in Berlin*. Berlin: Hande and Spener, 1984.

Fischer-Lichte, Erika. "Frauen erobern die Bühne: Dramatikerinnen im 20. Jahrhundert." In *Deutsche Literatur von Frauen*, vol. 2, ed. Gisela Brinker-Gabler, 379–93. Munich: Beck, 1988.

Fleißer, Marieluise. "Das dramatische Empfinden bei den Frauen [1930]." *Schreiben* 9, no. 29/30 (1986): 15–16.

———. *Gesammelte Werke*. 3 vols. Frankfurt: Suhrkamp, 1972.

———. *Purgatory in Ingolstadt*. Trans. Gitta Honegger. In *The Divided Home/ Land: Contemporary German Women's Plays*, ed. Sue-Ellen Case. Ann Arbor: University of Michigan Press, 1992.

Foucault, Michel. *The History of Sexuality*. Vol. 1, *An Introduction*. Trans. Robert Hurley. New York: Vintage, 1980.

Frauengruppe Faschismusforschung, ed. *Mutterkreuz und Arbeitsbuch*. Frankfurt: Fischer, 1981.

Frevert, Ute. *Frauen-Geschichte Zwischen Bürgerlicher Verbesserung und Neuer Weiblichkeit*. Frankfurt: Suhrkamp, 1986.

Frisch, Schelley. "'Alien Homeland': Erika Mann and the Adenauer Era." *Germanic Review* 63, no. 4 (Fall 1988): 172–82.

Fuchs, Christian, ed. *Theater von Frauen—Österreich: Elfriede Jelinek, Marie-Therese Kerschbaumer, Gerlinde Obermeir, Brigitte Schwaiger, Marlene Streeruwitz, Lisa Witasek*. Frankfurt: Eichborn, 1991.

Fuchs, Elinor, ed. *Plays of the Holocaust: An International Anthology*. New York: Theatre Communications Group, 1987.

Führich, Angelika E. *Aufbrüche des Weiblichen im Drama der Weimarer Republik: Brecht-Fleißer-Horvàth-Gmeyner*. Heidelberg: Carl Winter Universitätsverlag, 1992.

Gerhard, Ute. *Verhältnisse und Verhinderungen. Frauenarbeit, Familie und Rechte der Frauen im 19. Jahrhundert. Mit Dokumenten*. Frankfurt: Suhrkamp, 1978.

Gerhardt, Marlis. *Stimmen und Rhythmen: Weibliche Ästhetik und Avantgarde*. Berlin: Luchterhand, 1982.

Giehse, Therese. *Ich hab' nichts zu Sagen: Gespräche mit Monika Sperr.* Munich: Bertelsmann, 1973.

Giesing, Michaela. "Theater als verweigerter Raum: Dramatikerinnen der Jahrhundertwende in deutschsprachigen Ländern." In *Frauen Literatur Geschichte: Schreibende Frauen vom Mittelalter bis zur Gegenwart,* ed. Renate Möhrmann. Frankfurt: Suhrkamp, 1989.

Gisel-Pfannkuch, Susanne. "Die Pfeffermühle in der Schweiz 1933–1936." Unpublished MS, Munich City Library.

Goldberg, Marianne. "Artifice and Authenticity: Gender Scenarios in Pina Bausch's Dance Theater." *Women and Performance* (1989): 104–17.

Grimm, Reinhold. "Zwischen Expressionismus und Faschismus: Bemerkungen zum Drama der Zwanziger Jahre." In *Die Sogenannten Zwanziger Jahre.* Schriften zur Literatur, vol. 13, eds. Reinhold Grimm and Jost Hermand. Bad Homburg: Gehlen, 1970.

Grossman, Atina. "The New Woman and the Rationalization of Sexuality in Weimar Germany." In *Powers of Desire: The Politics of Sexuality,* ed. Ann Snitow, Christine Stansell, and Sharon Thompson. New York: Monthly Review, 1983.

———. *The New Woman, the New Family and the Rationalization of Sexuality: The Sex Reform Movement in Germany 1928 to 1933.* Ph.D. diss, Rutgers University, 1984.

———. "Satisfaction is Domestic Happiness." In *Towards the Holocaust: The Social and Economic Collapse of the Weimar Republic,* eds. Michael N. Dobkowski and Isidor Wallimann. Westport, Conn.: Greenwood, 1983.

Gürtler, Christa, ed. *Gegen den schönen Schein: Texte zu Elfriede Jelinek.* Frankfurt: Neue Kritik KG, 1990.

Habermas, Jürgen. "A Kind of Settlement of Damages (Apologetic Tendencies)." *New German Critique* 44 (Spring/Summer 1988): 25–39.

Handke, Peter. "Die Geborgenheit unter der Schädeldecke." In *Büchner-Preis-Reden, 1972–1983.* Stuttgart: Reclam, 1983.

Hanna, Gillian. "Feminism and Theatre." *Theatre Papers.* Dartington, Devon: Dartington College, 1978.

Haraway, Donna. "A Manifesto for Cyborgs: Science, Technology, and Socialist Feminism in the 1980s." In *Feminism/ Postmodernism,* ed. Linda J. Nicholson. New York: Routledge, 1990.

Hart, Lynda, ed. *Making a Spectacle: Feminist Essays on Contemporary Women's Theatre.* Ann Arbor: University of Michigan Press, 1989.

Hasecke, Ursula. "Die Kunst, Apokryphen zu lesen: Zu einigen Momentaufnahmen 'weiblicher' Imagination in der literarischen Arbeit Else Lasker-Schülers." In *Entwürfe von Frauen in der Literatur des 20. Jahrhunderts,* ed. Irmela von der Lühe. Berlin: Argument, 1982.

Hasenclever, Walter. "*Humanity.*" Trans. Walter Sokel and Jacqueline Sokel. In

Anthology of German Expressionist Drama, ed. Walter Sokel. Ithaca: Cornell University Press, 1963.

Hass, Ulrike. "Grausige Bilder. Große Musik. Zu den Theaterstücken Elfriede Jelineks." *Text und Kritik* 117 (January 1993): 21–30.

Hausen, Karin, ed. *Frauen suchen ihre Geschichte.* Munich: Carl Hanser, 1983.

Hedgepeth, Sonja M. "Betrachtungen einer Unpolitischen: Else Lasker-Schüler zu ihrem Leben im Exil." *Germanic Review* 62, no. 3 (Summer 1967): 130–35.

Hegel, Georg W. F. *Werke.* Vol. 15. Frankfurt: Suhrkamp, 1970.

Heller, Agnes. *Das Alltagsleben: Vesuch einer Erklärung der individuellen Reproduktion.* Trans. Hans Joas. Frankfurt: Suhrkamp, 1975.

Henning, Eike. *Zum Historikerstreit: Was heißt und zu welchem Ende studiert man Faschismus?* Frankfurt: Athenäum, 1988.

Hensel, Georg. "Ein Flickerlteppich in Braun." *Frankfurter Allgemeine Zeitung,* May 31, 1976.

———. "Gehemmte weibliche Kunstproduktion: *Clara S.*, eine 'musikalische Tragödie' von Elfriede Jelinek—Uraufführung in Bonn." *Frankfurter Allgemeine Zeitung,* September 19, 1982.

———. *Theater der siebziger Jahre: Kommentar, Kritik, Polemik.* Stuttgart: Deutsche Verlags-Anstalt, 1980.

Hermand, Jost, and Frank Trommler. *Die Kultur der Weimarer Republik.* Munich: Nymphenburger Verlagshandlung, 1978.

Hermann-Neiße, Max. *Kabarett: Schriften zum Kabarett und zur bildenden Kunst.* Frankfurt: Zweitausendeins, 1988.

Herzfelde, Wieland. "Else Lasker-Schüler: Begegnungen mit der Dichterin und Ihrem Werk." *Sinn und Form* 21, no. 6 (1969): 1295–1325.

Hessing, Jakob. *Else Lasker-Schüler: Biographie einer deutsch-jüdischen Dichterin.* Karlsruhe: von Loeper, 1985.

Heukenkamp, Ursula. "Das Frauenbild in der antifaschistischen Erneuerung der SBZ." In *Wen kümmert's, wer spricht?* ed. Inge Stephan, Sigrid Weigel, and Karin Wilhelm. Cologne: Böhlau, 1991.

Hildebrandt, Christel. "Dramatikerinnen in der DDR. Hoffnung auf Veränderung." *Schreiben* 9, nos. 29/30 (1986): 140–54.

Hildebrandt, Irma. *Warum schreiben Frauen? Befreiungsnotstand—Rollenhader— Emanzipation im Spiegel der modernen Literatur.* Freiburg: Herder, 1980.

Hoff, Dagmar von. *Dramen des Weiblichen: Deutsche Dramatikerinnen um 1800.* Opladen: Westdeutscher, 1989.

———. "Stücke für das Theater: Überlegungen zu Elfriede Jelineks Methode der Destruktion." In *Gegen den schönen Schein: Texte zu Elfriede Jelinek,* ed. Christa Gürtler, 112–19. Frankfurt: Neue Kritik KG, 1990.

Hoffmeister, Donna. "Access Routes into Postmodernism: Interviews with Innerhofer, Jelinek, Rosei, and Wolfgruber." *Modern Austrian Literature* 20, no.2 (1987): 97–130.

——. "Growing Up Female in the Weimar Republic: Young Women in Seven Stories by Marieluise Fleißer." *German Quarterly* 56, no. 3 (May 1983): 396–407.

hooks, bell. *Talking Back: Thinking Feminist, Thinking Black.* Boston: South End, 1989.

Horkheimer, Max. "Autorität und Familie." In *Traditionelle und kritische Theorie: Vier Aufsätze.* Frankfurt: Fischer, 1968.

Horkheimer, Max, and Theodor W. Adorno. *The Dialectic of Enlightenment.* Trans. John Cumming. New York: Continuum, 1972.

Hösch, Rudolf. *Kabarett von gestern und heute nach zeitgenössischen Berichten, Kritiken, Texten und Erinnerungen.* Vol. 2: *1933–1970.* Berlin: Henschel, 1972.

Hübner, Raoul. "'Klau mich' oder die Veränderungen von Verkehrsformen: Anstöße der Studentenbewegung." In *Literatur und Studentenbewegung: Eine Zwischenbilanz,* ed. W. Martin Lüdke. Opladen: Westdeutscher, 1977.

Hüfner, Agnes. *Straßentheater.* Frankfurt: Suhrkamp, 1970.

Huyssen, Andreas. "After the Wall: The Failure of German Intellectuals." *New German Critique* 52 (Winter 1991): 109–43.

Innerhofer, Roland. *Die Grazer Autorenversammlung (1973–1983): Zur Organisation einer "Avantgarde."* Cologne: Böhlau, 1985.

Irigaray, Luce. *Speculum of the Other Woman* [1974]. Trans. Gillian C. Gill. Ithaca: Cornell University Press, 1985.

——. *This Sex Which Is Not One* [1977]. Trans. Catherine Porter with Carolyn Burke. Ithaca: Cornell University Press, 1985.

Jäger, Gerd. "Episches Theater—hin zur Einfühlung." *Theater heute* 1 (January 1977): 4–8.

Janz, Marlies. "Falsche Spiegel: Über die Umkehrung als Verfahren bei Elfriede Jelinek." In *Gegen den schönen Schein: Texte zu Elfriede Jelinek,* ed. Christa Gürtler, 81–97. Frankfurt: Neue Kritik KG, 1990.

Jelinek, Elfriede. *Begierde & Fahrerlaubnis (eine Pornographie): Erster Text von vielen ähnlichen.* In *Blauer Streusand,* ed. Barbara Alms. Frankfurt: Suhrkamp, 1987.

——. *Die endlose Unschuldigkeit: Prosa-Hörspiel-Essay.* Schwifting: Schwiftinger Galerie, 1980.

——. "Ich möchte seicht sein." *Schreiben* 9, no. 29/30 (1986): 74.

——. *Krankheit oder Moderne Frauen.* Cologne: Prometh, 1987.

——. *Theaterstücke: Clara S.; Was geschah, nachdem Nora ihren Mann verlassen hatte; Burgtheater.* Cologne: Prometh, 1984.

———. *Totenauberg: Ein Stück*. Reinbek: Rowohlt, 1991.

———. *Wolken. Heim*. Göttingen: Steidl, 1990.

Kafka, Hans. "Dramatikerinnen erobern die Bühne." *Die Dame*, January 1933.

Kant, Immanuel. *Kritik der Urteilskraft und Schriften zur Naturphilosophie. Werke*. Vol. 10, ed. W. Weischedel. Frankfurt: Suhrkamp, 1957.

———. *Observations on the Feeling of the Beautiful and Sublime*. Trans. John T. Goldthwait. Berkeley: University of California Press, 1960.

Karasek, Hellmuth. "Auf dem Altar des männlichen Genies: Spiegel-Redakteur Hellmuth Karasek über das feministische Stück 'Clara S.' von Elfriede Jelinek." *Der Spiegel* 40 (1982): 236–39.

———. "Die Erneuerung des Volksstücks: Auf den Spuren Marieluise Fleißers und Ödön von Horvaths." In *Positionen des Dramas*, ed. Heinz Ludwig Arnold and Theo Buck. Munich: Beck, 1977.

Kässens, Wend. "Montagsszenen aus einem Büro." *Theater heute* 1 (January 1983): 38–41.

Katz, Esther, and Joan Miriam Ringelheim, eds. *Proceedings of the Conference "Women Surviving The Holocaust."* New York: Institute for Research in History, 1983.

Keiser-Hayne, Helga. *Beteiligt Euch, es geht um Eure Erde: Erika Mann und ihr politisches Kabarett die "Pfeffermühle" 1933–1937*. Munich: Edition Spangenberg, 1990.

Kiencke, Jutta E. "Die Dramen der Gerlind Reinshagen: Utopisches auf der Bühne." *Schreiben* 9, no. 29/30 (1986): 35–48.

Kiencke-Wagner, Jutta E. *Das Werk von Gerlind Reinshagen: Gesellschaftskritik und utopisches Denken*. Studien zur Deutschen Literatur des 19. und 20. Jahrhunderts 11. Frankfurt: Peter Lang, 1989.

Kipnis, Laura. *Ecstasy Unlimited: On Sex, Gender, Capital, and Aesthetics*. Minneapolis: University of Minnesota Press, 1993.

———. "Feminism: The Political Conscience of Postmodernism." In *Universal Abandon?* ed. Andrew Ross. Minneapolis: University of Minnesota Press, 1988.

Klapdor-Kops, Heike. "Dramatikerinnen auf deutschen Bühnen: Notwendige Fortsetzung einer im Jahr 1933 unterbrochenen Reflexion." *TheaterZeitSchrift* 9 (1984): 57–77.

———. *Heldinnen: Die Gestaltung der Frauen im Drama deutscher Exilautoren (1933–1945)*. Weinheim: Beltz, 1985.

Kleemann, Elisabeth. *Zwischen symbolischer Rebellion und politischer Revolution*. Würzburger Hochschulschriften zur Neueren Deutschen Literaturgeschichte, vol. 6. Frankfurt: Peter Lang, 1985.

Klier, Walter. "'In der Liebe schon ist die Frau nicht voll auf ihre Kosten gekommen, jetzt will sie nicht auch noch ermordet werden': Über die Schriftstellerin

Elfriede Jelinek." *Merkur: Deutsche Zeitschrift für europäisches Denken* 41 (May 1987): 423–27.

Klinger, Cornelia. "Déjà-Vu oder die Frage nach den Emanzipationsstrategien im Vergleich zwischen der ersten und zweiten Frauenbewegung." *Kommune* 12 (December 1986): 57–72.

Klüsener, Erika. *Lasker-Schüler*. Reinbek: Rowohlt, 1980.

Koonz, Claudia. *Mothers in the Fatherland: Women, the Family, and Nazi Politics*. New York: St. Martin's, 1987.

Kord, Susanne. *Ein Blick hinter die Kulissen: Deutschsprachige Dramatikerinnen im 18. und 19. Jahrhundert*. Stuttgart: Metzler, 1992.

———. "Fading Out: Invisible Women in Marieluise Fleißer's Early Dramas." *Women in German Yearbook: Feminist Studies and German Culture* 5 (1989): 57–72.

Kraft, Friedrich, ed. *Marieluise Fleißer: Anmerkungen Texte Dokumente*. Ingolstadt: Donau Courier, 1981.

Kramer, Helgard. "Veränderungen der Frauenrolle in der Weimarer Republik." *Beiträge feministischer Theorie und Praxis* 5 (1981): 17–25.

Kreuzer, Helmut. *Die Boheme: Beiträge zu ihrer Beschreibung*. Stuttgart: Metzler, 1968.

Kristeva, Julia. *Desire in Language: A Semiotic Approach to Literature and Art*. Trans. Thomas Gora, Alice Jardine, and Leon S. Roudiez; ed. Leon Roudiez. New York: Columbia University Press, 1980.

———. "Woman Can Never Be Defined." Trans. Marilyn A. August. In *New French Feminisms*, ed. and with introductions by Elaine Marks and Isabelle de Courtivron. New York: Schocken, 1981.

Kroetz, Franz Xaver. "Notwendiger Nachtrag zu *Sonntagskinder*." *Unsere Zeit*, October 14, 1976.

Krüll, Marianne. *Im Netz der Zauberer: Eine andere Geschichte der Familie Mann*. Zurich: Arche, 1991.

Kuckart, Judith. *Im Spiegel der Bäche finde ich mein Bild nicht mehr: Gratwanderung einer anderen Ästhetik der Dichterin Else Lasker-Schüler*. Frankfurt: Fischer, 1985.

Lacan, Jacques. *Écrits: A Selection*. Trans. Alan Sheridan. New York: Norton, 1977.

Lahann, Birgit. "'Männer sehen in mir die grosse Domina': Interview mit Elfriede Jelinek." *stern* 37 (September 8, 1988): 76–85.

Landes, Brigitte. "Zu Elfriede Jelinek's Stück: Krankheit oder Moderne Frauen. 'Wie ein Stück.'" *Schreiben* 9, no. 29/30 (1986): 89–95.

Lange, Wigand. *Theater in Deutschland nach 1945: Zur Theaterpolitik der amerikanischen Besatzungsbehörden*. Frankfurt: Peter Lang, 1980.

Langner, Ilse. *Dramen*. 2 vols. Ed. Eberhard Günter Schulz. Würzburg: Bergstadtverlag Wilhelm Gottlieb Korn, 1983.

Laqueur, Walter. *Weimar: A Cultural History, 1918–1933.* New York: Putnam, 1974.

Lareau, Alan. "The German Cabaret Movement During the Weimar Republic." *Theatre Journal* 43, no. 4 (December 1991): 471–90.

Lasker-Schüler, Else. *Gesammelte Werke.* 3 vols. Ed. Friedhelm Kemp. Munich: Kösel, 1962.

———. "*IandI.*" Trans. Beate Hein Bennett. In *The Divided Home/Land: Contemporary German Women's Plays,* ed. Sue-Ellen Case. Ann Arbor: University of Michigan Press, 1992.

———. *Lieber Gestreifter Tiger: Briefe von Else Lasker-Schüler.* Ed. Margarete Kupper. Munich, Kösel, 1969.

Lauretis, Teresa de, ed. *Feminist Studies/Critical Studies.* Bloomington: Indiana University Press, 1986.

———. "Sexual Indifference and Lesbian Representation." In *Performing Feminisms: Feminist Critical Theory and Theatre,* ed. Sue-Ellen Case. Baltimore: Johns Hopkins University Press, 1990.

———. *Technologies of Gender: Essays on Theory, Film, and Fiction.* Bloomington: Indiana University Press, 1987.

Leutenegger, Gertrud. *Lebewohl, Gute Reise: Ein dramatisches Poem.* Frankfurt: Suhrkamp, 1980.

Ley, Ralph. "Liberation from Brecht: A Marieluise Fleisser in Her Own Right." *Modern Drama* 31, no. 3 (September 1988): 340–51.

Linse, Ulrich. "'Geschlechtsnot der Jugend': Über Jugendbewegung und Sexualität." In *'Mit uns zieht die neue Zeit': Der Mythos Jugend,* ed. Thomas Koebner, Rolf-Peter Janz, and Frank Trommler, 245–309. Frankfurt: Suhrkamp, 1985.

Litzmann, Berthold. *Clara Schumann: Ein Künstlerleben.* 3 vols. Leipzig: Breitkopf and Härtel, 1918.

Löffler, Sigrid. "Was Habe Ich Gewußt?—Nichts." *Theater heute* 1 (January 1986): 2–6.

Lorde, Audré. "The Master's Tools Will Never Dismantle The Master's House." *Sister Outsider: Essays and Speeches.* Trumansburg, N.Y.: The Crossing, 1984.

Malina, Judith. "Director's Note to *IandI.*" Trans. Beate Hein Bennett. In *The Divided Home/Land: Contemporary German Women's Plays,* ed. Sue-Ellen Case. Ann Arbor: University of Michigan Press, 1992.

Mann, Erika. *Briefe und Antworten,* 2 vols. Ed. Anna Zanco Prestel. Munich: Edition Spangenberg, 1984.

———. "Lucky Hans"; "The Witch'; "The Cold." Trans. K. Sieg. In *The Divided Home/Land: Contemporary German Women's Plays,* ed. Sue-Ellen Case. Ann Arbor: University of Michigan Press, 1992.

Mann, Erika, and Klaus Mann. *Bilder und Dokumente*. Ed. Ursula Hummel and Eva Chrambach. Munich: Edition Spangenberg, 1990.

Mann, Klaus. *Der siebente Engel: Die Theaterstücke*. Reinbek: Rowohlt, 1989.

———. *Mephisto*. Trans. R. Smyth. New York: Random House, 1977.

Manning, Susan Allene. "An American Perspective on Tanztheater." *Drama Review* 30, no. 2 (Summer 1986): 57–79.

———. *Ecstasy and the Demon: Feminism and Nationalism in the Dances of Mary Wigman*. Berkeley: University of California Press, 1993.

Manning, Susan Allene, and Melissa Benson. "Interrupted Continuities: Modern Dance in Germany: An Historical Photoessay." *Drama Review* 30, no. 2 (Summer 1986): 30–45.

Marks, Elaine, and Isabelle de Courtivron. *New French Feminisms: An Anthology*. New York: Schocken, 1980.

Matthei, Renate, ed. *Grenzverschiebung: Neue Tendenzen in der deutschen Literatur der 6oer Jahre*. Cologne: Kiepenheuer and Witsch, 1970.

Mattis, Anita Maria. *Sprechen als theatralisches Handeln? Studien zur Dramaturgie der Theaterstücke Elfriede Jelineks*. Ph.D. diss., Vienna, 1987.

McGowan, Moray. *Marieluise Fleißer: Das Werk Marieluise Fleißers in biographischem und sozialgeschichtlichen Kontext*. Munich: Beck, 1987.

Meinhof, Ulrike Marie. *Bambule: Fürsorge - Sorge für wen?* Berlin: Wagenbach, 1971.

———. *Die Würde des Menschen ist antastbar: Aufsätze und Polemiken*. Berlin: Wagenbach, 1980.

Mennemeier, F. N., ed. *Modernes Deutsches Drama*. 2 vols. Munich: Wilhelm Fink, 1973.

Mewes, Horst. "The German New Left." *New German Critique* 1, no. 1 (Winter 1973): 22–41.

Meyer, Eva. *Architexturen*. Frankfurt: Stroemfeld/Roter Stern, 1986.

———. "Den Vampir Schreiben: Zu Elfriede Jelineks Theaterstück *Krankheit oder moderne Frauen*." In *Die Autobiographie der Schrift*. Frankfurt: Stroemfeld/Roter Stern, 1989.

———. *Zählen und Erzählen: Für eine Semiotik des Weiblichen*. Berlin: Medusa/Die Quere, 1983.

Michel, Karl Markus. "Ein Kranz für die Literatur." *Kursbuch* 15 (November 1968): 169–86.

Middell, Eike. "*IchundIch* von Else Lasker-Schüler." *Sinn und Form* 33, no. 4 (1981): 637–52.

Mitscherlich, Alexander, and Margarete Mitscherlich. *The Inability to Mourn: Principles of Collective Behavior*. Trans. B. Placzek. New York: Grove, 1975.

Mittenzwei, Werner. "Die Brecht-Lukács-Debatte." *Sinn und Form* 16 (1967): 235–71.

———. *Exil in der Schweiz: Kunst und Literatur im antifaschistischen Exil 1933–45.* Vol. 2. Frankfurt: Röderberg, 1981.

Möhrmann, Renate, ed. *Die Schauspielerin: Zur Kulturgeschichte der weiblichen Bühnenkunst.* Frankfurt: Insel, 1989.

Moníková, Libuše. *Unter Menschenfressern: Ein dramatisches Menü in vier Gängen.* Frankfurt: Verlag der Autoren, 1990.

Morris, Meaghann. *The Pirate's Fiancee: Feminism, Reading, Postmodernism.* London, New York: Verso, 1988.

Mosse, George. *Nationalism and Sexuality: Respectability and Abnormal Sexuality in Modern Europe.* New York: Fertig, 1985.

———. *Nazi Culture.* New York: Grosset and Dunlap, 1966.

Müller, Elfriede. *Damenbrise: Eine Theater-Komödie von heute. Theater* (special issue of *Theater heute*) 1989.

———. *Die Bergarbeiterinnen. Goldener Oktober: Zwei Stücke.* Frankfurt: Verlag der Autoren, 1992.

Müller, Heiner. *Explosion of a Memory: Writings by Heiner Müller.* Ed. and trans. Carl Weber. New York: PAJ Publications, 1989.

———. *Germania.* Trans. B. Schutze and C. Schutze; ed. Sylvère Lotringer. New York: Semiotext(e), 1990.

———. "Reflections of Postmodernism." *New German Critique* 16 (Winter 1979): 55–57.

Negt, Oskar, and Alexander Kluge. *Öffentlichkeit und Erfahrung: Zur Organisationsanalyse von bürgerlicher und proletarischer Öffentlichkeit.* Frankfurt: Suhrkamp, 1972.

Newton, Esther. *Mother Camp: Female Impersonators in America.* Englewood Cliffs: Prentice Hall, 1972.

Nolte, Ernst. "Vergangenheit, die nicht vergehen will." In *Historikerstreit: Die Dokumentation der Kontroverse um die Einzigartigkeit der nationalsozialistischen Judenvernichtung.* Munich, Zurich: Piper, 1987.

Nowoselsky-Müller, Sonia, ed. *ein mund von welt: ginka steinwachs. TEXT//S// ORTE//N//.* Bremen: Zeichen and Spuren, 1989.

Nussbaum, Laureen. "The German Documentary Theater of the Sixties: A Stereopsis of Contemporary History." *German Studies Review* 4, no.2 (May 1981): 237–57.

Ott, Rainer, and Walter Rösler. *Kabarettgeschichte: Abriß des deutschsprachigen Kabaretts.* Berlin: Henschel, 1981.

Papula, Dagmar, and Norbert Kentrup, eds. *Frauentheater.* Offenbach: Verlag 2000, 1982.

Patraka, Vivian M. "Contemporary Drama, Fascism, and the Holocaust." *Theatre Journal* 39, no. 1 (March 1987): 65–77.

Paulsen, Wolfgang, ed. *Die Frau als Heldin und Autorin: Neue kritische Ansätze zur deutschen Literatur.* Munich: Francke, 1979.

Pfister, Eva. "'Eine Wirklichkeit mußte sie haben': Über den Aufbruch der Marieluise Fleißer." In *Marieluise Fleißer: Anmerkungen Texte Dokumente,* ed. Friedrich Kraft. Ingolstadt: Donau Courier, 1981.

Piscator, Erwin. *The Political Theatre.* Trans. Hugh Rorrison. London: Avon, 1978.

Presber, Gabriele. *Die Kunst ist Weiblich: Gespräche.* Munich: Droemersche Verlagsanstalt, 1988.

Preuß, Patricia. "'Ich war nicht erzogen, daß ich mich wehrte': Marieluise Fleißer und ihr Werk in der Diskussion um weibliches Schreiben." *Germanic Review* 62, no. 4 (Fall 1987): 186–93.

Reinelt, Janelle. *After Brecht: British Epic Theatre.* Ann Arbor: University of Michigan Press, 1994.

———. "Beyond Brecht: Britain's New Feminist Drama." *Theatre Journal* 38, no. 2 (May 1986): 329–44.

Reinshagen, Gerlind. *Die Feuerblume. Spectaculum* 46 (1988).

———. *Die flüchtige Braut. Roman.* Frankfurt: Suhrkamp, 1984.

———. *Drei Wünsche frei: chorische Stücke.* Frankfurt: Suhrkamp, 1992.

———. *Gesammelte Stücke.* Frankfurt: Suhrkamp, 1986.

———. *Ironheart.* Trans. Sue-Ellen Case and Arlene A. Teraoka. In *The Divided Home/Land: Contemporary German Women's Plays,* ed. Sue-Ellen Case. Ann Arbor: University of Michigan Press, 1992.

Reinshagen, Gerlind, and Wend Kässens. "'Künftig werde ich noch weiter gehen.' Gerlind Reinshagen im Gespräch über ihr Stück *Eisenherz.*" *Theater heute* 1 (1983): 41–43.

Reinshagen, Gerlind, and Renate Klett. "Gespräch mit Gerlind Reinshagen." *Schreiben* 9, no. 29/30 (1986): 48–56.

———. "An Interview with Gerlind Reinshagen." Trans. Angelika Czekay. In *The Divided Home/Land: Contemporary German Women's Plays,* ed. Sue-Ellen Case. Ann Arbor: University of Michigan Press, 1992.

Reinshagen, Gerlind, and Horst Laube. "Der Mensch muß träumen: Gerlind Reinshagen und Horst Laube unterhalten sich über Theater und über das Theater der Reinshagen." *Theater heute* 17 (1975/76): 101–3.

Reinshagen, Gerlind, and Anke Roeder. "Theater as Counter-Councept: An Interview with Gerlind Reinshagen." Trans. Angelika Czekay. In *The Divided Home/Land: Contemporary German Women's Plays,* ed. Sue-Ellen Case. Ann Arbor: University of Michigan Press, 1992.

Riviere, Joan. "Womanliness as a Masquerade." *International Journal of Psycho-Analysis* 10 (1929): 303–13.

Roeder, Anke, ed. *Autorinnen: Herausforderungen an das Theater.* Frankfurt: Suhrkamp, 1989.

Roth, Friederike. "*Piano Plays.*" Trans. Andra Weddington. In *The Divided Home/Land: Contemporary German Women's Plays,* ed. Sue-Ellen Case. Ann Arbor: University of Michigan Press, 1992.

————. *Ritt auf die Wartburg.* Frankfurt: Verlag der Autoren, 1983.

Rouse, John. "Brecht and the Contradictory Actor." *Theatre Journal* 36, no. 1 (1984): 24–41.

————. *Brecht and the West German Theatre: The Practice and Politics of Interpretation.* Ann Arbor: UMI Research Press, 1989.

Rousseau, J. J. *Political Writings.* Trans. and ed. Frederick Watkins. New York: Nelson, 1953.

Rubin, Gayle. "The Traffic in Women: Notes Toward a Political Economy of Sex." In *Toward an Anthropology of Women,* ed. Rayna Reiter. New York: Monthly Review, 1975.

Rühle, Günther. "Die andere Seite von Ingolstadt: Wirkung und Umfang des Fleißerschen Werks." In *Marieluise Fleißer: Anmerkungen Texte Dokumente,* ed. Friedrich Kraft. Ingolstadt: Donau Kurier, 1981.

————. *Theater für die Republik.* Frankfurt./M.: Fischer, 1967.

————. *Zeit und Theater.* 3 vols. Berlin: Propyläen, 1972.

————, ed. *Materialien zum Leben und Schreiben der Marieluise Fleißer.* Frankfurt: Suhrkamp, 1973.

Rühm, Gerhard. *Die Wiener Gruppe. Achleitner, Artmann, Bayer, Rühm, Wiener: Texte, Gemeinschaftsarbeiten, Aktionen.* Reinbek: Rowohlt, 1967.

Russo, Mary. "Female Grotesques: Carnival and Theory." In *Feminist Studies/Critical Studies,* ed. Teresa de Lauretis. Bloomington: Indiana University Press, 1986.

Sachs, Nelly. *Zeichen im Sand: Die szenischen Dichtungen der Nelly Sachs.* Frankfurt: Suhrkamp, 1962.

Said, Edward. *Orientalism.* New York: Vintage, 1979.

Sauter, H.-J. "Interviews mit Barbara Frischmuth, Elfriede Jelinek, Michael Scharang." *Weimarer Beiträge* 27 (1981): 109–17.

Schiller, Friedrich. *Sämtliche Gedichte.* Vol. 1. Ed. H. G. Göpfert. Munich: Beck, 1965.

Schmidt, Henry J. *How Dramas End: Essays on the German Sturm und Drang, Büchner, Hauptmann, and Fleisser.* Ann Arbor: University of Michigan Press, 1992.

Schmitt, Hans-Jürgen, ed. *Die Expressionismus Debatte: Materialien zu einer marxistischen Realismuskonzeption.* Frankfurt: Suhrkamp, 1973.

Schmitz, Thomas. *Das Volksstück.* Sammlung Metzler 257. Stuttgart: Metzler, 1990.

Schneider, Peter. "Die Phantasie im Spätkapitalismus und die Kulturrevolution." *Kursbuch* 16 (1969): 1–37.

Schober, Siegfried. "Die neue Lust: Lust auf 'Schlimmes': Schriftstellerinnen entdecken das Obszöne." *stern* 18 (April 27, 1989): 66–72.

Schödel, Helmut. "Eisenherz, gebrochen." *Die Zeit,* November 26, 1982.

Schregel, Ursula, and Michael Erdmann. "Das Theater als letzte Bastion des Feudalismus?" *Theater heute* 26, no. 8 (1985): 28–33.

Schulze-Reimpell, Werner. "Sand im Geschreibe." *Theater heute* 2 (February 1989): 42.

Schwarzenbach, Annemarie. *"Wir werden es schon zuwege bringen, das Leben": Annemarie Schwarzenbach an Erika und Klaus Mann: Briefe 1930–1942.* Ed. Uta Fleischmann. Pfaffenweiler: Centaurus, 1993.

Schwarzer, Alice. "'Ich bitte um Gnade': Interview mit Elfriede Jelinek." *Emma* 7 (July 1989): 50–55.

Seiler, Manfred. "Die Frau, das Übermannte Wesen." *Theater heute* 11 (November 1982): 18–19.

Serke, Jürgen. *Frauen schreiben: Ein neues Kapitel deutschsprachiger Literatur.* Frankfurt: Fischer, 1982.

Sieg, Katrin. "Deviance and Dissidence: Subjects of the Cold War." In *Unnatural Acts: Theorizing the Performative,* ed. Sue-Ellen Case, Susan Foster, and Philip Brett. Bloomington: Indiana University Press, 1994.

———. "Equality Decreed: Dramatizing Gender in East Germany." *Women in German Yearbook* 9 (1993): 113–26.

———. "The Representation of Fascism in Gerlind Reinshagen's *Sunday's Children.*" *Theatre Studies* 36 (1991): 31–44.

———. "The Revolution Has Been Televised: Reconfiguring History and Identity in Post-Wall Germany." *Theatre Journal* 45, no. 1 (March 1993): 35–47.

———. "Subjectivity and Socialism: Feminist Discourses in East Germany." *Genders* (1995).

Silverman, Kaja. *The Subject of Semiotics.* Oxford: Oxford University Press, 1983.

Sokel, Walter. *Anthology of German Expressionist Drama.* Ithaca: Cornell University Press, 1963.

Specht, Kerstin. *Lila. Das Glühend Männla. Amiwiesn: Drei Stücke.* Frankfurt: Verlag der Autoren, 1990.

————. *The Little Red-Hot Man.* Trans. Guntram H. Weber. In *The Divided Home/Land: Contemporary German Women's Plays,* ed. Sue-Ellen Case. Ann Arbor: University of Michigan Press, 1992.

Spielmann, Yvonne. "Überlegungen zu feministischer Theaterästhetik." *Theater-ZeitSchrift* 9 (1984): 78–86.

Spivak, Gayatri Chakravorty. "French Feminism in an International Frame." In *In Other Worlds: Essays in Cultural Politics.* New York: Routledge, 1988.

Stefan, Verena. *Häutungen: Autobiografische Aufzeichnungen Gedichte Träume Analysen.* Munich: Frauenoffensive, 1975. English translation: *Shedding.* Trans. J. Morre and B. Weckmueller. New York: Daughters, 1978.

Steinwachs, Ginka. "das gaumentheater des mundes" [1983]. In *ein mund von welt: ginka steinwachs,* ed. Sonia Nowoselsky-Müller. Bremen: Zeichen and Spuren, 1989. Translated as "The Palatheatre of the Mouth," by K. Sieg. In *Women in Theatre: German Women Playwrights on Theatre.* New York: Goethe House, 1991. Photocopy.

————. "Das Theater als oralische Anstalt." Originally published as "Wie finde ich Stand und leiste so Widerstand." *Die Schwarze Botin* 23 (1984).

————. *Erzherzog-Herzherzog Oder: das unglückliche Haus Österreich heiratet die Insel der Stille.* Munich: Raben, 1985.

————. *George Sand.* Trans. Jamie Owen Daniels and Katrin Sieg with Sue-Ellen Case. In *The Divided Home/Land: Contemporary German Women's Plays,* ed. Sue-Ellen Case. Ann Arbor: University of Michigan Press, 1992.

————. *George Sand: Eine Frau in Bewegung, die Frau von Stand.* [1980]. Reprint. Berlin: Ullstein, 1983.

————. "Konzept der Dichtungsmaschine." *Sprache im technischen Zeitalter* 55 (1975): 204–8.

————. "Monsieur-Madame." *Schreibheft* 21 (1983): 89–93, and 22 (1983): 104–9.

————. *Mythologie des Surrealismus oder die Rückverwandlung von Kultur in Natur: Eine strukturale Analyse von Bretons.* Berlin: Luchterhand, 1971.

————. *Tränende Herzen: Ein sentimentales Frauenstück.* Cologne: Schauspiel Cologne, 1978.

Stephan, Inge. "Zwischen Provinz und Metropole—Zur Avantgarde-Kritik von Marieluise Fleißer." In *Weiblichkeit und Avantgarde,* ed. Inge Stephan and Sigrid Weigel. Berlin: Argument, 1987.

Stürzer, Anne. *Dramatikerinnen und Zeitstücke: Ein vergessenes Kapitel der Theater .geschichte von der Weimarer Republik bis zur Nachkriegszeit.* Stuttgart: Metzler, 1993.

Sullivan, Esther Beth. *Emplotment: A Feminist Analysis of Narrative on Stage.* Ph.D. diss. University of Washington, 1989.

tax, sissi. *marieluise fleißer: schreiben, überleben. ein biographischer versuch*. Frankfurt: Stroemfeld/Roter Stern, 1984.

Theweleit, Klaus. *Male Fantasies*. 2 vols. Trans. Stephen Conway, Erica Carter, and Chris Turner. Minneapolis: University of Minnesota Press, 1987.

Tröger, Annette. "Die Dolchstoßlegende der Linken: 'Frauen haben Hitler an die Macht gebracht:' Thesen zur Geschichte der Frauen am Vorabend des Dritten Reichs." In *Frauen und Wissenschaft: Beiträge zur Berliner Sommeruniversität für Frauenforschung, Juli 1976*, ed. Gruppe Berliner Dozentinnen. Berlin: Courage, 1977.

Tyson, Peter K. "Else Lasker-Schüler's *Die Wupper*: Between Naturalism and Expressionism." *AUMLA: Journal of the Australasian Universities Language and Literature Association* 64 (November 1985): 144–53.

Ueding, Gert, ed. *Literatur ist Utopie*. Frankfurt: Suhrkamp, 1978.

Wandor, Michelene. *Carry on, Understudies: Theatre and Sexual Politics*. London: Methuen, 1981.

Weber, Betty Nance. "Gerlind Reinshagen: Versuch eines Portraits." In *Die Frau als Heldin und Autorin*, ed. Wolfgang Paulsen. Bern: Francke, 1979.

Weigel, Sigrid. *Die Stimme der Medusa: Schreibweisen in der Gegenwartsliteratur von Frauen*. Reinbek: Rowohlt, 1989.

Weiss, Peter. "The Material and the Models [1968]," *Theatre Quarterly* 1, no. 1 (January–March 1971) 41-45.

Wiedenmann, Ursula. "Frauen im Schatten: Mitarbeiterinnen und Mitautorinnen. Das Beispiel der literarischen Produktion Bertolt Brechts." In *Deutsche Literatur von Frauen*, 2 vols., ed. Gisela Brinker-Gabler. Munich: Beck, 1988.

Wiener, Meir. "Else Lasker-Schüler." In *Juden in der deutschen Literatur: Essays über zeitgenössische Schriftsteller*, ed. Gustav Krojanker. Berlin: Welt, 1922.

Wiesmayr, Elisabeth. *Die Zeitschrift "manuskripte" 1960–1970*. Königstein: Anton Hain, 1980.

Wilke, Sabine. "Zerrspiegel imaginierter Weiblichkeit: Eine Analyse zeitgenössischer Texte von Elfriede Jelinek, Ginka Steinwachs und Gisela von Wysocki." *TheaterZeitSchrift* 33/34 (1993): 181–203.

Willett, John. *The New Sobriety: Art and Politics in the Weimar Period 1917–33*. London: Thames and Hudson, 1978.

Wittig, Monique. *The Straight Mind and Other Essays*. Foreword by Louise Turcotte. Boston: Beacon Press, 1992.

Wurst, Karin A., ed. *Frauen und Drama im achtzehnten Jahrhundert*. Cologne: Böhlau, 1991.

Wysocki, Gisela von. "Der Aufbruch der Frauen: Verordnete Träume, Bubikopf und 'sachliches Leben.' Ein aktueller Streifzug durch SCHERL's Magazin, Jahrgang 1925, Berlin." In *Massenkommunikationsforschung: Produktanalysen*, vol. 3, ed. Dieter Prokop. Frankfurt: Fischer, 1977.

———. *Die Fröste der Freiheit: Aufbruchsphantasien.* Frankfurt: Syndikat, 1980.

Young, Frank W. "Elfriede Jelinek—Profile of an Austrian Feminist." In *Continental, Latin-American and Francophone Women Writers: Selected Papers from the Wichita State University Conference on Foreign Literature, 1984–1985,* ed. Eunice Myers and Ginette Adamson, 97–105. Lanham, New York: University Press of America, 1987.

Zipes, Jack D. "Documentary Drama in Germany: Mending the Circuit." *Germanic Review* 42 (1967): 49–62.

Index